Murders and Acquisitions

Murders and Acquisitions

Representations of the serial killer in
popular culture

Edited by
ALZENA MACDONALD

B L O O M S B U R Y
NEW YORK • LONDON • NEW DELHI • SYDNEY

Bloomsbury Academic

An imprint of Bloomsbury Publishing Plc

1385 Broadway   50 Bedford Square
New York   London
NY 10018   WC1B 3DP
USA   UK

www.bloomsbury.com

Bloomsbury is a registered trade mark of Bloomsbury Publishing PLC

First published 2013

Library of Congress Cataloging-in-Publication Data
Murders and acquisitions : representations of the serial killer in
popular culture / edited by Alzena MacDonald.
pages cm
ISBN 978-1-4411-7630-1 (hardback) – ISBN 978-1-4411-9292-9 (paperback) –
ISBN 978-1-4411-5485-9 (e-pub) 1. Serial murderers in mass media.
2. Serial murderers in popular culture. I. MacDonald,
Alzena, editor of compilation
P96.S44M87 2013
302.23′4–dc23
2013020323

ISBN: HB: 978-1-4411-7630-1
PB: 978-1-4411-9292-9
e-PDF: 978-1-4411-7702-5
e-Pub: 978-1-4411-5485-9

Design by Newgen Knowledge Works (P) Ltd., Chennai, India
Printed and bound in the United States of America

To my children,
Jed and Nate D'Costa;

my parents,
Allan and Zenobia MacDonald;

and

my mentors,
Professor Jon Stratton and Dr Ann McGuire.

Contents

Figures

Acknowledgments

Murders and Acquisitions is the fruit of exciting research and collegiality with 13 fine scholars, namely Sara L. Knox, Robert Cettl, Kumarini Silva, Danielle Rousseau, Mark Bernard, Christina Lee, Oliver Carter, Louis Bayman, Janice Baker, Philip L. Simpson, Sofia Bull, David Buchbinder, and Ann Elizabeth McGuire. I extend to these learned people my humble thanks for their insightful contributions to this anthology and warm support to complete this project.

My sincere thanks to Katie Gallof—editor extraordinaire at Bloomsbury Publishing (New York)—for her professionalism, enthusiasm, and friendly guidance. Tremendous thanks to the Critical Textual Studies research cluster within the Faculty of Humanities at Curtin University, especially Rachel Robertson, for providing me with the necessary funds to purchase the images included in this book.

My heartfelt thanks to Christina Lee—my delightful and brilliant colleague, friend and kindred spirit—for inspiring me to undertake this project. I am forever grateful for all the invaluable advice she has provided me on this scholarly journey. A big thank you to my dear friend Kara-Jane Lombard for assisting me to format references and being a great listener. Special thanks to Kristen Phillips (my 'Special K') for her ongoing kindness, and intellectual and emotional strength.

I would like to thank my colleagues in the School of Media, Culture, and Creative Arts, in particular Steve Mickler and Ron Blaber, for their strong support.

For their uplifting presence in my life, I thank my beautiful friends Elaine Meyer (my BFF), Emmanuella Murray, Marilyn Lobo, Suvas Lobo, Carly Parker, Melissa Mitsikas, Arvind Agrawal, and Liam Lynch.

My unending love and thanks to the two brightest lights in my life, Jed and Nate D'Costa, for your sweet affection and joyous energies, and also to my beloved parents, Allan and Zenobia MacDonald, for raising me to have a quest for knowledge and always encouraging my educational pursuits. Finally, I extend my eternal gratitude to my mentors, Jon Stratton and Ann McGuire, for their wisdom, care and unfailing support which has enriched my life beyond measure. I dedicate this collection to all of them.

1

Dissecting the "Dark Passenger": Reading Representations of the Serial Killer

Alzena MacDonald

> Serial killers are so common . . . that you can't swing a dead cat
> without hitting one.
>
> ADAM BUCKMAN, 2008

It seems a truth universally acknowledged that the serial killer has achieved an overwhelming ubiquity in popular culture. In 1978, John Carpenter's *Halloween* seduced cinema-goers with menacing images of a knife-crazed, masked villain, Michael Myers, stalking and, then, one-by-one, brutally hacking his teenage victims to their direful deaths. Myer's harrowing chaos awakened the small, sleepy town of Haddonfield, Illinois, and transformed it into a murderer's playground. Peter Hutchings (1996, 90, 92) notes that the despotic nature of *Halloween* "has been seen by many critics as inaugurating a new type of horror"; a horror that gave birth to reinvigorated "'killing machines'" now known as serial killers. Following *Halloween*'s positive reception, serial killing became a recurrent narrative theme, and myriad representations of the acts and the people who perform them became increasingly pervasive in the news media, literature, television, and film.

The growth and popularization of representations of the serial killer in the late 1970s and throughout the 1980s can be attributed to the discursive construction of serial killing in the mid-1970s. The discourse emerged around the time that Robert Ressler, the cofounder of the Federal Bureau of Investigation's renowned Behavioral Science Unit at Quantico, coined the term 'serial killer' in what he refers to as a "'naming event'" (Seltzer 1998, 16). The serial killer, however, "is not a single deliberate act of invention, but a complex process of accumulation of ideas and representations" (Warwick 2006, 554). The serial killer, then, is a discursive construct; a figure that has been reified in popular culture. As this collection showcases, it is appropriated in various ways to articulate anxieties—spoken and unspoken—and to make "certain acts . . . intelligible and meaningful for us" (Cameron 1994, 151). The numerous earlier portrayals of serial killers ('true crime' accounts and fictional) are strongly informed by the reported detestable and bewildering behaviors of real-life criminals. Serial killers such as John Wayne Gacy ('Killer Clown'), Ted Bundy, and David Berkowitz ('Son of Sam') had become household names and widely infamous by the end of the 1970s, specifically in the United States where they were 'active'. Their repugnant rape and abuse of women and children were reviled by society. It is unsurprising, then, the serial killer became "the 1980s movie monster *par excellence*" (Hutchings 1996, 91) with prominent exemplar films including *Calendar Girl Murders* (1984), *Nightmare on Elm Street* (1984–91), *The Deliberate Stranger* (1986), *Manhunter* (1986), *Henry: Portrait of a Serial Killer* (1986), *The Case of the Hillside Stranglers* (1989), and, of course, the expansion of the *Halloween* franchise (parts II–V) throughout the decade.

Undoubtedly, serial killing received its most unforgettable exhibition in Jonathan Demme's *The Silence of the Lambs* (1991) which became "a central point of reference in the renewed concern with serial homicide" (Jenkins 1994, 75). The film enjoyed massive critical and box-office success, and its winning three Academy Awards signaled an official acceptance of 'serial killer' films. In "The Serial Killer in Cinema," Kimberley Tyrrell (2001, 274) identifies that "the representation of the serial killer fluctuates across films, from hero to monster, from inevitable by-product of culture to an explicable force of nature, from irredeemable to pitiable." We are often positioned ambivalently viz-à-viz the serial killer who, traversing a spectrum of character forms, is embodied diversely. We may find ourselves confronted with a loathsome, well-styled narcissist—like Patrick Bateman who has a postmodern penchant for consumption—or we may be charmed by a crime-crusader—like Dexter Morgan who is romanticized as a 'knight with knives'. In the last two decades, the serial killer and serial killing has featured heavily in films including, but not limited to, *To Catch a Killer* (1991), *Natural Born Killers* (1994), *Se7en* (1995), *Copycat* (1995), *Fallen* (1998), *Summer of Sam* (1999), *The Bone Collector* (1999), *American Psycho* (2000), *Taking Lives* (2004), *Disturbia* (2007), *Funny Games* and its remake (1997 and 2007 respectively), *The Killer Inside Me* (2010), *The Call* (2013), and the *Scream* (1996–2011) and *Saw* (2004–)

franchises; television series such as the *Law and Order* (1990–) and *CSI* (2000–) franchises, *NCIS* (2003–), *Criminal Minds* (2005–), *Bones* (2005–), *Dexter* (2006–), *The Following* (2013–), and *Hannibal* (2013–); and novels such as *The Lovely Bones* (2002), as well as being the subject of a plethora of 'true crime' books focusing on the lives and exploits of real-life serial killers.

Multiple murder, however, is not a new 'activity' in the social. In *Serial Murder: An Elusive Phenomenon*, Steven A. Egger (1990, 29) contends that historical research "refutes the notion that serial murder is a contemporary phenomenon." He argues that individuals who are responsible for the murders of many people have probably always been among us in the 'real' world, even if not cinematically. Taking a sociological approach, Elliot Leyton (1986, 269) claims that multiple murderers are "very much men of their time," whose individual histories are enmeshed with social histories. For example, the preindustrial multiple murderer was most often an aristocrat, who murdered members of the 'rebellious' peasantry that threatened to usurp his authority (Leyton 1986, 273). In the industrial era, the major trend was the 'new bourgeois' who, operating as a 'middle-class' functionary, murdered social 'deviants' in an attempt to enforce a conservative "moral order" (Leyton 1986, 276). In the mature industrial era (post-World War Two) the multiple murderer is most often a failed middle-class subject who, feeling excluded from the normative social, wreaks "vengeance on the symbol and source of his excommunication" (Leyton 1986, 287–8). Given that there exists a social typography to multiple murder, and in light of the prevalence of serial killer representations, it seems reasonable to claim that the serial killer has achieved 'popular' status as a (western) "culture industry."

While the experience of sequential killings is not particular to late capitalist society, its representation is. Although serial killers and serial killing now feature in almost every aspect of contemporary media, until relatively recently no terminology or discourse was available to articulate its practice, and hence there existed no language to adequately speak its representation. Prior to the invocation of the term 'serial killer', labels such a 'repeat killer' or 'stranger killer' were employed to refer to a person who committed murder repeatedly. The concurrent use of various terms indicates an epistemological struggle to delineate a definition. This was a result of an ongoing cultural angst to come to terms with performances of cruelty that fall under the rubric of 'incomprehensible' and 'irrational'. The need for a unanimously employed label for menacing behavior underscores the desire to disarm serial killing as a source of cultural anxiety—for "that which is named is robbed of the power to threaten" (Hutchinson 1974, 46). The word "serial" seems most appropriate as it signifies the episodic pattern in which each instance of violence climaxes in murder while also connoting the anticipation of an offence or offences to follow. In terms of its representation, this label seems apt in a "mass culture [that] offers us a tradition of seriality in literature, film and television" (Coughlin 2000, 104).

Conceptualizations of serial killing have historically been in flux too. Egger (1990) claims that there are very few empirically determined definitions as most literature assumes that the terms "serial murder" and "serial murderer" are well understood within the culture. His seminal explanation, devised in 1983, reads as follows:

> Serial murder occurs when one or more individuals—in most known cases, male—commit a second murder and/or subsequent murder; is relationshipless (victim and attacker are strangers); occurs at a different time and has no connection to the initial (and subsequent) murder; and is frequently committed in a different geographic location. (Egger 1990, 4)

Robert Ressler, however, describes serial killing as "murder of separate victims with time breaks between victims, as minimal as two days to weeks or months. These time breaks are referred to as a 'cooling off period'" (quoted in Egger 1990, 5). Both these definitions focus on behavioral pattern, however Levin and Fox (1985) regard the serial killer as an individual who searches for and preys upon victims "whom he can rape and sodomize, torture and dismember, stab and strangle" (quoted in Egger 1990, 5). This latter definition understands serial killing as imbricated with acts of violence imposed on bodies, prior to murder itself, which has become a taken-for-granted aspect of serial killing tableaus. Our familiarity with the serial killer's domain of violence is an effect of a steady flow of representations generated by mass media (Egger 1998, 85). If the genre so crudely highlights our corporeality by confronting us with images of torn-open bodies and ritualistic viciousness imposed on people, especially women, the question begs: why is gratuitous assault so popular in our culture?

In *The Killers Among Us: An Examination of Serial Murder and its Investigation*, Egger (1998) argues that serial killing is spectacularized by the mass media in its discursive production of a genre that satisfies the culture's obsessions with violence. Violence is not a recent site of cultural consumption, entertainment or artistic muse. In *The Aesthetics of Murder* Joel Black (1991, 3) recounts Edmund Burke's interest in the enthusiasm of an eighteenth-century public who had gathered to witness the execution of Lord Lovat. Burke had pondered: "What work of art could compete with the reality of such a spectacle?" The mass media's gratuitous depictions of corporeal afflictions is indicative of the "effacement of the boundary between art and everyday life, the collapse of the distinction between high art and mass/popular culture" (Featherstone 2007, 64) that is characteristic of postmodernism. As murder is experienced aesthetically via mass media representation, the serial killer, despite his unsavoury activities, can be regarded as an artist—"a performance artist or anti-artist whose specialty is not creation but destruction" (Black 1991, 14). The aestheticization of serial killing provides a space where private desire and public fantasy converge to an extent that the culture's appetite for violence may be sated via the positioning of the viewer to read the shocking realism as if it were "an art form" (Egger 1998, 90).

Serial killing is discursively produced by and within a media-managed culture that is simultaneously hyperreal and aesthetic. Black (1991, 9) argues that while the mass media exposes us to "artistic presentations of violence," its mediation of actual events such as murder transgresses the lucidity of 'reality' to enter the domain of the "quasi-fictional" (Black 1991, 10). In *Using Murder* Philip Jenkins (1994, 81) remarks that, "in coverage of serial murder, the boundaries between fiction and real life were often blurred to the point of non-existence." Similarly, Egger proposes that, in the processes of informing the public, the media does not relay accurate reports but, rather, offers audience-fabricated accounts that construct a reality that effectively perpetuates a generic myth about serial killers and their 'work'. Egger (1998, 88) notes that central to these portrayals is the notion of the profile—a summary of the offender's "criminal background, his motivation, the type of victim he selects, and how the police will eventually catch him." Depictions of the Federal Bureau of Investigation as "experts on the phenomenon of serial killing," and responsible for the creation of the profile, function to validate the purported authenticity of these accounts (Egger 1998, 89).

The serial killing genre, in its enduring propagation by the film industry (primarily Hollywood), has become synonymous with uninhibited slaughter and a style of murder that is articulated in fine detail, often involving the playing out of a repertoire of sadistic games performed on vulnerable bodies that showcase the nightmares of our imaginations. The generic history of this cultural figure is located in the Jack the Ripper murders (Stratton 1996, 92) that took place in lower socioeconomic areas of Whitechapel in Autumn 1888. The five crimes attributed to the never-identified 'Jack' have been immortalized via a plethora of blood-curdling recollections of the bodies of female prostitutes found lying in slums—their abdomens ripped open from breastbone to pelvis, intestines thrown over the shoulders. The gruesome representation of the 'Ripper' murders has informed the mythology of the serial killer as an intelligent *male*, elusive, and obsessed with 'doing things' to and with bodies.

In postmodern culture, the body has become *the* pre-eminent site of spectacle or representation, "most insistently, as spectacle or representation of crisis, disaster, or atrocity" (Seltzer 1995, 130). This is realized nowhere more fully than in the discourse of serial killing, as serial killers, in both their generic construction and practice, take pleasure in violating bodies: rape, dissection, and cannibalism. Ed Gein, who terrorized Wisconsin in the 1950s, engaged in grave-robbing, murder, flaying, and cannibalism (Stratton 1996, 92). In the 1960s case of Albert Henry DeSalvo (the 'Boston Strangler'), it was reported that "[e]leven of his victims had been sexually assaulted; most died by strangulation, and their bodies had been desecrated and placed in bizarre positions after they were slain" (Kelleher and Kelleher 1998, ix). In searching the home of Jeffrey Dahmer, who targeted homosexual men in the Milwaukee area in the years 1978–91, police discovered hacked-off male genitalia in kettles and metal drums. With the fury of media attention serial killers receive, they shift instantly from obscurity to infamous icon, despite apparent public and legal condemnation. In 1992 public interest in Dahmer's trial, and more probably his savage exploits, was so great it was telecast live on national cable television. The violence committed by serial killers in the 'real world' is essentially abhorred but it is also *experienced* as intoxicating to the point that "the only remedy for us . . . is to get to grips with the fear by enjoying it" (Hutchinson 1974, 13).

It can be argued that the prominence, near celebration, of the serial killer in popular culture is symptomatic of late capitalism, and yet, also, it is the quintessential cultural figure utilized to critique this context of re-production. In "Kill and Kill Again," Richard Dyer (1997, 14) acknowledges that "[s]erial killing is often taken to be the crime of our age." Both the emphasis on the killer's seriality—the repetitive, episodic nature of the murders—and the constant *recycling* of narratives of serial killing are surely an effect of an economic milieu of rampant production and consumption. In late capitalism, "the world as we encounter it, including ourselves and the products of our labour, is transformed into a series of objects" (Bewes 2002, xi). This generic objectification, this *über*-commodification, of bodily spectacle is a function of the postmodern aesthetic that Jameson (1991) identifies as the "cultural dominant" synonymous with late capitalism. He elucidates on the 'silent' effects of postmodernism in relation to the present economic condition:

[T]his whole global, yet American, postmodern culture is the internal and superstructural expression of a whole new wave of American military and economic domination throughout the world: in this sense, as throughout class history, the underside of culture is blood, torture, death, and terror. (Jameson 1991, 5)

If, as Jameson proposes, there is a logic about the inevitable 'naturalized' corporeal destruction of those living in late capitalism, then serial killing remains the discourse most suited to stage the "underside" of culture as he describes it.

In recognizing that the serial killer remains a pervasive part of everyday life, *Murders and Acquisitions* chooses not to meditate further on *why* the serial killer is so popular but, instead, examines the potent instrumentality of this cultural figure. The collection is not underpinned by any notion of the serial killer as a stable category but, rather, treats it as a shifting cultural form whose nuances, offered via popular representations, beg to be evaluated for what they bring to light about our transient culture: the anxieties that are transparent and, perhaps more importantly, those that are not. Jon Stratton (1996, 77) has remarked: "It is possible that the concern with the serial killer is a discursive effect, a product of a generic construction which thematizes concerns within the population at large." This collection takes seriously this 'possibility', and thus undertakes a diverse exploration of the ways in which representations of the serial killer function to address concerns and preoccupations specific to their context of production.

The contributions within this anthology evaluate the ways in which the serial killer is imagined, articulated, and engaged with in popular culture. The chapters which comprise this book examine the serial killer at the level of *representation*—necessarily implicating a critical analysis of power relations undergirded by ideology. They explore how the serial killer is (re)appropriated in various cultural contexts and *fictional* narrative forms via the mediums of film, television, the novel, and fan production. There are, however, necessary limits placed on the scope of this project to ensure a continuity of overarching themes. The material contained herein does not venture to analyze representations of the serial killer produced by the news media, as its categorization as a nonfiction genre situates such representations as outside the focus of this book. This collection mobilizes a broad spectrum of cultural theory and performs rigorous textual analysis to examine the sophisticated ways the serial killer, as a cultural figure, is deployed to mediate and/or negotiate cultural anxieties including those relating to the nation-state, late capitalism, and categories of gender, sexuality, class, and 'race'. In its strive to make meanings of a range of narrative (re)appropriations of the serial killer, *Murders and Acquisitions* recognizes the "*continuing* invention of the serial killer, who is the necessary figure that is imagined to stabilize such confusion, even when confusion is [the] very condition from which he is created" (Warwick 2006, 567; emphasis mine).

The first chapter by Sara L. Knox argues the serial killer is a cultural product and resource that can be 'faked'—narrated and performed—to suit institutional purposes. To demonstrate this, Knox discusses in detail two examples of such invention. The first pertains to the crimes of Henry Lee Lucas. It is illustrated how police coaxed Lucas's seemingly verbose confessions to over 600 murders to assuage pressure to close unsolved case files. The second account relates to a particular narrative trajectory of the fifth and final season of HBO's TV series *The Wire*, in which the existence of a serial killer is fabricated for professional gains. This chapter showcases the malleability of the serial killer as a *cultural construct*, and the possibilities for leveraging it to achieve bureaucratic 'successes'.

My own contribution examines the discursive construction of the serial killer as a mythic synecdoche of the modern State by focusing on the films *Kiss the Girls* (1997), *The Watcher* (2000), and *Untraceable* (2008). It takes as its theoretical departure point Max Weber's conceptualization of the modern State as marked by a centralized bureaucratic administration and the legitimacy to use violence at will. This chapter argues that the generic traiting of the serial killer as a *man* who performs acts of surveillance and ruthless violence can be read as a representation of the terror that permeates surveillance society—which, no doubt, has intensified post-9/11.

Robert Cettl offers a critical reading of Shaun Costello's pornographic film *Forced Entry* (1973) to explore the ways its serial killer narrative functions to critique patriarchal masculinity, in particular its validation of male sexual power. With a specific focus on the rape-murder set piece, Cettl discusses a poignant paradox of patriarchy: the violent performance of masculinity it privileges and simultaneously seeks to pathologize and eradicate. The serial killer's violence in *Forced Entry* highlights a flawed patriarchy as it affects men (and women).

Discursively, serial killers are almost always 'white' males. The assumed 'maleness' of the serial killer serves to reinforce patriarchal notions of female public activity—particularly female violence—as a disruption to 'natural' order. Traditionally, aggression and violence are associated with masculinity which, within patriarchal constraints, is to be embodied by men. Kumarini Silva and Danielle Rousseau address this dominant gendering of the serial killer by exploring how *Monster* (2003), a highly acclaimed film about serial killer Aileen Wuornos, engages issues of feminine performance, sexual 'deviance', gender and violence, and criminal psychopathy. Applying feminist and criminological theory, it is argued that Wuornos is represented as both victim and perpetrator. In patriarchal terms, she is deemed masculine and sexually aberrant. The film rearticulates her non-feminine mannerisms and behavior as psychopathy, indeed as *monstrous*.

'Race' "is rarely figured as an important or constitutive element of the serial killer film" (Tyrell 2001, 276). Mark Bernard attends to this lack by examining the role of race in the *Saw* franchise (2004–10). He argues that through the course of seven films, which contain more twists than a Hitchcock suspense, the white Jigsaw killer, the film's primary antagonist, takes revenge on people because he feels invisible, and therefore unappreciated, in the social. Jigsaw selects victims he considers to be 'seen' (and therefore given attention) in society—people of color, women, and members of the working class—and stages traps which mutilate and ultimately kill them. Drawing on the seminal work of cultural theorist Richard Dyer, Bernard discusses how this sense of invisibility is located in the serial killer's 'whiteness', which the killer understands to be a site of disadvantage, instead of understanding his 'unmarked-ness' as empowering.

Christina Lee examines *American Psycho*'s blatant commentary on consumer culture. The apparent superficiality of Patrick Bateman, a serial killer with a commodity-fetish larger than life, epitomizes the gross depthlessness that marks postmodern culture (Jameson 1991). Bateman's appetite to consume extends to people, who he objectifies and treats as excess thus legitimating their disposal by whatever means necessary: ax, chainsaw, knife, nail gun. Lee reads this representation of the serial killer as a product of 1980s American culture which imbibed Gordon Gekko's adage: "greed is good." She makes the point, too, that the serial killer is now fetishized as a cultural by-product. It is this association between murder and material gain facilitating consumption, identified as symptomatic of our contemporary economic environment, which inspires the title of this book, *Murders and Acquisitions*.

The commodification of the serial killer is further explored by Oliver Carter, who presents a case study of the fan-produced (re)imaginings of the *giallo* film. As Carter explains, the typical *giallo* film narrative—a non-Anglophone form of representation—features a black-gloved serial killer murdering beautiful women in graphic and often highly sexual(ized) ways. This chapter focuses on the *Fantom Kiler* (1998–2008) series of films, an example of what Carter terms "slash production," to highlight key political and economic factors that impact on the making and distribution of these extremely violent and sexualized fan productions, and the ways in which the serial killer is rearticulated in this genre to produce disturbing affects for viewing pleasure.

Adopting the Romantic notion of "killer-as-artist" put forward by Joel Black, Louis Bayman demonstrates, with reference to a broad range of films, how the serial killer is frequently represented as having a particular relationship to *taste*. The serial killer, such as in the form of Jean-Baptiste Grenouille (in *Das Parfum* (2006)), has been depicted as having a crafted sensibility or sensitivity. He may also be imbued with a pronounced preoccupation with artistic production and/or performance in the vein of Hannibal Lecter. Bayman argues that this affinity with art enables the serial killer to embody cultural fears about deviance and cruelty, and the consequences of failing to maintain order and rationality.

Continuing an exploration of the relationship between serial killing and affect, Janice Baker approaches serial killing as a form of cinematic horror that repositions the viewer away from the logic of reason through a dismantling of subjectivity via 'modifications' to bodies. With a particular attention to the representation of serial killing in the museum space—theoretically a locus of modern rationality and order—Baker applies Deleuze's conceptualization of the cinematic image (as opposed to psychoanalytic theory) to argue that serial killing, in its disruptions of the body, induces an affective response for its viewership. This corporeal response is not located in an objectification of the viewer that is fixed to their Oedipal desires. Instead, moving through a discussion of classic films such as *Waxworks* (1924) and *House of Wax* (1953), Baker illustrates how serial killing narratives set in the museum can be philosophically understood as functioning to detach desire from subjective formation and to rupture any such encoding of identity.

Philip L. Simpson reads *The Strangers* (2008) as speaking to post-9/11 American middle-class anxieties about homeland security, and attendant concerns about class and gender. He contends that the film both employs a 'home invasion' narrative (already well established in the American cultural consciousness, principally via the mediation of the 'Manson Murders') and evidences a homage to the 1970s 'slasher' film to express cultural apprehensions about the perceived threat posed by unknown Others. In *The Strangers*, the representation of apparently random serial killing in the domestic sphere enables an exploration of a national fear of Others, both foreign and domestic.

Sofia Bull examines the popular forensic crime drama *CSI: Crime Scene Investigation* (2000–) to highlight significant implications for (re)conceptualizing the serial killer following the series's post-9/11 shift in the figure of the "expert investigator" from the profiler to the criminalist. The criminalist, who relies on the purportedly more objective discourse of forensic science as a method of detection, is often shown explaining the serial killer's criminality to be a result of 'aberrant' genetics. Previously, the profiler had determined psychological impact of social experiences as principally producing 'deviance'. Bull argues that as well as opening a narrative space to interrogate recent developments in genetics, this change in 'type' of expert investigator facilitates a removal of responsibility for criminality from the social and, instead, (re)locates it within the body of the *individual*, thus enabling a scientific identification of the serial killer as domestic Other—much like the terrorist is 'detected' by supposedly rational means as foreign Other.

Concluding *Murders and Acquisitions* is David Buchbinder and Ann Elizabeth McGuire's meditation on how and why contemporary audiences derive pleasure from the brand of justice implemented by Dexter in the eponymous narrative series by Jeff Lindsay. The authors focus on the first novel *Darkly Dreaming Dexter* (2004) which, they argue, is loaded with "doublings and dualisms." Dexter is characterized as a 'Jekyll and Hyde' detective of sorts—blood-spatter analyst by day, serial killer by night. Reading Dexter as a *homme fatal*, the chapter locates Dexter's 'masculine' charm as at the intersection of the three meanings of this term: fate, death, and seduction. Through a close reading of Lindsay's prose, Buchbinder and McGuire identify Dexter's murderous urges as analogous to sexual impulse. In order to control his temperament, Dexter kills only those whom he decides, in alignment with his father's moral code, deserve to die: unremorseful criminals who have fallen through the cracks of police and legal bureaucratic processes. In this duality, Dexter is marked as 'different'; his killing has a pathologized purpose. In a post-9/11 context, the perversity of Dexter's punishments is consumed enthusiastically by an audience for which retribution—and its consequent eruptions of gore, horror, and death—is normalized and legitimated.

References

Bewes, Timothy. 2002. *Reification: Or the Anxiety of Late Capitalism.* New York: Verso.

Black, Joel. 1991. *The Aesthetics of Murder: A Study in Romantic Literature and Contemporary Culture.* Baltimore: John Hopkins University Press.

Buckman, Adam. 2008. "Psych Out: Adam Loses his Mind Over 'Mentalist'." *New York Post*, September 23. www.nypost.com/p/entertainment/tv/item_6WQWsyO1XdSvcOkepdnAwM.

Cameron, Deborah. 1994. "Sti-i-i-i-ll Going . . . The Quest for Jack the Ripper." *Social Text* 40: 147–54.

Coughlin, Paul. 2002. "Getting Away with Murder: *American Psycho* and *Henry: Portrait of a Serial Killer*." *Metro Magazine* 124/125: 100–5.

Dyer, Richard. "Kill and Kill Again." *Sight and Sound* 7(9): 14–17.

Egger, Steven A. 1990. "Serial Murder: A Synthesis of Literature and Research." In *Serial Murder: An Elusive Phenomenon*, edited by Steven A. Egger, 3–34. New York and London: Praeger Publishers.

—. 1998. *The Killers Among Us: An Examination of Serial Murder and its Investigation.* New Jersey: Prentice-Hall.

Featherstone, Mike. 2007. *Consumer Culture and Postmodernism*, 2nd edn. London: Sage.

Hutchings, Peter. 1996. "Tearing Your Soul Apart: Horror's New Monsters." In *Modern Gothic: A Reader*, edited by Victor Sage and Allan Lloyd Smith, 89–103. New York: Manchester University Press.

Hutchinson, Tom. 1974. *Horror and Fantasy in the Cinema.* London: Roxby.

Jameson, Fredric. 1991. *Postmodernism, or, the Cultural Logic of Late Capitalism.* Durham: Duke University Press.

Jenkins, Philip. 1994. *Using Murder: The Social Construction of Serial Homicide*. New York: Aldine De Gruyter.

Kelleher, Michael D., and C. L. Kelleher. 1998. *Murder Most Rare: The Female Serial Killer*. Westport, CT: Praeger.

Leyton, Elliott. 1986. *Compulsive Killers: The Story of the Modern Multiple Murderer*. New York: New York University Press.

Lindsay, Jeff. 2005 [2004]. *Darkly Dreaming Dexter*. London: Orion Books.

Sebold, Alice. 2002. *The Lovely Bones*. New York: Little, Brown and Company.

Seltzer, Mark. 1995. "Serial Killers 2: The Pathological Public Sphere." *Critical Inquiry* 22(1): 122–49.

—. 1998. *Serial Killers: Death and Life in America's Wound Culture*. New York and London: Routledge.

Stratton, Jon. 1996. "Serial Killing and the Transformation of the Social." *Theory, Culture and Society* 13(1): 77–98.

Tyrrell, Kimberley. 2001. "The Serial Killer in Cinema." *Alternative Law Journal* 26(6): 274–77.

Warwick, Alexandra. 2006. "The Scene of the Crime: Inventing the Serial Killer." *Social & Legal Studies* 15: 552–69.

Filmography

American Psycho. DVD. Directed by Mary Harron. 2000; Santa Monica, CA: Lionsgate Home Entertainment, 2005.

The Bone Collector. DVD. Directed by Phillip Noyce. 1999; Universal City, CA: Universal Studios Home Entertainment, 2001.

Bones. Television. Produced by Kathy Reichs, Emily Deschanel, and David Boreanaz. Los Angeles, CA: Fox, 2005–.

Calendar Girl Murders. DVD. Directed by William A. Graham. 1984; Westlake Village, CA: Trinity Home Entertainment, 2005.

The Call. Directed by Brad Anderson. 2013; Culver City, CA: TriStar Pictures.

The Case of the Hillside Stranglers. VHS. Directed by Steve Gethers. 1989; Beverly Hills, CA: Delta Library Company, 1990.

The Cell. DVD. Directed by Tarsam Singh. 2000; Los Angeles, CA: New Line Home Entertainment, 2000.

Copycat. DVD. Directed by Jon Amiel. 1995; Burbank, CA: Warner Home Video, 1995.

Criminal Minds. Television. Created by Jeff Davis. New York, NY: CBS, 2005–.

CSI: Crime Scene Investigation. Television. Produced by Jerry Bruckheimer. Santa Monica, CA: CBS, 2000–.

The Deliberate Stranger. DVD. Directed by Marvin J. Chomsky. 1986; Burbank, CA: Warner Home Video, 2010.

Dexter. Television. Produced by Showtime Networks. New York, NY: Showtime, 2006–.

Disturbia. DVD. Directed by D. J. Caruso. 2007; Universal City, CA: Dreamworks, 2007.

Fallen. DVD. Directed by Gregory Hoblit. 1998; Burbank, CA: Warner Home Video, 1998.

The Following. Television. Produced by Rebecca Dameron and Michael Strick. Los Angeles, CA: Fox, 2013.

Funny Games. DVD. Directed by Michael Haneke. 2007; Burbank, CA: Warner Home Video, 2008.

Funny Games. DVD. 1997. Directed by Michael Haneke. 1997; New York, NY: Fox Lorber, 1999.

Halloween. DVD. Directed by John Carpenter. 1978; Beverly Hills, CA: Anchor Bay Entertainment, 1997.

Hannibal. Television. Produced by Carol Dunn Trussell. New York, NY: NBC, 2013.

Henry: Portrait of a Serial Killer. DVD. Directed by John McNaughton. 1986; Orland Park, IL: MPI Media Group, 1998.

The Killer Inside Me. DVD. Directed by Michael Winterbottom. 2010; Orland Park, IL: MPI Media Group, 2010.

Kiss the Girls. DVD. Directed by Gary Fleder. 1997; Hollywood, CA: Paramount Home Entertainment, 1998.

Law and Order. Television. Produced by Dick Wolf and Joseph Stern. New York, NY: NBC, 1990–.

Manhunter. DVD. Directed by Michael Mann. 1986; Beverly Hills, CA: MGM Home Entertainment, 2007.

Monster. DVD. Directed by Patty Jenkins. 2003; Culver City, CA: Sony Pictures Home Entertainment, 2004.

Natural Born Killers. DVD. Directed by Oliver Stone. 1994; Santa Monica, CA: Lionsgate Home Entertainment, 2000.

NCIS. Television. Produced by Donald P. Bellisario and Avery C. Drewe. New York, NY: CBS, 2003–.

Nightmare on Elm Street. DVD. Directed by Wes Craven. 1984; Los Angeles, CA: New Line Home Entertainment, 1999.

Saw. DVD. Directed by James Wan. 2005; Santa Monica, CA: Lionsgate Home Entertainment, 2005.

Scream. DVD. Directed by Wes Craven. 1996; Burbank, CA: Walt Disney Studios Home Entertainment, 1997.

Se7en. DVD. Directed by David Fincher. 1995; Los Angeles, CA: New Line Home Entertainment, 2004.

The Silence of the Lambs. DVD. Directed by Jonathan Demme. 1991; Los Angeles, CA: Orion Pictures Corporation, 1997.

The Strangers. DVD. Directed Bryan Bertino. 2008; Universal City, CA: Universal Studios Home Entertainment, 2008.

Summer of Sam. DVD. Directed by Spike Lee. 1999; Burbank, CA: Walt Disney Studios Home Entertainment, 1999.

Taking Lives. DVD. Directed by D. J. Caruso. 2004; Burbank, CA: Warner Home Video, 2004.

The Watcher. DVD. Directed by Joe Charbanic. 2000; Universal City, CA: Universal Studios Home Entertainment, 2003.

To Catch a Killer. DVD. Directed by Eric Till. 1991; Chatsworth, CA: Image Entertainment, Inc., 1999.

Untraceable. DVD. Directed by Gregory Hoblit. 2008; Culver City, CA: Screen Gems, 2008.

2

'Made-up and Made-over': Faking the Serial Killer and the Serial Killer Fake

Sara L. Knox

Introduction

In the decades since the peak of the serial killing crisis of the 1980s and early 1990s—an era that saw the trials of some of the biggest names in the pop cult pantheon of killers[1]—serial killing has become "something to do (a lifestyle, career, or calling)," and the serial killer, as Mark Seltzer (1998, 4) puts it, identifiable "as something to be (a species of person)." The serial killer still routinely features large in the true crime genre, and is drawn frequently in those genres that have made his (or, less frequently, her) name: the thriller, detective noir and, his exemplary realm, horror (Simpson 2000; Hutchings 2001). So, too, is the figure of the serial killer well exercised in contemporary cultural theory. It is taken as representing the threat of repetition to symbolic order—what Philip Jenkins (2002, 2) terms the "singular evil of seriality itself"; a crisis of distinction as much cultural as psychopathological, as signified by the threat of likeness and doubling, that typicality beneath which strangeness lurks (Stratton 1996; Seltzer 1998, 40–1). The serial killer can also be read as an embodiment of the monstrous (Jenkins 1994, 2002; Simpson 2000) and, as an elaboration of these concepts, the dark sublime, that is, if serial killing offers the most aesthetic and "scenical" of killings (to use Thomas De Quincey's term, retaining its irony) then it is that kind of murder most fitted to representation (Black 1991, 52–60). It is in this latter context that I'd like to carry forward Seltzer's insight that the serial killer has become "something to be" and serial killing "something to do" to examine the narrative and performative compulsions in the tale of murder as serial killing, that is, not only the shaping pressure exerted by institutional cultures and practices, but also the sheer giddy liveliness of the tale of murder, where—to paraphrase the English proverb—it is words, not blood, that will out.

If the serial killer has clear currency and visibility as a category of "something to be" then it also follows that the role of killer becomes available to actual persons; a fact that complicates the logical accounting of forensics as exemplified by serial killer typologies. The identification of a given criminal as a 'serial killer' must come after the fact of the killing/s, even if the killer exists only speculatively—as a 'profile'—before they are captured. It might therefore be supposed that typological categories are based on forensic fact: fact as it applies to the crime in question and/or to crimes *like* the crime in question. The assignment of a crime to its correct typological place, and a criminal to type, relies on precedent and classification by likeness of kind: on the extrapolation *from* type *to* type. These iterations of type circulate as cultural products (handbooks for writers in the crime genre, for instance, that offer tips for the portrayal of a credible serial killer) but so too do they circulate as templates for identity.

It is this easy iteration of type—its circulation as cultural product; as actual and potential identity—that makes inevitable the fake, and the faked, serial killer. This chapter explores elements of invention—what goes into making a serial killer—and the institutional and cultural uses to which that invention can be put. My starting point is a discussion of the case of Henry Lee Lucas, whose claim to have killed more than 600 people over the ten years proceeding his arrest in 1983 was readily accepted by State and Federal investigators, regional and national press, and the wider public. Secondly, I would like to unpack one dramatization of the process by which a serial killer is invented, and the uses to which that empty figure is rhetorically put. By examining the controversial plot pivot point of the closing season of HBOs critically acclaimed drama series *The Wire* (in which Detective McNulty fakes a serial killer to bring on a 'red ball' investigation[2]) I propose an inflammatory paraphrasing of Voltaire, that is, *if the Serial Killer did not exist, it would be necessary to invent him.* The serial killer proposes as much as he disposes, not only are his (and I use the pronoun advisedly) killings an engine of narrative, but—institutionally speaking—he is, at times, an opportunity too good to miss.

Invention

In the summer of 1983, itinerant odd-jobs man, Henry Lee Lucas, was in the jail cells in Montague County, Texas.[3] He'd been arrested by the County

Sheriff, W. F. 'Hound Dog' Conway and Texas Ranger Phil Ryan for unlawful possession of a firearm. Lucas had been in the custody of the two men previously. Conway and Ryan had had Lucas under a close eye for more than eight months, believing him responsible for the disappearance and death of a local lady, Kate Rich, with whom Lucas and his common-law wife Becky Powell had been living. Conway and Ryan also suspected Lucas of murdering Powell, despite his protestations that the girl had hopped a ride at a truck stop and left him. Once again they had Lucas behind bars, but still lacked the evidence necessary to tie him to the disappearance of both women (Shellady and Hansen, 1994).

After four days in the cells, Lucas broke down, telling the deputy on guard that he'd "done some bad things"—including having killed Rich and Powell. He elaborated in a written statement: "I've been killing ever [sic] thing I can for the past 10 yeas [sic] dogs cats. . . . I did not want to do these things but I can't stop I have tryed [sic] to but can't once my mind takes over." Lucas's admissions to a compulsion for killing women had a maudlin sub-text: in killing Powell he'd lost his "only true friend and wife." He concluded the statement with the plea, "[w]hat ever inside me I hope will leave me alone" (quoted in Shellady and Hansen 1994, 13–16).

Over the next two days Lucas expanded on the history of violence implied by his first confession; an elaboration both quantitative and qualitative as the would-be killer indicated his responsibility for a wide range of cases, while at the same time broadening and deepening his narrative of the murders most immediately pressing: that of Kate Rich and Becky Powell. Lucas told how "he got the urge to kill" Rich while driving her to Ringold in his old blue Ford:

> I had a brown handle butcher knife laying in the seat next to me and I got it in my right hand and stuck it all the way in Kate's left side. Kate fell over against the door. . . . I opened the door . . . and she fell half way out of the car. I stepped over her and pulled her down the embankment. She bled some in the car and a lot on the ground. I immediately undressed her and layed out her clothes next to her. I got naked and screwed her until I finished. . . . As far as I know, the knife could have stayed in the car. (Quoted in Shellady and Hansen 1994, 338)

Lucas then told how he and Becky Powell had been out one day, sitting on a blanket in a pasture. They'd argued and Becky had hit him. Feeling she never would "grow up or take responsibility," he took the "meat cutting, carbon knife with an ivory bone handle [that they] kept . . . handy in case someone came up on us" and, "before" he "knew it," had "hit her in the chest part":

Becky didn't say a word, she was gone before I knew it. . . . then I took advantage of her. . . . I don't know why I get something out of that but I do. I then took the knife and cut her head off, arms off and then her head off. I cut her legs off at the hips. I'm not sure but I think I left her legs whole. I cut the trunk of her body in two parts. I stuffed her body in 3 pillowcases except her legs and hips. I started to drag her and bury her but change my mind and left her scattered out of a 50 foot square. As far as the Knife, it may be there yet. (Quoted in Shellady and Hansen 1994, 341–2)

Lucas's account of murdering Rich and Powell editorialized on the *business* of killing and body disposal: "everybody says people bleed alot but they don't bleed that much" (quoted in Shellady and Hansen 1994, 342); that a body don't come to much more than "a five gal bucket of ashes" (Shellady and Hansen 1994, 340) when you burn it right down in a woodstove, and that the worse it smells the better it's likely to burn (Shellady and Hansen 1994, 340). Embellishments like these illustrate Lucas's 'style' as a false-confessor; that show why he could so easily figure himself as one of America's worst serial killers, and why that self-styling would be so widely—and easily— accepted. These flourishes of detail and the meditative tone with which they are delivered suggest expertise and dedication, the surrealized professional interest of a man dedicated to his work. The baroque detail also marks Lucas as a man not too particular about facts. People do bleed a great deal, but that rather depends where you stab them. And nobody can burn a body down to a small amount of ash if they're using an old woodstove to do it. Nor does how a corpse smells have much to do with the rate at which it burns. Lucas's formula for throwing off the issue of the murder weapon is likewise revealing: for all he knows it "could have stayed" in the car (the Rich murder) or "might yet be" in the field where he'd scattered bits of Becky Powell. That vagueness contrasts with his precise descriptions of the knives he used to kill the women: so looming are these tools that he gives a capital to the word "Knife" in his statement about Powell's death. It is as if Lucas hasn't decided yet whether the knife is or isn't "there." He has realized the murder weapon better than the killing itself because the knife is a prop in an unfinished narrative: unfinished because it's in the process of being invented.

Lucas's confessions are informed by an established discourse about serial killing. In 'making himself up' and in forming his persona as drifter-killer, Lucas was acting out an already established cultural script, but so too was that persona and its script instantiating the institutional context for its reception. Rather than incredulity at the extent and ferocity of Lucas's killings, from the outset his interrogators collaborated with, and encouraged, Lucas's confessions. They, too, took their cues from a script as lurid as it was compelling. After making his statement about the deaths of Rich and Powell, Lucas went on in a rush about the many other women he'd killed so he could have sex with them. Ranger Phil Ryan later admitted he'd been skeptical at the time, but what had he done with his skepticism? He'd opted "to test Lucas by making up murders" (Shellady and Hansen 1994, 20). This was a significant move on Ryan's part, and like Lucas's hallmark style of high-violence described in a meditative tone, with lurid detail inserted to enliven the narrative, Lucas's interrogators gave as good as they got. "'Every day',", Ryan recalled:

> I would invent one [murder], and I would say, "Alright, what about this one?" A high percentage of the time [Lucas would come back with], "Yeah, yeah, I did that." I knew he was lying because there was no such case. *But what do you do*? (Quoted in Shellady and Hansen 1994, 20; emphasis mine)

Having proved to himself that Lucas has no idea what he's talking about, does Ryan put a stop to things? Does he go on the record with his doubts? No, he does not. He shrugs off his doubts. The phrase "what do you do?" points to the good institutional reason for letting Lucas's false confessions slide: when the two cases of nearest interest to them rest on a confession, they can't afford doubt cast on the credibility of the confessor. In larger terms "but what do you do?" means: if someone's willing to roll over for an open case, you let 'em. A confession is an opportunity too good to miss.[4]

But Ryan does not just let the inventive Lucas run on, he shapes the direction of the confession, and the result is the escalation of the murder narrative, quantitatively and qualitatively, and the increase of its reach and potency. Ryan himself discovers good institutional reasons for hearing out Henry, and for believing him. Taking cues from the Federal Bureau of Investigation's bureaucratic claims on the investigation of serial killing (Jenkins 1994), and the (re)definition of the threat of the serial killer to stress the reach of such crimes, not just over time (repetition) but across geographical space, Ranger Phil Ryan offered the cooperative Lucas scenarios that fit well with both the categorical and the literal violence of the serial killer. But in Ryan giving Lucas an inch, the putative killer takes a mile. Ryan asks if Lucas had "ever cut a woman's head off and moved it away from the body" (Shellady and Hansen 1994, 20) and Lucas raises the stakes without a pause, answering that not only had he done this, he'd once "carried a head all the way to Arizona."[5] And, after he was indicted for the murder of Kate Rich, Lucas passed on to Ryan a "series of sketches of women's heads" he'd made while trying to remember the head he'd taken to Arizona, and thrown out of his car window. It is not coincidental that references to dismemberment became a staple in the stories Lucas would subsequently tell lawmen over the next weeks and months; confessions the lawmen hoped would close the open cases they'd brought Lucas to look at. (To 'look at', literally: Lucas drew identifying detail about victims from files left invitingly open on the desk in front of him, giving new meaning to the term 'open case file').

Lucas's building up of his stories of post-mortem sexual attacks on the bodies of women, then of dismemberment and the spreading around of the body parts, reflects in content the process by which the confessions—and his reputation or 'profile' as a killer—was being constructed. The narrative structure of Lucas's confessions to murder—claims not only on the open cases, but also about the nature of serial killing itself—mirrored the context of the confessions' production: they are cut-ups, pastiche, stories reassembled from a diverse array of component parts. Fact is drawn from the pages of case files; while the style of violence and the killing 'demeanour' came from the already well-publicized serial killing careers of murderers like Kenneth Bianchi, John Wayne Gacy, Ted Bundy, and Ed Kemper.[6] By the early 1980s the characteristics of contemporary serial violence and serial killers, as a predatory class, had already been taken up by popular culture through crime fiction, film, and television portrayals of serial killing. For example, the first three of Lawrence Sanders's best-selling 'Deadly Sins' novels offered portrayals that built upon existing popular knowledge about the 'psychopath', the 'psycho killer', and the 'sex maniac'. Even the semi-literate Henry Lee Lucas had a deep cultural well of stories from which he might draw.

Aspects of Lucas's confessions are extracted from near sources. The story of the head carried all the way to Arizona and then thrown out of a window resonates in subtle ways with stories elsewhere in circulation—like the by-then well-canvassed confessions of Ed Kemper, a man who knew how to tell a good story about his own compulsions. It is hard not to hear echoes in Lucas's confessions—right from the outset with his "what ever inside me I hope will leave me alone"—of what was then one of the longest running murder trials in the United States, that of 'Hillside Strangler' Kenneth Bianchi. Bianchi's lawyers invoked the insanity defense and the accused performed confusion on the stand and claimed to be the victim of one of the nastier multiple personalities to which 'he' was host. The notoriety of the trial, and its complexity, was increased by the admission of testimony gained under hypnosis, so that a central discursive thread of the trial was of 'shadow' truths and realities. So too was the story of David Berkowitz, 'Son of Sam', by then, well-rehearsed by the press, who took up the theme of the killer's claims of demonic possession with relish.[7] Lucas was no reader but he did watch a lot of television: indeed, for periods of his life that was pretty much all he did. An idiosyncratic store of stories and images shape the universe from which

Lucas's florid confessions came, some with no relationship to the subject of killing but that give tone and texture to his accounts.

Lucas's litanies about a life spent on the move, driving from state to state, covering impossible distances, and carting body parts with him, seems to refer to a world in which all sorts of things are magically possible, like that memorable Dristan advertisement, with its refrain about "sending your sinuses to Arizona!" In this, an enormous black suitcase swoops into the sufferer's living room, closing upon and vanishing him—sinuses, head, body and all—then whisking off to deposit the sufferer on the patio of a desert hotel. In both the fro-shot and the to-shot the image of the suitcase looms in place of the man—luggage large enough for a spot of corpse-carrying, like the leaking suitcase that Henry—in John McNaughton's mythologizing serial killer bio-pic of Lucas, *Henry: Portrait of a Serial Killer*—leaves standing at the side of the road at the film's end. While an advertisement for nasal decongestant clearly has nothing whatsoever to do with the business of serial killing, its image repertoire offers an icon suggestive not of relief but of oppression—the sinister frame (see Figure 2.1) showing a backlit head, the face a shadowed blank over-laid by a stylized representation of the nasal passages.

FIGURE 2.1 *"Send your sinuses to Arizona": Dristan advertisement (1960), Adclassix.com.*

If we replace the phrase "Dristan Tablets" with 'Serial Killer' the image makes no less sense, for its iconographic particulars are by now familiar to us from the cover art of true crime books and genre fiction, and from film posters. The image of the faceless man who can be in one place at one time and then hundreds of miles away is a fitting precursor for the drifter killers of the 1970s and 1980s, among them that claimant for world title, Henry Lee Lucas.

The more direct source for Lucas's self-styling as a killer was the already canvassed confessions of killers like Ed Kemper. In Elliot Leyton's retelling of Donald Lunde's portrait of Kemper, 'the Co-ed killer', we find the subject of post-mortem violence and disposal of the body:

> . . . taking Polaroid photographs of his actions, he decapitated Luchessa, disrobed and dissected Pesce, and sexually assaulted various body parts. Later, he drove into the mountains with Pesce's body in a plastic bag, and buried it, disguising the site with techniques he had learned from the Boy Scouts of America. He kept the heads of both women for a time, but then threw them into a ravine. (Leyton 1986, 45)[8]

That description of the body dump sight is almost impossible to read—to sound in the head—in anything but the breathless voiceover of a Crime and Investigation Network primetime documentary. This kind of narrative of baroque violence may not have been as familiar then as now, but it was nevertheless—from the point of view of law enforcement, and of media and their public—what shaped the plausibility of Lucas's confessions. The day after he had talked to Lucas, Sheriff Boutwell told reporters that Lucas had killed women "all over" and that "he would dismember the bodies and carry the pieces around with him in his car" (Shellady and Hansen 1994, 25).[9] That description recalls the killings of Ed Kemper, ala Lunde, ala Leyton—and it also recalls a good number of other serials killers not named Ed. It recalls, it should also be noted, the kinds of killing behaviors that are least typical of serial killings (and serial killers) in general, but most popularly associated with them. As if this was not baroque enough as a narrative of violence, Boutwell upped the ante a few days after this initial statement to the press, telling how Lucas (quoted in Shellady and Hansen 1994, 26) "sometimes buried" his victim's bodies, and "sometimes burned their bodies and sometimes dismembered them and carried pieces of the bodies with him in his car." For the lawmen hearing Lucas's confessions, the shape and style and tone of previous killers' accounts of killing would have shaped the way they heard Lucas, and—if we are not to take them as completely cynical in the motivations—must have given an air of credibility to what he was telling them.

By this kind of sampling of the possible cultural and narrative stock for the telling of a career in serial killing, we can begin to see both the variety of that stock—it is a deep well—and to understand the role of pastiche in such tellings, the way in which Lucas shaped his tales of murder *and* the grounds for the credulity of those listening to him. One of the most incredible aspects of Lucas's confessions—the wide variety of ways in which he claimed to have killed his victims—gained credibility in proportion to its very outlandishness. Henry Lee Lucas was not just a serial killer but was a digest of possible methods of serial killing and his narratives of violence form a compendium of techniques. Lucas was serial killing embodied. As I've argued elsewhere (Knox 2004a; 2004b) there was a constituency for Lucas's tales of murder. The credulity of that constituency was shaped by the long tail of the representation of murder (see Halttunen 1998; Biressi 2001), a tradition that stands in curious relation to the classifying and organizing typologies of the human sciences, which nevertheless feed into it. By "curious relation" I mean that one tends toward synthesis, aggregation and borrowing, and the other toward analysis, sorting and identification: ostensibly opposing logics. But Lucas's narratives of killing appeal to both traditions, and he is the *product* of both. There is a bleed between the fictional and the real, and their modes (see Picart and Greek 2009), but there's also a great deal of instability about what counts as real and, on the other hand, the facticity of analytical systems. The undergirding of fact to Lucas's confessions is appallingly light, but that seems not to matter. The sheer baroque ferocity of the violence narrated creates its own aura. So it is not merely, as Nixon (1998, 223) argues about the "gothic postmodern," that the "horror of the real" cannot be argued without recourse to the fictional but that the "horror of the real" lies in the sobering sense that horror is not all that horrifying. It is entertaining, and it is an invitation: to representation and to agency, personal and collective. The horrors of serial killing have a constituency, and one that is not simply reducible to those exemplary subjects of the vicarious, audience and reader.

More specifically, the confessions offered an opportunity, institutionally and bureaucratically, to make sense of the horror of serial killing both retrospectively and prospectively. Lucas's telling of his crimes gathers into one killing career all the variations of cruelty and compulsion that have been canvassed in the case studies of serial killers preceding him. That was a making of retrospective sense of the killing, in the light of types of killers and killings already infamous. But so too were Lucas's confessions a prospective 'making sense' in terms of the institutional context for the confessions: they 'made sense' of open cases, 'made sense' of the Texas Rangers expertise and efficiency, just as they 'made sense' of the local sheriff department's suspicion of drifters, of outsiders to the community. Lucas's confession of depredations on a community, and across state lines, is not a narrative solely of his own making. It is one put together from his cultural knowledge of serial murder and from his responses to the prompts and hints and cajolery of his interrogators. Lucas tells his tales of murder, playing to his interrogators' expectations and fears. The process of narrative construction can be seen in numbers of documented exchanges between Ranger Phil Ryan and Lucas, of which the following is but one example:

> Ryan asked Lucas if he had ever gone into a house. Lucas answered "I went into a trailer house." When asked where, he said, "Out west Texas." How had he killed her? "Strangled her," Lucas said, "but not with my hands, something in the trailer." (Shellady and Hansen 1994, 27)

A couple of months later Lucas would tell investigators that he had a photographic memory, and that was why he knew so much, remembered so much. And, more importantly: "the more I talk about it [his murders], the clearer the picture" (quoted in Shellady and Hansen 1994, 36–7). What Lucas is describing is the process of narrative texturing: he knows so much because he's the author of the tale. But we must also keep in mind the fact that Lucas is an 'author' under pressure to produce a certain *kind* of narrative. The collaborative process of invention can be most clearly seen in the findings of the Texas Attorney-General's investigation into the techniques of the 'Lucas Task Force' and the reliability of the Lucas confessions. When the Attorney-General's chief criminal investigator deposed Lucas at length on the way he had been questioned in those busy months after his first confession, Lucas was as ever blandly eloquent, but this time about the contingency of the production of his own tales of murder:

> . . . we were talking to [Lucas] about how he would start of [sic] saying "Well, I stabbed them." And that didn't seem to please, then he would say: "Well, then I shot them," and if that didn't please, "well, I choked them." (Mattox quoted in Shellady and Hansen 1994, 126)

Both the would-be killer and his interrogators had stakes in the 'story' (or 'case', as the credulous had it) building, and in how it would be told; investments not reducible to practicalities (for Lucas, the comforts of special treatment in jail, and chaperoned jaunts intra- and interstate to body-dump sites, and for the investigators, the ability to close score upon score of open homicide cases). In the early months of questioning, the 'Lucas task force' described Henry's strange peccadilloes, habits and phobias that seemed to tie him directly to the 'Orange Socks' murder (Lucas protested to hate wearing socks, but left the bodies of the women he'd supposedly killed in nothing but their socks (Shellady and Hansen 1994, 42)); habits and phobias that there was no evidence of, outside of Lucas's own view of himself. It is still impossible to say whether such quirks were true, Lucas's invention, or a baroque elaboration of the pathologies the investigators expected to see. Both the fabulist and the constituency for his tales worked the same store of raw narrative material; the cultural stuff out of which the figure of a killer could be formed. It is the capacity of the confessions to make good institutional sense that compels credulity or, at the least, leads law enforcement not to air their doubts in public. In all the talk about Lucas's *compulsions*—over the years in which he was believed to be a killer and then the years during which those beliefs were debunked—what was elided is the productive drive of the confessions, and the opportunities they afforded. The institutional horizon to the confessions worked to make them stick, even in the face of contrary fact. Lucas offered the numbers: 360 dead, across the continental United States. And those numbers proved too tempting in the beginning blush of a decade characterized by zero-tolerance, law and order policing, and moral panic. The narrative of compulsion that is Lucas's confessions is, therefore, partly a portrait of pathology and its personification (that is, Lucas acts the killer) but it is also a portrait of institutional pathologies, of police work beyond its limits: temptations and compulsions of quite another kind.

Contingency

> I can't make shit up, can I? It is what it is.
>
> (Det. MCNULTY, *The Wire* 2008)

The possibility of 'making shit up' is less the preoccupation of the fifth season of *The Wire* than the probability—the inevitability—that the made up shit will fly. There are, among all the other important plot streams, two parallel stories of fakery that unfold over the season's 13 episodes. Detective McNulty tampers with a crime scene, then subsequently invents forensic and circumstantial evidence to suggest a serial killer is at work in Baltimore killing homeless men, and acting out sexually on their corpses. McNulty's scheme is inextricably connected to the story of Scott Templeton, an investigative reporter for *The Baltimore Sun*, who capping a series of invented informants and embroidered on-the-record quotes, reinvents himself as the only reporter to be directly contacted by the killer of homeless men.

Both McNulty and Templeton have their ethical foils. McNulty's fellow homicide detective, Bunk Moreland—like McNulty, 'natural-born murder po-leese'—deplores McNulty's scheme. Returning to his now no longer funded investigation of the 22 bodies found in 'the vacants' (the Marlo gangs' drug murders that feature in Season Four), Bunk explains, "I'm a murder police. I work murders. I don't fuck with no make-believe . . . [I'm] working this shit like I'm supposed to" (*The Wire* 2008). And at *The Baltimore Sun* the 'old school' editor of the City Desk has a dossier on Templeton's fabrications, the sources that can't be confirmed or that don't exist. As far as the editor of the city desk is concerned, Scott Templeton is a particular kind of reporter: one of those guys who "start small, with a quote here and there that they clean up, and then it's a whole anecdote, and eventually they're seeing amazing shit. . . ." (*The Wire* 2008).

The institutional contexts for the lies of McNulty and Templeton are, on the face of it, alike. The fact-finding and fact-checking processes of a reputable daily newspaper should, like that of careful police work, hinge on reliability. Indeed, it is the threat to the credibility of sources that so animates Templeton's editor. The professionalism of newspaper journalism is what is at stake—professionalism is much at risk from expedient managerial policies as from the rogue investigative strategies of one ambitious reporter. Just as Templeton imperils the basic contract of investigative journalism, McNulty's scam puts the business of careful police work at risk: natural-born murder police are meant to solve and close cases, within the limits and conditions of their work. In the Baltimore Homicide Department those limits and conditions are a budget blowout, backlogs in the processing of lab work, and none of the paid overtime so essential to the running of a surveillance investigation. That a natural born murder police works in a state of permanent and cynical tension with his superiors is to be expected. McNulty's foul-mouthed disdain for the stupidity and cupidity of his superiors makes his doing the job well all the more necessary and satisfying. But he puts all this at risk when he reverses the logics and processes of detection to invent a case rather than solve one. He is not working backwards from an outcome: he is making shit up; using his skills to subvert the art of good police-work. McNulty's cynicism has both lost context and widened its reach: it approaches the pathological.

What McNulty is doing is finding good institutional reasons for screwing with the very facet of the institution he is most bound by, and most respects: the art of real detective work. Like Lucas's interrogators, McNulty too has found the temptation of the numbers (all those open cases) too difficult to resist. So he honours the spirit of policing, but not its letter: an ethical balancing act that is awkward, to say the least. When Detectives McNulty and Kima Greggs are sent to the Bureau to get a profile on a killer that McNulty knows does not exist (Episode 8, "Clarifications"), McNulty scoffs at profiling as useless and a waste of time—but nevertheless sees himself in the FBI profile of the killer (white male, not college educated but "nonetheless feels superior to those with advanced education" . . . employed in bureaucratic or public service "from which he feels alienated" . . . "has problem with authority," and . . . "deep-seated resentment against those who've impeded his progress professionally" (*The Wire* 2008)). He sits listening, shifty-eyed and with his jaw working agitatedly, and the cast of his eyebrows tells the story of the profile hitting its mark: that he is "a high-functioning alcoholic" who has "difficulty sustaining relationships" (*The Wire* 2008). To the renegade detective's ear, the profile strings together empty truisms about the serial killer, but it has also identified the shadow-side of his own not inconsiderable gifts. The trumped-up crime scene is a *virtuoso* performance, "a demonstration to the authorities"[10] and a demonstration of authority: "an opportunity for" McNulty, the killer's author, "to assert his superiority and intellectual prowess" (*The Wire* 2008). (It is precisely that kind of thing that got McNulty banished from homicide to the river police at the end of Season One). Earlier in the season, another aspect of this same typological 'bleed' can be seen. In Episode Seven the lack of affect, compulsion, and sense of superiority of the (author of the) serial killer is made clear when Griggs vents to McNulty about the grief of the family of the latest 'victim' of the serial killer (that victim is a homeless man that McNulty himself has abducted and left happily ensconced in an out-of-state shelter). Griggs complains of having to sit there with those "salt of the fuckin' earth" people telling them why their "eldest . . . met his end being bit on and fucked with by some sick motherfucka who used him for jerk off purposes" (*The Wire* 2008). McNulty squirms at hearing this but his discomfort is nothing compared to his suffering in the scene immediately before. Grateful to have had the cost of two nights' surveillance for another case put onto the overtime sheets for the serial killer investigation, one of McNulty's fellow detectives tells him, "You're doing good here, Boss" (*The Wire* 2008). McNulty bridles in shock, saying, "*What* did you just call me?" He can bear the idea of collateral damage (the needless suffering of the family who think their son has been murdered), but can't take the loss of his role as outsider in the team: how can he both *bite* the hand that feeds and *be* that hand?

What's underlined in the scenes discussed above are the costs—ethical and otherwise—of a categorical crisis. The moral, ethical and practical distinction between the scamming reporter (Templeton) and the scamming detective (McNulty) dissolves at the point where both seem to slide into sociopathy: willing to blink at the collateral damage caused by the scheme, in the grip of an overmastering sense of self and rightness of purpose, and following the course of rogue individualism. McNulty and Templeton refuse bureaucratic processes, procedures, and protocols, but nevertheless follow an idealized notion of their own profession: one so idealized it can only be served by transgression. Templeton is self-serving: he wants to make it as an investigative reporter, to get to the big time on the *Washington Post.* But that pursuit of the Pulitzer also shows a fealty to the profession's exemplum. McNulty, by comparison, is perpetrating a fraud (a victimless crime with an invented perpetrator) to wrest municipal funding from a Baltimore City school system in crisis by presenting the mayor and his subordinates with a 'worse' disaster than the state of school funding. The beneficiary of the scam is not McNulty; he even sets himself up to fail at something where success is very dear to him—the ability to close a case. The two scams are also enacted differently: Templeton creates his inventions by himself. McNulty has confederates, he is still working procedurally in that sense. As McNulty's hoax case develops there is a widening circle of cops 'in the know': the other homicide detectives quickly learn that McNulty is the go-to guy for getting overtime, cars and materiel. In this way, those 'in the know' are letting it happen—indeed, they're getting something out of it. By contrast the people 'in the know' about Templeton's scheme 'know' because they've made the effort to confirm their doubts and suspicions. And they most certainly do not profit, or approve.

But to see the distinction this way is to miss, as Lester Freamon puts it, "following the money trail" (*The Wire* 2008). Both schemes profit the institutions defrauded (a bump in sales and the prestige of a Pulitzer for the newspaper, the closing of cases and improved quarterly crime stats for the department) as both are enacted in the context of a fiscal blowout. *The Baltimore Sun* is downsizing, and the managing editor, Klebanow, and executive editor, Whiting, are not only firing employees, they are eager for stories that can increase sales, and aren't willing to look too closely at the factual particulars of a scoop. Like Ranger Phil Ryan listening to Henry Lee Lucas's claims to have killed women all over the United States, the managing editors of the newspaper are not thinking too hard about the gift they've been given. They're saying to themselves: "But what do you do?" McNulty's scam also provides unexpected dividends to the municipality being milked by the hoax (the Mayor, for instance, gets leverage in a political struggle between himself and the sitting Governor).

It is significant that both acts of fakery are set against a backdrop of scarcity and absence, for this underlines what Mark Seltzer (1998, 108) suggests is the "empty circularity . . . at the level of construction and self-construction" of the serial killer. It is not accidentally the tale of a serial killer at loose in

Baltimore that tempts Templeton into making his leap from the embroidery of fact to pure invention. Like McNulty, he has more than enough cultural material out of which he might 'make shit up', and the results of his invention, not surprisingly, turn out to be narratively consistent with McNulty's, even though both men are engineering their fakes independently. Everything remains to be found in both narratives, everything is there for the taking, and there is no core of the real to contend with the fake. There is a nullity at the center of the story (viz. there is no serial killer), but that is only the most obvious of the phantasms from which the scam is made. The homeless, from which the class of the victims is drawn, are not a constituency: they are a nonconstituency (as the Mayor discovers, making great political capital out of their defense). Even the signature of the killer's *modus operandi* is a symbol of absence: the ribbon wrapped around the wrist ordinarily signals a prompt for something else: something that needs to be remembered or done. Around such absences "making shit up" is not only possible, it's inevitable: there is only the shit.

The logic, and necessity, of 'making shit up' works conceptually elsewhere in the season. At the close of the scene in which Greggs complains to McNulty about having to talk to the next of kin of the most recent homeless victim, she plucks up her car keys and tells McNulty she's "gotta run" as she's "got shit to assemble." With a derisive look at McNulty, she adds, "You didn't tell me about that part of it, did you muthafucka?" (*The Wire* 2008). Greggs has to go home to put together the cot she's bought from Ikea. And—as we see later in the episode—that shit just won't hang together. The scene with Greggs balancing the bi-fold of instructions, dowels, and component pieces, and getting more and more frustrated as one part assembled results in another collapsing, shows how things that are meant to work—that are designed to fit together, and hold—don't.[11] Things fall apart: the Western District's patrol cars; the homicide detective's pool cars; the newspaper business; the crime stats (that the Mayor's assistant wants 'juked' just for the quarter running up to the Mayor's gubernatorial bid); the schools; the DA's case against the corrupt Senator; and the municipal budget. These are all things that should fit together, and hold—but they don't, and it's into the void of that collapse that flows the living stuff of invention (McNulty's and Templeton's scams), a flow that, ironically, props up the working of the system.

What the fifth season of *The Wire* so artfully dramatizes are the compulsions of narrative, and its institutional contingency. By representing the symbolic, moral, and literal economies that ask—indeed require—the invention of the serial killer, we can see how empty the category of the serial killer is; how empty, and yet, how malleable: a nothing from which a great deal can and must be made.

Notes

1 John Wayne Gacy, Ted Bundy, Denis Nilsen, Ed Kemper, and the Hillside Stranglers, Kenneth Bianchi and Angela Buono, were all killing throughout the 1970s, and were tried for their crimes in the 1980s. Jeffrey Dahmer was brought to trial in 1992 for killings committed throughout the 1980s.

2 A 'red ball' case is one that draws political and media attention, and that also therefore demands both a quick and massive response from the police charged with the investigation. A 'red ball' case means that all the staff of a given department, the full roster of homicide detectives, will be committed to the case.

3 The following account of the facts of Lucas's arrest and confessions is derived from the most reliable factual source I have been able to find—the as yet unpublished book length study by Brad Shellady, one of the investigators paid by Lucas's defense team, and Gunnar Hansen. For an extended analytic comparison of the facts of the case and the myth, see Knox (2004b).

4 The Lucas confession spree came in the decade prior to the increase of critical scrutiny (from academic experts and legal representatives who aired their doubts in appellate courts around the United States) of the system's tendency to produce wrongful convictions through the extortion of false confessions, too great reliance on unreliable eyewitness testimony, poor forensic practice, and endemic problems with the inadequate legal defense of those who stand to lose the most from a conviction: three out of four of these elements are relevant to the Lucas case. The gazumping forensic certainty of DNA evidence that so shaped the controversy over false convictions belongs to a period after Lucas, and it is hard to imagine Phil Ryan so airily saying "but what do you do?" in that later—much changed— forensic universe.

5 Ryan may have been drawing on the kind of violence already made famous by Donald Lunde's (1976) portrait of serial killer Ed Kemper.

6 Philip Jenkins (1994, 92) notes the increased production and steady sales of true crime literature, an increase that spiked in the 'crime' decade of the 1980s, and an increase characterized by the high proportion ("between a third and half the output") of such works devoted to the subject of serial murder. He also notes that the mid-1970s cases of Ed Kemper and Dean Corll caused a mini-spike in the numbers of book-length studies.

7 The theme of the serial killer's demonic possession has been kept alive by serial killer fiction (see Simpson 2000, 19–21) but also by a lively fundamentalist religious scholarship in the United States that argues that cases of actual demonic possession are routine, and that some of the worst are what the secular state has tried as the serial crimes of sociopaths (see, for instance, Livingstone 2004; Pacey 2004).

8 Leyton's (1986) *Hunting Humans* was not published until a few years after Lucas's confessions, but he draws his account from Kemper's confessions in Lunde's 1976 study *Murders and Madness*.

9 Sheriff Boutwell was one of the earliest of the law enforcement officers to question Lucas in the hope he could close an open case (the murder of the woman known on the file as 'Orange Socks', and the murder for which Lucas would subsequently be convicted and sentenced to death).

10 The phrase is Ed Kemper's (the 'Co-Ed Killer'). See Elliot Leyton, *Hunting Humans* (1986, 68).

11 The scene with Greggs and the Ikea furniture also explicitly pairs her and McNulty as types. In an earlier season we've seen McNulty's own lost battle with the makings of his son's bedroom furniture from Ikea. The two suffer, and react, the same way. And necessarily so for the structure of the drama: it is Greggs who blows the whistle on McNulty's and Freamon's scam.

References

Biressi, Anita. 2001. *Crime, Fear and the Law in True Crime Stories*. Basingstoke: Palgrave.

Black, Joel. 1991. *The Aesthetics of Murder: A Study in Romantic Literature and Contemporary Culture*. Baltimore: Johns Hopkins University Press.

Halttunen, Karen. 1998. *Murder Most Foul: The Killer and the American Gothic Imagination*. Cambridge: Harvard University Press.

Hutchings, Peter. 2001. *The Criminal Spectre in Law, Literature and Aesthetics: Incriminating Subjects*. London and New York: Routledge.

Jenkins, Philip. 1994. *Using Murder: The Social Construction of Serial Homicide*. New York: Aldine de Gruyter.

—. 2002. "Catch Me Before I Kill More: Seriality as Modern Monstrosity." *Cultural Analysis* 3: 1–17. Accessed December 17, 2012. http://socrates.berkeley.edu/~caforum/volume3/vol3_article1.html.

Knox, Sara. 2004a. "A Gruesome Accounting: Mass, Serial, and Spree Killing in the Mediated Public Sphere." *Journal for Crime, Conflict and the Media* 1(2): 1–14.

—. 2004b. "The Confessions of Henry Lee Lucas: High Numbers and Higher Stakes." In *Famous American Crimes and Trials* (vol. 5), edited by Frankie Y. Bailey and Steven Chermak, 35–52. Westport, CT: Praeger.

Leyton, Elliot. 1986. *Hunting Humans: The Rise of the Modern Multiple Murderer*, London: Penguin.

Livingstone, John. G. 2004. *Adversaries Among Us*. Fort Bragg, CA: Lost Coast Press.

Lunde, Donald T. 1976. *Murder and Madness*. San Francisco: San Francisco Book Co.

Nixon, Nicola. 1998. "Making Monsters, or Serializing Killers." In *American Gothic: New Interventions in a National Narrative,* edited by Robert K. Martin and Eric Savoy, 217–36. Iowa City: University of Iowa Press.

Pacey, Steven. 2004. *Deceptive Lights: The History and Imminent Collapse of Satan's Empire*. Lincoln, NE: iUniverse.

Picart, Caroline J., and Cecil Greek. 2009. "The Compulsions of Real/Reel Serial Killers and Vampires: Toward a Gothic Criminology." In *Dracula, Vampires, and Other Undead Forms: Essays on Gender, Race, and Culture,* edited by John Edgar Browning and Caroline Joan Picart, 37–62. Lanham, MD: Scarecrow Press.

Seltzer, Mark. 1998. *Serial Killers: Death and Life in America's Wound Culture.* New York: Routledge.

Shellady, Brad, and Gunnar Hansen. 1994. "Things Only the Killer Knew: The Framing of Henry Lee Lucas." Unpublished manuscript in the possession of the author.

Simpson, Philip L. 2000. *Psycho Paths: Tracking the Serial Killer through Contemporary American Film and Fiction.* Carbondale: Southern Illinois University Press.

Stratton, Jon. 1996. "Serial Killing and the Transformation of the Social." *Theory, Culture and Society* 13(1): 77–98.

Filmography

The Wire. Television. Produced by Ed Burns and Joe Chappelle. New York, NY: HBO, 2002–2008.

3

Serial Killing, Surveillance, and the State

Alzena MacDonald

You want to know all about me, don't you? . . .
I lived with them all that June. I lived in the attic.
I was watching. . . .
And then I decided to declare myself. . . .
Just a little pinprick. There. Kiss me.

NICK RUSKIN AKA "CASANOVA" in *Kiss the Girls*, 1997

The opening credits of *Kiss the Girls* appear on a dimly lit, black background. A climate of *terror* mounts as the piercing strains of a violin, which pre-empt the anguished cries of a young woman, are heard. In a close-up shot, crackling flames frame the image of the *unknown* woman, who is wearing only her delicate night-gown as she moves casually around her second-level bedroom. She is being watched, but she doesn't know.

The audience does, and we are invited to partake in this act of lewd voyeurism via camera perspective and the seductive, retrospective narration of the watcher. The faceless male, who later refers to himself as "Casanova," recounts the annunciation of his presence to the 'object' of his gaze; how he viciously injected her with a sedative drug—"just a little pinprick." As the plot unravels we learn that *watching* is a part of his ritualistic preparation for kidnapping his unsuspecting female victims. After 'declaring' himself, he imprisons the women; his sex slaves, his concubine, in a subterranean lair where he rapes them repeatedly prior to *murdering* them—punishment for some apparent 'transgression' of trust. The watcher, who we are initially positioned to identify with through flashback rhetorical address, is a serial killer. For viewers familiar with the codes and conventions, characterization and *mise-en-scène* of the serial killer narrative, this representation of the serial killer as performing acts of surveillance and ruthless violence exists in the consciousness of those fluent in its 'language'. This chapter focuses on the generic reification of the serial killer in three filmic representations: *Kiss the Girls*, *The Watcher* (2000), and *Untraceable* (2008). It offers a response to the begging question: what is the ideological investment of such repetitive representation? What cultural anxieties are articulated via these persisting elements of character? While being definitive traits of the serial killer, surveillance and (legitimacy to use) violence are also foundational tenets of the modern State. According to Max Weber, the modern State is founded on the monopoly of the *legitimate use of violence* within a given territory and *centralized bureaucratic administration* is a necessary feature of political and social organization (Held 1989, 39–44). Acknowledging this discursive parity between serial killer and the State, this chapter argues that, in its generic construction, the serial killer can be read as a synecdoche of the modern State.

In popular culture, the serial killer is thought of as a male predator "who relentlessly stalks his prey in a series of compulsive acts that must inevitably end in murder" (Kelleher and Kelleher 1998, x). The act of stalking which is referred to in this definition implies an on-going pattern of tracking and spying, a process by which information on the movements of a potential victim is collated and ultimately used to control them. For example, the serial killer in *The Watcher*, David Allen Griffin (Keanu Reeves), is shown to be logging into a diary the daily activities of the women he stalks—his soon-to-be victims. Sharing a crash profile on the 'perp', FBI detective Joel Campbell (James Spader) tells his psychiatrist: "After he [Griffin] picks his target, he'll watch her for weeks. He'll study every detail of her routine: when she goes home, when she goes to sleep." Throughout the film the killer's voyeurism is delineated by a changing camera angle which shifts the narrative perspective from omniscient to that of Griffin. Through his eyes (and heavy breathing) we fixate upon his young, attractive victims, we move with him as he makes his silent murderous approach, and as he carefully tracks the detection progress of his nemesis, Campbell.

The serial killer is oft-configured as cataloguing the private acts of his potential victims in a prelude to murder. This behavior acquires certain cultural significance when understood in terms of the State's bureaucratic surveillance practices. In *The Political Illusion*, Jacques Ellul (1972, 141) declares that "[a] modern state . . . is primarily an enormous machinery of bureaus." The deployment of bureaucratic strategies in the late eighteenth century is a key marker of the disciplinary formation of the modern State. One kind of strategy was surveillance, which was regarded as necessary to manage an increasingly urban society precipitated by emergent capitalism (Dandeker 1990, 116–17). Surveillance, as defined by Anthony Giddens (1995, 169), "refer[s] to two connected phenomena. First, to the accumulation of 'information'—symbolic materials that can be stored by an agency or collectivity. Second, to the supervision of the activities of subordinates by their superiors within any collectivity." Surveillance, as exhibited in the figure of the serial killer, involves "the focused, systematic and routine attention to personal details for purposes of influence, management, protection or direction" (Lyon 2007, 14).

The act of watching *incognito* is a *bona fide* characteristic of the serial killer, both expected by viewers and characters within the diegesis. In *The Watcher*, a title which signposts this generic feature, Detective Campbell angsts: "What are the odds he's watching us right now?" Similarly, in *Kiss the Girls*, Washington DC detective and forensic psychologist Dr Alex Cross (Morgan Freeman) says: "If [he's] not [here], he's watching. I guarantee you." Watching as a means of social control can be understood in terms of Michel Foucault's (1979) conceptualization of 'disciplinary power', which is thought to be continuously and anonymously exercised, rather than possessed, and is imbricated with knowledge. This power–knowledge relationship is fundamental to the modern practice of surveillance, which is thought to discipline the individual purely via observation. In *Power/Knowledge* Foucault (1980) identifies Jeremy Bentham's Panopticon as the model for disciplinary power that was designed to solve the problems of surveillance within modern industrial societies.

The Panopticon is a 'diagram' of a ring of prison cells surrounding a centrally positioned tower in which stands an overseer. Each prison cell has two windows, the exterior allowing daylight in, and the interior facing the windows of the tower. This configuration enables the visibility of bodies and gestures, under a system of centralized observation, *without* the object's knowledge. Foucault asserts that in this model of 'visibility' the exercise of power and the registration of knowledge are simultaneously achieved by a continuous, dominant overseeing 'gaze'—without knowledge, power cannot be exercised without force (Deleuze 1988, 26). The internalization of the 'omniscient', penetrating, inspecting gaze is sufficient to ensure that the individual becomes a willing and competent judge of her/himself, and thus becomes a model for the internalization of the 'gaze' of the [State] authorities (Staples 1997, 28). Disciplinary power operates without "need for arms, physical violence, [or] material constraints" (Foucault 1980, 155) to produce self-controlled, docile bodies.

The serial killer, in its synecdochic relationship to the State, signifies "a technique of power/knowledge that creates and exploits a new kind of visibility, of organizing people so that they can be seen, known, surveilled and controlled" (Hillier 1997, 139). At the denouement of *Kiss the Girls*, the killer, Detective Nick Ruskin/Casanova, on the pretext of giving security advice to his lone escapee, Dr Kate McTiernan (Ashley Judd), reveals the surveillance methods he enacted prior to attempting to kill her (see Figure 3.1).

KATE: "What does taking your garbage out the morning of have to do with anything?"

NICK: "Night before, anyone can tear through it. . . . Think about it. A guy could come by, say, Tuesday night, three in the morning, dump your trash in one of those 30-gallon plastic sacks. Haul it down to an abandoned lot and bingo! There it is. What a lady eats, how often she shaves. He can even tell a lady's time of the month. Anything you want to know. What kind of lipstick she wears, and used condoms. How often she's gettin' it? Twice a week? Three times? The same guy, different guys? Of course, that doesn't apply to you. Let's face it. In your case, it's been quite awhile. Not since that, that surgeon. What? Six, seven months ago? You were special, Kate. Do you have any idea how much time I gave you? Months. Yes, months."

FIGURE 3.1 *Internalizing the 'gaze': Kate (Ashley Judd) senses being watched in* Kiss the Girls *(1997), Paramount/Rysher. Photographer: K. Wright. The Kobal Collection.*

Serial killers are discursively constructed as performing surveillance; gathering information about their (potential) victims which will be useful to gain control and exercise power.

As an 'invisible' watcher the serial killer demonstrates that bureaucratic surveillance is a practice conducive to the exercise of power. This is thematically expressed in *The Watcher:* Griffin lures Detective Campbell into a cunning cat and mouse game in which he mails Campbell a photo of his next victim giving him a day to ascertain her whereabouts. Each girl is considered to be 'loner', a marginalized subject. This exemplifies Jon Stratton's (1996) claim that postmodern serial killers "choose as their victims down-and-outs, hitchhikers and so on who are, at that moment, outside the social" (82). Despite Detective Campbell's media broadcasting of the various "Jane Does," the killer succeeds in executing their murders and eluding the police on several occasions. The killer's strike rate is unblemished because, in effect, these women fall out of the surveillance network and are, therefore, not noticed. The serial killer exercises a form of disciplinary power, which is not extended to individuals. The State is 'Big Brother' but our inability to 'see' one another makes us all vulnerable to and reliant on the State. The discursive construction of the serial killers as a visual *virtuoso* represents this dependency and the terror it creates.

Furthermore, in its synecdochic relationship to the State, serial killers are frequently depicted as residing or performing their depraved deeds in the privacy of a 'bad place', an off-limits jurisdiction. For example, in *The Silence of the Lambs* (1991) Jame Gumb, the killer whom the FBI are trying to track, adorns the skins he has flayed from his victims' bodies to parade his transvestism in the basement of his home. In *The Cell* (2000), the killer's private sanctuary is an underground, sadomasochistic chamber in which he suspends himself from the ceiling over his victims' corpses by threading small metal rings through the flesh on his back. In *Kiss the Girls*, cop-killer Nick Ruskin inhabits a covert cave in the woods which his co-conspirator describes as "subterranean Gothic." The residences of the killers are 'secret houses' which hold the mysteries and evidences of their crimes. These secluded spaces, where the killers' monstrous delusions are unleashed and played out freely, signify that the State—its bureaucracy and legitimacy to commit violence—is often exempt from the rigour of its own surveillance.

The serial killer can be read as representing anxieties about living under the State's bureaucratic 'gaze'. Henri Lefebvre (2000, 147) contends that terror is the "logical and structural outcome of an over-repressive society" coordinated by a general strategy which he identifies with State bureaucracy. In the bureaucratic deployment of everyday life "terror is diffuse, violence is always latent" (Lefebvre 2000, 147). The disciplinary transformation of the modern state marked a transition from public and tortuous of punishment to institutionalized forms of anonymous social control via surveillance. Forms of corporeal and capital retribution—public flogging, hanging, decapitation, and burning at the stake—were replaced with the development of modern disciplinary technologies, such as the asylum and penitentiary. Informed by principles of rationality, these institutions sought to deter and reform by reconstructing the 'deviant' into the 'ideal' moral, autonomous individual. While "discipline in the modern period achieves a decorporealized discretion" (Seltzer 1998, 129), the State, as Weber posits, retains legitimacy to use violence at any time.

In modernity, State bureaucracy replaces the Church as moral disciplinarian, making the 'individual' feel guilty and ensuring their consent. It is thought that the internalized 'gaze' functions ideologically to eliminate any individual's duplicity in relation to the State. The repressive nature of the bureaucratic State is maintained by both ideological "*persuasion* and *compulsion* (punishment, laws and codes, courts, violence kept in store to prevent violence, overt violence, armed forces, police . . .)" (Lefebvre 2000, 144). Terror is the logical outcome as the State's "persuasion turns into compulsion" (Lefebvre 2000, 159). As bureaucracy functions to acquire knowledge of the subject population, it binds the 'individual' into an ongoing practice of excessive nonviolent writing through the process of filling out forms and questionnaires. Bureaucracy operates as a "system" that has a "hold on every member separately" (Lefebvre 2000, 147), while submitting every member to that system. Terror is extensive, yet we don't recognize it in any physical form. In Gramscian terms, the hegemonic power of the modern State is undergirded by its ability to persuade the population to *consent* to its bureaucratic processes. When the people do not consent, the State retains legitimacy to use violence as a "means of coercion" to *force* compliance (O'Kane 1996, 19) to the limitations of living in a monitored social. In its representation as performing surveillance and committing acts of extreme violence, the serial killer functions as a mythic synecdoche of the State, an embodiment of the terror that permeates everyday life in a bureaucratic surveillance society.

In *Kiss the Girls*, the serial killer's treatment of his female victims typifies the exercise of disciplinary power and the threat of violence that it implies. Detective Dr Cross profiles Ruskin as a 'collector'. Surveying the case files, he says: "I bet these women are alive," later explaining that this "demonstrates his power; his dominance." As he must attend his respectable job as a Durham detective, Ruskin cannot be physically present to monitor his many simultaneous victims, and therefore imprisons each one alone in an underground cell with a viewing grate that can only be opened by him from the exterior tunnel-side. In this quasi-panoptic maze, Ruskin has control over when he can see his victims, but a right to visibility is removed from them. He instructs the helpless women never to call out. The women obey his command as they do not know when Ruskin will return, when he may hear them, and what he will do to them if he does. For fear of retribution, Ruskin's captives internalize his gaze, his watchful authority as though he is always there. The vulnerable women are silenced, and become docile bodies, at the mercy of a sadomasochistic murderer.

Viewers are privy to Ruskin's impending capture of Kate. We are offered scenes of Kate walking while being trailed and watched by a shadowed male figure. When Ruskin adds Kate to his "collection," she asks: "What do you want from me?" He rasps: "Everything." Ruskin personifies the nature of the State that, ironically, *demands* consent and total complicity. However, when Kate dares to disregard her captor's authority and calls out from her individual dungeon—refusing to consent—she learns that she is one of many women trapped by the tunnel walls at the mercy of an "enthusiastic rapist." The audience witnesses how the killer's brand of 'disciplinary power' turns to a violent rage—to force—after Ruskin somehow discovers her disobedience. Moving toward her with drug-filled syringe, he threatens Kate: "Didn't I warn you about breaking the rules." She begs: "I'll do anything you want." Assured of his dominance and power, he exclaims: "I know you will." As he approaches, however, Kate uses her well-honed kick-boxing skills to attack Ruskin and, following a frenetic chase through the woods, is able to make a near-death escape.

State surveillance can be understood as a response to burgeoning urbanization; serving to make known, and thus control, the subject population. In "Urbanism as a Way of Life," sociologist Louis Wirth (1938, 20–1) argues that urbanization engenders a loss of community and social alienation. He describes the development of the modern, 'soul-less' city as resulting in the "substitution of secondary for primary contacts, the weakening of bonds of kinship, and the declining social significance of the family, the disappearance of neighbourhood and the undermining of the traditional basis of social solidarity." According to Wirth, in the city, the new locus for the increasingly dense settlement of "socially heterogeneous individuals" (Wirth 1938, 8), there will still be face-to-face contact, but they will be "impersonal, superficial, transitory, and segmental" (Wirth 1938, 12). Bureaucratic surveillance serves to make the whereabouts of, and connections between, persons known to the State, which is particularly useful in counteracting criminal activities. However persons living within the social remain relatively anonymous to each other, and quite literally comprise the 'society of strangers' that Wirth, and earlier also Georg Simmel (1950) in 1903, envisioned. This perception of the social as an evasive space is articulated by Griffin in *The Watcher* when he asks rhetorically: "It's amazing, isn't it. We're all stacked right on top of each other, but we don't really notice each other, do we?"

In the postmodern representation of serial killers, the city is still very much depicted as the hub of hidden agenda and intrigue; a personal amusement park for the serial killer to pursue his perverse pleasures. Stratton (1994, 11) observes that "[t]he idea of mapping the city is a metaphorical expression of this surveillance." Just as the mysteries of the city are the domain of state surveillance, it is also the passion and addiction of the serial killer. "The fact that serial killing is a criminal phenomenon primarily of the twentieth century emphasizes the effect that the anonymity of the modern city and the reification of mass culture has had on the life of the individual" (Coughlin 2000, 104). In its synecdochic relation to the State, serial killing, like surveillance, are focused on bodies in cities. In her PhD dissertation, Jennifer Reburn (2012) addresses the significance of the surveillance of urban space in serial killer films in relation to men and masculinity. She argues that in the 1990s serial killer films emphasized "the vast labyrinthine city" (2012, 120). She notes that:

> The general landscape of many of the 1990s films, particularly those set in urban areas, is monitored and mapped in various ways. Of the thirty-one 1990s films, twenty-four are located in cities, these settings highlighting difficulties in scrutinising heavily populated areas. These cities are often nightmarish, claustrophobic and dystopian. (Reburn 2012, 124)

This is true of *The Watcher*, a film loaded with a plethora of fast action shots of the killer scouring and coveting spaces of metropolitan Chicago. These scenes mimic the mechanized application of state bureaucracy that gazes at citizens in a random fashion. This "methodical, technology-driven, impersonal gaze . . . is fixed on our bodies and their movements" (Staples 1997, 4). Scenes of concrete skyscrapers, flashing lights, helicopter fly-overs, subways, street-walks, and high-speed chases through busy, traffic-infested streets, married with an edgy soundtrack, provide a frenzied, (over)stimulated urban setting for the depiction of crimes affecting the *corpus*. Seltzer (1995, 129) argues that this kind of "spectacular public representation . . . has come to function as a way of imagining and situating, albeit in a violently pathologized form, the very idea of 'the public' and more exactly, the reactions of bodies and persons to public spaces." Serial killing is the definitive public activity.

Given the serial killer's fascination with the city, this cultural figure can be understood as a regeneration of another: the flâneur. The flâneur received 'his' most "famous eulogy" (Tester 1994, 1) in the writings of Charles Baudelaire. Walter Benjamin (1983) in *Charles Baudelaire: A Lyric Poet in the Era of High Capitalism*—his much celebrated analysis of Baudelaire's work—locates the flâneur's pervasiveness to nineteenth-century Paris. The flâneur is the man who performs flânerie, that is, a casual activity of strolling within the newly created metropolis, gazing, looking at people, and taking pleasure in the sites and spectacle of the city. He is considered the observer of the interactions of daily life but he does not merge with the crowd. Baudelaire's flâneur can be read as a "perambulating Panopticon" (Mazlish 1994, 50), an all-seeing man of the masses, an extension or personification of the silent State bureaucratic apparatuses that govern. Modernity's flâneur is distinguished from the masses in the sense that he is "the man *of* the crowd as opposed to the man *in* the crowd" (Tester 1994, 3). Similarly, in the postmodern context, "[t]he serial killer is often described as abnormally normal, an everyman, a citizen X melting into the background" (Coughlin 2000, 102).

The serial killer can be conceptualized as a cultural reincarnation of the flâneur; a "secret spectator" (Tester 1994, 7). Benjamin's (1983) argument that the flâneur 'died' in the nineteenth century is based on the supposition that the breadth of capitalist markets left no space conceptually for him to explore. The rhetoric of flânerie can be used to read the serial killer as one who soaks up the essences of the people without their knowledge in order to gain an audacious sense of power. In its imitation of flânerie, the serial killer similarly reverberates the practices of bureaucratic surveillance performed by the State. He engages in acts of surveillance in urban spaces so 'he' might attain knowledge of, and thereby gain *power* over, 'his' victims. To paraphrase Benjamin (1983, 41): "No matter what trail the serial killer may follow, every one of them will lead him to *commit* a crime."

Like the flâneur, the serial killer is configured as male. The dominant representation of serial killers as being *men* that indulge in voyeurism and violence can also be located in the discursive construction of the modern State. First, "[m]en watching men manipulate and control the apparatuses of surveillance that the post-security society has come to rely on" (Denzin 1995, 186). Furthermore, violence committed by the 'male' killer is an ideological imperative for, as Weber contends, the State is considered to be "a relation of men dominating men, a relation supported by means of legitimate (i.e. considered to be legitimate) violence" (quoted in O'Kane 1996, 5). In these ways, the myth of the serial killer, characterized by the parameters of patriarchal governance, can be regarded as an ultra-personification of the State and its ideological regulation of everyday life.

The maleness of the serial killer preserves the domination of men in the public sphere and his violence reifies aggression as a 'male' trait. From a feminist position, the construction of serial killing is considered an expression of male aggression against women. The terms *gynocide* and/or *femicide* have been coined to describe the repetitious killing of women, thus casting the female as the object of the serial killer's desire (Jenkins 1994, 139). Kelleher and Kelleher (1998, x–xii) acknowledge that, although the culture tends to efface her presence in fictional representations, the female serial killer does in fact exist; it is simply the bias of the media that 'silences' her activity. In the seldom instance of her representation, the female serial killer is often depicted as operating in the private domain. Alternatively, the female serial killer may be depicted as working alongside a male partner, as his underrated, relatively passive accomplice. Examples of women involved in such crime 'partnerships' include Catherine Birnie who committed four calculated murders in Perth, Australia, in 1986 with her de facto husband, David Birnie. Another such case is that of Rosemary West who was convicted of ten murders that she committed with her husband Fred West in Gloucester, England, in the 1970s. As Stratton (1996, 85) notes, "[m]uch of the horrified reaction to these women comes from their transgression of the caring roles assigned to them in the patriarchally ordered social." Certainly such was the response to Aileen Wuornos who killed seven of her male sex clients in Florida in 1989 and 1990.

The framing of the serial killer's savage violence as having a relationship to the State has its origins in the modern rationalization of crime. In modernity, it was thought that murder was always committed with motive, for motiveless crime was a transgression against reason and this threatened the social order (Stratton 1996, 80). Repetitious murder by one individual was best understood as the work of an "'over-socialized'" individual, a vigilante who reinforced the bourgeois moral and social order, by murdering 'deviant' women (McLaren 1993, xiv). A classic example is the case of Jack the Ripper, who in the late-nineteenth century terrorized the streets of London gutting five or six sex-workers. The serial killer's lust to flagellate and mutilate bodies could be 'rationalized' by rethinking a person who commits these acts as a misguided, but essentially law-preserving, citizen. From a sociopolitical perspective, there is a fundamental continuity between the modern and postmodern social in that the organization of society is sustained by the surveillance of the State. This conceptualization of the serial killer as a moral functionary remains highly pertinent; today best illustrated in the character of Dexter Morgan. A forensic blood analyst who works for the Miami Metro Police Department, Dexter is enabled via having access to bureaucratic systems to also moonlight as a meticulous murderer. He harnesses his "dark passenger" to drain society of its despicable dregs: murderers (ironically so), paedophiles and rapists.

The postmodern genre of serial killing continues to explicate the terror of bureaucratically managed society. The serial killer's acts of watching inevitably culminate in strong physical contact, characteristically reaching their crescendo in vicious homicide; epitomizing the fact that violence is "the most flagrant manifestation of power" (Arendt 1972, 134). The killer's *modus operandi* is intimate and invasive, and violence is a weapon for ensuring their complete and undivided domination and control. For example, in *The Watcher*, Griffin, who is said to be responsible for 11 murders, speaks with his female victim to familiarize himself with her persona in the hours prior to brutally strangling her with piano wire. This kind of act of sadism, that the serial killer typically uses to manipulate his unsuspecting victims, represents the terror of the State's hegemonic power. The State, through its deployment of bureaucratic instruments, sees and thus 'knows' its subject population and can choose when and how to act upon our bodies without warning.

The State's hegemonic power is anchored in its ability to sanction law-preserving or lawful violence and killing (Benjamin 1979, 287; Stratton 1996, 81). Murder, the unlawful killing of a person by another, is therefore deemed a crime against the State, and the State retains the right to punish those who commit such a crime (Benjamin 1979, 287; Stratton 1996, 81). It is in the illegitimate and demonized seizure of violence that the serial killer makes his most critical commentary. In postmodernity, the social is considered to be uncontainable and unknowable; the site of disorder, as opposed to the modern social. The notion that there exist connections between individuals is redundant, and therefore the idea of motiveless murder itself becomes reasonable. Serial killing is thought of as the epitome of motiveless murder; the serial killer the archetypal random offender that may strike without hesitation or regard for his victims. In its very construction, as a mythic synecdoche of the State, the motiveless nature of the serial killer's crimes can be seen as articulating cultural fears about the unforeseeable occurrence of State violence.

This cultural anxiety has intensified acutely following the terrorist attacks in New York City and the Washington, D.C. area on September 11, 2001 (commonly reduced to the loaded signifier '9/11'). The anxieties in relation to State violence are, at the least, twofold. In the first instance, as an effect of trauma, we have been conditioned to be tense about potential future random acts of violence carried out by foreign nation-States (or those who claim to work on their behalf) on the 'homeland'. However, we may be equally anxious about the possible *consequences* exacted by the State as a result of 'terrorist' activity: increased surveillance and a culture of warfare. Surveillance studies scholar David Lyon (2002, 1) elucidates the impact of 9/11 on bureaucratic surveillance practices:

> September 11 prompted widespread international concern for security in the face of global terrorism, seen terrifyingly in the suicide plane attack on the World Trade Center in New York, and the damage inflicted on the Pentagon. Already existing surveillance was reinforced at crucial points, with the promise of more to come. Many countries rapidly passed laws permitting unprecedented levels of policing and intelligence surveillance, which in turn draws upon other sources such as consumer records.

It has been argued (Whitaker 1999; Boyne 2000; Lyon 2001; Koskela 2003; Muir 2012) that in post-9/11 surveillance society, the Panoptic model of disciplinary power, which "communicated through the material structures of the built environment" (Muir 2012, 264), has been replaced by a control model that emphasizes automated, digital surveillance practices. Post-9/11 society is comprised of increasingly "[t]echnically mediated communities . . . characterized by both watching and a high awareness of being watched" (Marwick 2012, 379), although people may remain "unaware how comprehensive others' knowledge of them actually is" (Lyon 1994, 5).

With such apprehension marking the post-9/11 milieu, it seems reasonable to ask whether the *gravitas* of the serial killer has been usurped by the (male) cultural figure of the terrorist? David Schmid (2005, 61) contends that serial murder has retained its popularity in the globalized aftermath of 9/11. He attributes the serial killer's continued anti-hero status to the fact that serial killer narratives have become comfortingly familiar and "ritualistic," thus serving as "a way to present the figure of the terrorist to the American public." Prima facie, 'the terrorist' appears more political, and therefore unmanageable. The serial killer, however, as a product of culture, is a highly political, embodied expression of ideological investments that is mobilized contextually and variously.

The serial killer's synecdochic relationship to the State is consolidated post-9/11 with serial killer films highlighting surveillance mechanisms as central to the execution of crimes. Reburn (2012, 232) argues that "[t]echnologies of surveillance are particularly important in these films, amplifying the monitoring powers of the serial killer and incorporating anxieties regarding these technologies." In *Untraceable*, the serial killer hosts a website called KillWithMe.com, which he uses to stage his sinful sadism. As the film's title suggests, the killer evades Special Agent Jennifer Marsh (Diane Lane) and her team of detectives through savvy control of technology: a constantly changing IP address prevents his website from being shut down. The killer, whose identity is ultimately uncovered to be Owen Reilly, is enraged because he believes that people have capitalized on the filming of his father's suicide. He consciously appropriates surveillance technologies, in particular via the internet, to make a deadly cultural critique of a corporate culture that is not only complicit in acts of suffering and exploitative consumerism but that appears to have an insatiable appetite for it. Seeking revenge, Reilly incarcerates his victims in elaborate torture contraptions and connects a live-feed to his website so the public can watch each convulsing person's demise. Surprisingly, these hellish scenarios aren't, in themselves, the pinnacle of perversion. The psychological 'twist' is the killer's invitation to "kill with me"—the more 'hits' the site receives, the faster the victim is submitted to an agonizing death.

Reilly's first murder—exsanguination precipitated by intravenous anticoagulant—attracts over 37,000 watchers; or, as Special Agent Marsh terms them, his "accomplices." His second victim is burnt to death by heat lamps while cemented to the floor. The third victim is submerged up to his neck in increasingly concentrated sulfuric acid, and dies with 24.5 million 'participants'. It is clear Reilly feels no empathy. "As well as incorporating contemporary concerns regarding surveillance, particularly after 9/11 and during a time of rapid technological advances, these films [such as *Untraceable*] connect the killer's surveillance skills to a dispassionate, depersonalised form of serial killing" (Reburn 2012, 80). In a declaration that demonstrates Reilly's detachment and reinforces the serial killer as a synecdoche of the State, through seizing control of the right to violence and acts of watching (bureaucratic surveillance) that legitimates State power, he informs one victim: "You know I'm only doing to you what they're going to do to me. Only they'll use potassium chloride and they won't let very many people watch." *Untraceable* literalizes Watts's explanation that "State violence, whether it be murder, rape, surveillance, incarceration or psychological *terror*, is one of the ways that states touch their 'subjects', 'citizens', or 'victims' most intimately, most corporeally" (Watts 1997, 36; emphasis mine). It is the State's capacity to expose its citizens to violence—whether by engaging in warfare or using its right to punish—that incites terror, and "one of the ways the modern state remains an embodied presence in our lives" (Watts 1997, 34).

Poignantly, *Untraceable* depicts that watching people is a not passive activity but, rather, a social foreplay to action. In a moment of truth, Reilly points out: "You know if no one was watching right now, you'd just be sitting in water. But the whole world wants to watch you die, and they don't even know you." This film's proposal of 'internet users as killers' foregrounds the imbrication of watching and violence; as both watching and violence exert a pressure on bodies. This actuality is particularly resonant for post-9/11 society in which citizens are frequently interpellated by government to 'be on alert for terrorist activity', 'report unaccompanied packages left in buses', and 'call such-and-such a hotline if you see a *suspicious person*'. We are constantly hailed to partake in surveillance and to act as agents of the State. It seems then that, post-9/11, we have realized the adroitness of Benjamin's (1983, 40) supposition: "In times of terror, when everyone is something of a conspirator, everybody will be in a situation where he has to play detective." The implication is that once agencies of the State are advised of incriminating behavior, they will commence investigative processes. We, the panicked citizenry, are placed in a position of social and political responsibility for maintaining 'our way of life'; to look out for those who threaten our ideologically defined boundaries and enable their extermination (literally) if necessary.

The generic construction of the serial killer works from within the suffocating terror that suffuses everyday life: the tensions of living within a monitored social, in which one must behave in a docile manner, and the unsettling fear that harm may befall oneself at the State's pleasure. The serial killer's representation as an information-gathering voyeur and perpetrator of violence (that the State keeps in abeyance) parades the dynamics of the underlying principles of State power. In its representational relation to the State, the serial killer embodies the disembodied terror of a bureaucratic society in which no one is immune to the State's stronghold of surveillance and no one is free from the reach of the State's legitimacy to appropriate violence without warning. Our increased realization post-9/11 that we are all viable targets of unprovoked State-endorsed havoc—domestic (implemented under the guise of 'protection') as well as foreign—produces an even greater climate of intimidation. In executing a series of abominable acts, the serial killer (re)actualizes terror and is a cultural personification of the threat of violence that is naturalized in the formation of the State. The serial killer, through spectacularized displays of horror, expresses the repressed, but ever-present, cultural anxieties of living in a modern State in which the "inevitable processes of bureaucratization [are] the 'steel-hard cage' against whose bars we can only scratch our fingers vainly" (Giddens 1995, 176).

References

Arendt, Hannah. 1972. *Crises of the Republic*. New York: Harcourt Brace.
Benjamin, Walter. 1979. "Critique of Violence." In *One-Way Street and Other Writings*, translated by Edmund Jephcott and Kingsley Shorter, 132–56. London: NLB.

—. 1983. *Charles Baudelaire: A Lyric Poet in the Era of High Capitalism*. London: Verso.

Boyne, R. 2000. "Post-Panopticism." *Economy and Society* 29: 285–307.

Coughlin, Paul. 2002. "Getting Away with Murder: *American Psycho* and *Henry: Portrait of a Serial Killer*." *Metro Magazine* 124/125: 100–5.

Dandeker, Christopher. 1990. *Surveillance, Power and Modernity*. Cambridge, UK: Polity.

Deleuze, Gilles. 1988. "A New Cartographer (*Discipline and Punish*)." In *Foucault*, translated and edited by Sèan Hand, 22–44. London: Athlone.

Denzin, Norman. 1995. *The Cinematic Society: The Voyeur's Gaze*. London: Sage.

Ellul, Jacques. 1972. *The Political Illusion*, translated by Konrad Kellen. New York: Vintage.

Foucault, Michel. 1980. "The Eye of Power." In *Power/Knowledge: Selected Interviews and Other Writings 1972–1977 by Michel Foucault*, edited by Colin Gordon, 146–65. Sussex: Harvester.

Giddens, Anthony. 1995. *A Contemporary Critique of Historical Materialism*, 2nd edn. Houndsmills, Basingstoke: Macmillan.

Held, David. 1989. *Political Theory and the Modern State: Essays on the State, Power and Democracy*. Cambridge, UK: Polity.

Hillier, Jean. 1997. "Foucault's Gaze." In *Foucault: The Legacy*, edited by Clare O'Farrell, 139–54. Kelvin Grove: Queensland University Press.

Jenkins, Philip. 1994. *Using Murder: The Social Construction of Serial Homicide*. New York: Aldine De Gruyter.

Kelleher, Michael D., and C. L. Kelleher. 1998. *Murder Most Rare: The Female Serial Killer*. Westport, CT: Praeger.

Koskela, Hille. 2003. "'Cam Era'—the Contemporary Urban Panopticon." *Surveillance & Society* 1(3): 292–313.

Lefebvre, Henri. 2000. *Everyday Life in the Modern World*. London: Continuum.

Lyon, David. 1994. *The Electronic Eye: The Rise of Surveillance Society*. Minneapolis: University of Minnesota Press.

—. 2001. *Surveillance Society: Monitoring Everyday Life*. Buckingham: Open University Press.

—. 2002. "Editorial. Surveillance Studies: Understanding Visibility, Mobility and the Phenetic Fix." *Surveillance & Society* 1(1): 1–7.

—. 2007. *Surveillance Studies: An Overview*. Cambridge, UK: Polity.

Marwick, Alice E. 2012. "The Public Domain: Social Surveillance in Everyday Life." *Surveillance & Society* 9(4): 378–93.

Mazlish, Bruce. 1994. "The Flâneur: From Spectator to Representation." In *The Flâneur*, edited by Keith Tester, 43–60. London and New York: Routledge.

McLaren, Angus. 1993. *A Prescription for Murder: The Victorian Serial Killings of Dr. Thomas Neill Cream*. Chicago: University of Chicago Press.

Muir, Lorna. 2012. "Control Space?: Cinematic Representations of Surveillance Space between Discipline and Control." *Surveillance & Society* 9(3): 263–79.

O'Kane, Rosemary H. T. 1996. *Terror, Forces and States: The Path from Modernity*. Cheltenham, UK; Brookfield, USA: Edward Elgar.

Reburn, Jennifer. 2012. "Watching Men: Masculinity and Surveillance in the American Serial Killer Film 1978–2008." Glasgow Theses Service, http://theses.gla.ac.uk/.

Schmid, David. 2005. "Serial Killing in American After 9/11." *The Journal of American Culture* 28(1): 61–9.

Seltzer, Mark. 1995. "Serial Killers 2: The Pathological Public Sphere." *Critical Inquiry* 22(1): 122–49.

—. 1998. *Serial Killers: Death and Life in America's Wound Culture.* New York and London: Routledge.

Simmel, Georg. 1950 [1903]. "The Metropolis and Mental Life." In *The Sociology of Georg Simmel*, translated by Kurt Wolff, 409–24. New York: Free Press.

Staples, William. 1997. *The Culture of Surveillance: Discipline and Social Control in the United States.* New York: St. Martin's Press.

Stratton, Jon. 1994. "(S)talking in the City: Serial Killing and Modern Life." *Southern Review* 27(1): 7–27.

—. 1996. "Serial Killing and the Transformation of the Social." *Theory, Culture and Society* 13(1): 77–98.

Tester, Keith. 1994. "Introduction." *The Flâneur*, edited by Keith Tester, 1–21. London and New York: Routledge.

Watts, Rob. 1997. "States of Violence, States of Trust: Violence in the Gulag Century." *Arena Magazine* 32 (Dec./Jan.): 34–7.

Whitaker, Reg. 1999. *The End of Privacy: How Total Surveillance is Becoming a Reality.* New York: The New Press.

Wirth, Louis. 1938. "Urbanism as a Way of Life." *The American Journal of Sociology* 44(1): 1–24.

Filmography

The Cell. DVD. Directed by Tarsam Singh. 2000; Los Angeles, CA: New Line Home Entertainment, 2000.

Kiss the Girls. DVD. Directed by Gary Fleder. 1997; Hollywood, CA: Paramount Home Entertainment, 1998.

The Silence of the Lambs. DVD. Directed by Jonathan Demme. 1991; Los Angeles, CA: Orion Pictures Corporation, 1997.

Untraceable. DVD. Directed by Gregory Hoblit. 2008; Culver City, CA: Screen Gems, 2008.

The Watcher. DVD. Directed by Joe Charbanic. 2000; Universal City, CA: Universal Studios Home Entertainment, 2003.

4

Forced Entry: Serial Killer Pornography as a Patriarchal Paradox

Robert Cettl

The *serial killer* film has had a tremendous influence on contemporary American culturesince it was widely popularized by Jonathan Demme's *The Silence of the Lambs* (1991) (Wolf and Lavezzi 2007, 199). Subsequent mass media glamorization led to an arguable romanticization of the serial killer. Wolf and Lavezzi (2007) argue, in their comparison of screen fiction with criminal case studies, that this near-mythic elevation of the serial killer is a recent development. However, Jane Caputi (1989, 445) isolated such a trend as originating with the mythification of 'Jack the Ripper' as patriarchal *hero* in the early twentieth century. She argues that this kind of mythification has a dual function: "to terrorize women and to empower and inspire men" (Caputi 1989, 445). Richard Dyer (1997, 14) similarly notes that contemporary "serial killer fictions condemn the slaughter of women, of course, yet also provide opportunities for misogyny." He suggests that "[t]he misogyny within such identification or admiration may be explicit woman-hating, a dwelling and a getting off on the killer's dominance and destruction of women, or it maybe a fascination more with his power" (Dyer 1997, 17). This reading of the serial killer is reframed when narratives are structured by pornographic aestheticization of rape-murder.

According to some feminist theorists, such as Andrea Dworkin (1981), author of *Pornography: Men Possessing Women*, male expressions of force and intimidation are what mark 'pornography' as a site of sexualized gender inequality. She contends that "[p]ornography, like heterosexual sex in general, is merely an extreme form by which men exercise power over women" (Wolfe 1990, 28). Catherine MacKinnon (2010, 510), a feminist and legal theorist, isolates filmed sex- and rape-murder (snuff) as informed by patriarchal ideology which sexualizes women as desired objects. She argues that such sexualized power is "the drug of male supremacy" (MacKinnon 2010, 504).

Taking a critical approach that shifts away from the anti-porn/anti-censorship debates, Linda Williams (1989) in *Hard Core* offers a seminal exploration of pornography as 'a body genre', evaluating its history and contribution to a discourse of sexuality. Williams "urges that we take pornography seriously, which does not mean that we like it, or that we believe it is art . . . Williams wants us to learn the rules of the pornographic genre" (Wolfe 1990, 30). By familiarizing ourselves with 'the rules' we can (re)consider its cultural message—for, as Jameson (1983, 141) explains, genre is a "socio-symbolic message, or, in other terms . . . an ideology in its own right." Likewise, Susanne Kappeler (1986, 1–2) in *The Pornography of Representations* makes the following declaration:

> It is my contention that the feminist argument about pornography would significantly advance if we were to shift the ground of the argument. Representation, therefore, not "real-life sex," should be the wider context in which we analyse this special case of representation: pornography.

From these theoretical points of departure, we can legitimately address the cultural instrumentality of pornography. This chapter, then, (re)examines Shaun Costello's film *Forced Entry* (1973) to argue that its particular 'pornographic' (sexually explicit) aestheticizations of rape-murder within a serial killer narrative function to critique patriarchy by highlighting a paradox in relation to hegemonic masculinity.

Patriarchy derives from the Greek "rule of (or by) the father" (Buchbinder 2012, 66). Traditionally, the term has been used to describe the power men assume over women. It is also a state of affairs that refers to male control of social institutions. In *The Origin of the Family, Private Property and the State*, Engels (1884) locates the origins of patriarchy within the capitalist mode of production (Bullock, Stallybrass, and Trombley 1988, 632). The patriarchal structuring of the social in the eighteenth century, then, is a discursive effect of modernity. Bourgeois ideology saw the positioning of men in the public sphere, and women in the private, as necessary to maintain capitalist relations. "Patriarchy . . . is today less an overt, explicit social structure than a rather nebulous set of discursive strands that constitute for people in the culture an order and way of thinking" (Buchbinder 2012, 68). The discourse of feminism identifies the ways in which women have been subjected to patriarchal authority. But, as patriarchy constitutes various discursive formations, which have been naturalized in the social context, it follows that men too are victims of its organizational structures that interpellate them into an idealized subject position. Seidler (1989, 8) advises:

It is important not to lose sight of the fact that there is a principle of non-identity between institutionalized power of men as a sex, and the experience of particular individual men. This means that, whilst acknowledging the force of its contribution on other levels, we need to see that the radical feminist assumption that the world is organized to the unconditional benefit and fulfilment of men is inadequate as an analysis of the relations between men and women.

While the patriarchy interpellates women to be passive, docile, and sexually submissive subjects, it simultaneously demands that men be active, aggressive, and sexually dominant.

Essentialist ideologies interpellate us to see our sex and also our gender as natural, so that the sexual conduct and roles we are to assume are taken for granted. Such ideologies reinforce patriarchal structures, and notions of phallic power. From a constructivist perspective, Cliff Cheng (1999, 296) acknowledges gender as a "socially constructed ideal of what it means to be a woman or man." The set of expectations, attitudes, behavior, and gestures assigned to members of each biological/anatomical sex (Buchbinder 1998) becomes naturalized in our culture. Gender distinctions—what is considered 'masculine' and 'feminine' —are, therefore, ideological. However in recognizing that gender is a learnt practice, then we can understand gender as a performance. In "Men Victimizing Men," Messerschmidt (1998, 130) explains that the concept of masculinity itself "can only be understood as a fluid, relational and structural construct." Hegemonic masculinity is always constructed in relation to various subordinated masculinities as well as in relation to women. It is a culturally idealized form of masculinity in a given historical period.

Applying these insights to critique an early analysis of pornography, David Buchbinder (1991, 55) argues that:

Perhaps the most disturbing aspect of Dworkin's analysis of pornography and its effect on male behaviour is its essentialist implication of a misogynist violence inherent in maleness itself. Not only does such a position simply dismiss the possibility that such violence is constituted historically and socially as a characteristic of masculinity, but logically it also implies that such violence is inevitable and ineradicable.

Ironically, in its aestheticization of rape-murder, *Forced Entry*, as will later be made evident through close analysis of the film, demonstrates that these essentialist ideologies are equally oppressive to men as they are to women. There is a certain pressure "to become a man's man—phallocentric, patriarchal, and masculine. Moreover, once the 'pressure' has become internalized, a part of one's sense of self, then failure to live up to the ideal can have painful, even catastrophic consequences" (Jefferson 1994, 12). *Forced Entry* heightens the intensity of such possible consequences. It dramatizes them through graphic rape-murder to make the culture aware of the limits of its own (patriarchal) construction.

The pornographic genre is a cultural product of patriarchal capitalism, and although it "exists where sex and politics meet" (Wolfe 1990, 27), it is not always simply invested in reproducing its power relations; indeed, it may be read as critiquing the same. Robert Jensen and Gail Dines (1998, 70) contend that

> Pornography is produced and circulated in a male-dominant society in which sexualised violence against women and children is routine. Pornography is a genre produced primarily for men as a masturbation facilitator. Whatever interpretations of the pornographic text one makes, they must be made within that context: Pornography is a product made primarily by men, primarily for men, in a patriarchal society.

While acknowledging that men may enjoy pornography, Alan Soble presents an alternative point that it is "'not an expression of males' power, but their lack of power, a defensive adaptation to the social advances of women" (Berger, Searles, and Cottle 1991, 58). In the model ordinance drafted by Dworkin and MacKinnon (1988, 132), pornography is defined as follows: "'Pornography' means the graphic sexually explicit subordination of women through pictures and/or words." Drucilla Cornell (2001, 51) finds this definition insufficient as it "fails to distinguish between materials that depict women as dehumanized sex objects for educational purposes (like the movie *The Accused*—which I [Cornell] consider nonpornographic) and materials that degrade women for males' sexual entertainment and/or sexual gratification." Adopting a similar position, this chapter considers the cultural work performed when 'pornographic' rape-murder is employed as a set piece in a serial killing narrative.

Popular 'mainstream' serial killer cinema since the 1960s has given the character of the 'profiler' at least equal importance in the narrative as the serial killer (Cettl 2003). Dyer (1997, 14) describes the profiler as "the genius-like investigator." The profiler, as a character within the crime genre, represents

State authority: law, order, morality, and the policing of sexual deviance. The profiler is separated from the ordinary police officer by virtue of their knowledge of, and expertise in, behavioral science—they alone are considered to have the ability to identify the serial killer. Correspondingly, the mainstream serial killer film is defined less by the sensationalized romanticizing of the serial killer figure than by the assignation of a central character triptych—serial killer, police officer, and profiler (Cettl 2003)—within which to morally and sociopolitically contextualize the serial killer's aberrance as sexually abject.

As a product of the pitting of profiler against serial killer, one of the genre's central thematic dichotomies emerge: patriarchal authority versus male performances of masculinity. 'Mainstream' representations of serial rapist-killers, such as those offered by the *Law and Order* (1990–) and *CSI* (2000–) franchises, depict the serial killer's crimes as baffling to policemen and then, through focus on the profiler figure, contextualize them in terms of (1) individual sexual behaviorism, and (2) authoritarian response to the threat of such pathological sexual aberration. The profiler figure anchors this latter assessment and, in as far as the profiler intuits the serial killer's sexual pathology, often concludes that rape-murder is abject behavior. In this, the profiler is a functionary of the authoritarian institution charged with policing sexual aberration and regulating 'acceptable' expressions of male sexuality within a patriarchal framework. Yet, in as far as the serial killer's crimes sexually subordinate women, the patriarchy that regulates such individual male 'aberration' is ironically that which also perpetuates the same subordination of women at a systemic sociocultural level through the aesthetics of 'pornography' (Dworkin 1981; MacKinnon and Dworkin 1997; Dines 2010). Therein lies the inherent sociopolitical and moral ambivalence of the serial killer film as genre. Its second, and irreconcilable, paradox is that the sociopolitical apparatus of patriarchy is charged with abjecting the very masculinity which, by subordinating women to the point of their extermination, epitomizes that same patriarchal authority.

Correspondingly, the pornography genre's defining set piece is that which dramatizes (and aestheticizes) this apparent paradox—patriarchal masculinity's omnipresent, but taboo, sexual pathology—rape-murder as an extreme performance of male sexuality. If the rape-murder set piece is aestheticized from the killer's point of view, the film's inspiration is determined to be 'pornography', both in its sexual explicitness and the equation of sexual power and pleasure as socially contingent on male supremacy, that is, achieved via patriarchy's subordination of women (Cameron 1990, 795). Time and again the genre stylizes scenes of rape-murder in ways that emphasize the aberrational enormity of the sexualized subordination of women by the (usually male) killer. For the killer, this kind of sexual performance is transcendent, yet for patriarchy to retain its guise of legitimacy and power such deviance must be eliminated—though less to protect women than to protect the façade of patriarchal authority from (over)exposure of its inherent oppression of women in all its ugly forms: socially, politically, economically, and sexually.

Within this context of critique of patriarchy, the serial killer can be read as epitomizing a sociopolitical system that sexualizes the subordination of women. Sexualized murder is the ultimate expression of patriarchal authority, eroticizing the male's power over life and death of the subordinated female (Dworkin 1981). By stylizing (and ambivalently sexualizing) rape-murder as a concurrent display of behavioral authenticity, psychological profile, and sociopolitical allegory for sex/gender dynamics, the rape-murder set piece in serial killer cinema dramatizes and deconstructs gender power relations. The filmic showcasing of the role of sexual violence, as an aspect of patriarchal male sexuality, registers the hypocrisy of patriarchy which simultaneously demonizes sex-/rape-murder as deviant yet relies on a masculine, if not male, performance of violence/force to retain its authority.

The rape-murder set piece, rather than just being evidence of the killer's danger to patriarchal moral authority, is a psychodrama of male sexuality. The result is a disturbing moral ambivalence and relativism that underlies an increasing number of serial killer films, beginning in the 1970s, which subvert convention by deconstructing the designation of the serial killer as aberrant sexual abject. Herein, the emphasis on rape-murder as a set piece has purpose akin to that described by Linda Williams (1999, 123–4) in her analysis of sexually explicit spectacle in pornography. She argues that sexually explicit spectacle serves a similar narrative function as song/dance in musicals. Specifically, Williams (1999, 155) discusses the sex scene in narrative film pornography as akin to the song/dance number's utopian function in the musical genre. In Williams's (1999, 170) study of the "integrated utopia," where the sex scenes emerge from the narrative, as is the case in *Forced Entry*, Williams asserts that the sex scene is used as discursive negotiation—"for power and within pleasure." It is in this negotiation that *Forced Entry* becomes metatextual in its staging of a 'pornographic' rape scene as political discourse: pathology and patriarchy. Little surprise, therefore, that *Forced Entry*, which was the first serial killer narrative to expose the irreconcilable dichotomy between abject male sexuality and patriarchal masculinity, was a pornographic film. Pornography is, after all, one genre where patriarchal authority has an explicitly sexual signifier (the 'cum shot'/ejaculating penis).

In *Forced Entry*, a nameless Vietnam veteran (Harry Reems), plagued by his war experiences (illustrated by repeated archival stock-footage flashbacks), works in a gas station as a pump attendant. He records the address details of female customers who appeal to his taste in women (specifically, those whose authority and independence he resents) only to stalk them, invade their homes, explicitly rape them (orally, vaginally, and anally), and then kill them with his knife after threatening, forcing, and coercing them with his pistol. The film begins with the ending: male police detectives attending the death of the killer—the camera zooming in on his corpse's exposed brain tissue. It is a deliberate camera movement suggesting that the remainder of the film—a protracted flashback to the killer's behavior and prior victims—is a contemplation of pathology within patriarchy. Bleak, wretched irony and subversion are Costello's techniques. The film's protagonist wears a baseball cap emblazoned with the US flag, and he is first seen hiding away his gun and preparing his knife standing under a business sign which reads "Joe's Friendly Service." The black and white archival footage of the Vietnam War that intercuts at key points in the film—as the protagonist works himself up toward rape-murder—suggests the killer's identity and definition of masculinity is largely a product of wartime affectivities. The film establishes Reems as a symbolic American fighting man, a stateside GI Joe, who needs an Other against which to define an image of patriarchal masculinity so offered the American male. The film's sexually explicit staging of three rape-murders dramatizes the process whereby Reems performs patriarchal masculinity in the domestic setting; an extended homage to a nationalism that seduced him to exterminate, that is, abject, any body that is reified as Other.

Rape-murder is a narrative strategy which provides a space for male sexuality to be showcased as monstrous; a grotesque display of male supremacy which is the product of a patriarchal demonization of women as Other. It is unsurprising that Reems's victims are independent women; the apparent beneficiaries of second-wave feminism. Assumed to be empowered by the sexual revolution, from a patriarchal perspective that demands their subordination, these women are now deemed to have the capacity to emasculate. The rape-murder is the punishment assigned; exercising power by intimidation, force, and obliteration of the objectified Other is the ultimate means to systemically subordinate.

The rape scenes are, thus, extremely explicit. The penis is the serial killer's weapon as much as his knife: nonconsensual sexual penetration is followed by furious stabbing—the knife is an extension of the penis. Reems uses the equally phallicized gun as a means of controlling his victims—forcing them to fellate him as he holds the gun to their heads (an image now forbidden in adult cinema). The female victims' protests are lost on Reems, who demands the subordination of women made possible only through rape as an expression of patriarchal validation: raping women makes him a *man*. His masculinity and sexuality are succinctly defined and symbolized by the central trope of pornography as a genre: the erect, ejaculating penis. In its sexual explicitness,

Forced Entry is ambivalent about any eroticism in its scenes of rape-murder. In fact, the director inserts occasional disorienting point-of-view shots which function to destabilize any empathetic male viewer identification with the killer, thus making traditional anti-porn, feminist denouncement of this film highly problematic despite its explicit sexual violence and sexualized violence.

It is also within *Forced Entry* that the serial killer film confronted the behavioral reality of the serial killer in unflinching photo-realist terms; this cinematic treatment seemingly addressing a cultural 'crisis in masculinity'. In *Taking It Like A Man* David Savran (1998, 5) asserts that:

> [A] new masculinity became hegemonic in the 1970s because it represents an attempt by white men to respond to and regroup in the face of particular social and economic challenges: the re-emergence of the feminist movement; the limited success of the civil rights movement in redressing gross historical inequities; . . . the rise of the lesbian and gay rights movements; the failure of American's most disastrous imperialist adventure, the Vietnam War; and perhaps most important, the end of the post-World War Two economic boom and the resultant steady decline in the income of white working- and lower-middle-class men.

In *Forced Entry* there is no moral framework within which to contextualize the serial killer as an aberration to patriarchal authority, as abject. Indeed, it is the most radical serial killer film to emerge from the 1970s as the serial killer is here representative of patriarchal authority in such a way as to make the bridging figure of the profiler, present in traditional narratives, functionally irrelevant.

Aware that the film would employ violent rape scenes which escalate to murder, Costello concluded that for the *pornographic* serial killer film to fit within the obscenity rulings, and the moral expectations now demanded by US courts in order to validate 'socially redeeming merit' in sexually explicit material, the killer would have to die at the end and be seen to be punished for his crimes. Only such poetic justice could absolve the film from being considered obscene according to patriarchy's legalized moralism. In short, the serial killer's sexuality had to be depicted as abject, and any allegorical assertion (through aesthetic depictions of rape-murder) of such sexuality as an affront to patriarchal authority was forbidden. What was labeled obscene was subversive political allegory—using sexually explicit aesthetics as political speech. This irony offended Costello: the same patriarchal authority that demanded a moral message to emerge from explicit sex films in order to not be 'obscene' was the very same authority that in Vietnam was responsible for such atrocities as the My Lai Massacre and the napalming of innocent Vietnamese children (as shown in the archival stock photos interspersed throughout *Forced Entry*). Costello highlighted this paradox between moral virtue (democratic and capitalist as it was) and Vietnam-era American war policy by utilizing the horrors of the Vietnam War as the sociopolitical background for *Forced Entry*'s deconstruction of patriarchal 'aberration'.

In *Forced Entry*, patriarchy is a war-mongering institution that holds rape-murder as an expression of consummate masculinity, demonizing women as Other in sexist parallel to racist war policy. The depiction of this patriarchal paradox became the underlying moral ambiguity behind the aesthetics of violent pornography. The film both experientially validates patriarchal authority and the expository denouncement of the same. The ejaculating penis—shown in *Forced Entry* first shooting ejaculate directly into the camera lens—is overtly sexual yet an assault on the viewer's sensibilities; inherently disorienting to any male viewer, as they are, in fact, 'cum on'. Ironically, this dialectic meaning produced by sexually explicit imagery as political speech debunked precisely the literalist theory concurrently advanced by Dworkin in their denouncement of pornography. Where Dworkin argued mimesis (demanding that an explicit rape depicted within photorealistic aesthetics was equivalent to an actual rape), Costello contested this literalism. He saw pornographic iconography in the serial killer film as having a specifically postmodern potential to play a discursive role in sociopolitical criticism of patriarchal masculinity and male sexuality. 'Pornography' in *Forced Entry*, rather than being the expression of patriarchal subordination of women, became the aesthetic for the analysis of it. It did, indeed, represent rape, but in no way validating it, instead critically engaging with it through specific aesthetic choices.

In *Forced Entry* Costello turned pornography into self-conscious political discourse: thus, as the killer rapes and murders women, his thrusting and ejaculating penis is intercut with yet more stock footage of Vietnam atrocities—the serial killer does to its sexual Other in private microcosm what patriarchy does in macrocosm to its political-cultural Other. As Nicole Ward Jouve (1986) explains:

> While popular culture positions the killer as epitomising certain masculine ideas . . . feminist responses have argued that the killer conversely demonstrates a failing masculinity which must be bolstered through violence. . . . Instead of being understood as isolated aberrance, they can instead be seen as motivated by an inability to correspond to gender roles. His extreme violence committed against women who are constructed as the site of sex and sin suggests a hatred of femininity which exposes his own sense of masculine insecurity. (Quoted in Reburn 2012, 47)

Serial killers as a representation of patriarchy speak its instabilities, inconsistencies, and hypocrisies. The aestheticizations of rape-murder serve as an analogy for patriarchy's desire to maintain and exercise (phallic) power. Patriarchy is, hence, a sexually pathological authority.

With the serial killer figure allied to patriarchy at the level of violence and systemic subordination of the gendered Other, there is little need for a continued police or law enforcement presence within the narrative. The serial killer represents patriarchal authority in a way that conventional narratives hold for the symbolic status of the profiler. The killer's power is exercised and, by extension, patriarchal masculinity performed via rape-murder—the objectification, consumption, and obliteration of the subordinated Other. Thus, since *Forced Entry*, aestheticized rape-murder has become an established plot element of the serial killer film genre. As a narrative strategy rape-murder is less moral aberration than a visual representation of patriarchal masculinity and male sexuality. To these effects, Costello brought a variety of staging techniques to the three rape-murder set pieces within *Forced Entry*. Within the killer's pattern of stalk, rape, and murder, Costello used the rape-murder set piece to chart the process surrounding the repetitious quality of the killer's behavior. Thus, although the rape-murder set piece functions as a dramatization of the killer's extreme performances of patriarchal masculinity, the variety between such set pieces qualifies this in psycho-social terms of gender analysis. Reems behaves in much the same way in each rape-murder set piece—the serial killer demands routine and repetition (that is, sexualized ritual) within which there is some room for improvisation—but the highly distinctive differences in the depiction of the female victims are revelatory of patriarchy's gender socialization. Here, the film's allegorical strength is enhanced by the actresses' portrayals of rape victims, that is, their self-conscious, deliberated assessment of sexually objectified victimology.

The killer's first victim is an independent woman first seen naked as she initiates sex with her boyfriend (played by Costello himself). The woman is clearly in charge but sex act is loving: she wishes to make love with 'her man' who responds with due loving tenderness and affection. The scenes, though still sexually explicit, are in no way 'pornographic' in terms of any Dworkin-based definition. The sexual activity is watched by the killer from outside—the point of view here is of the stalker as a precursor to rape-murder. The first sex act depicted is fellatio, shown as a tender act wherein women's sexuality is drawn to the control of the phallus through oral stimulation. Fellatio in this context is an expression of active sexual control, the male being a passive recipient and the woman the active partner. The woman here is depicted as sexually expressive, though not aggressive. Male supremacy and women's sexual subordination is restored only when the killer later invades the house and holds the woman captive at gunpoint.

In mocking inversion of the preceding intimacy of fellatio, in which the male was lying down on his back and the woman on top and dominant in the frame, the killer now stands and forces the woman to kneel. Gun to her head, he unzips his fly and orders her to fellate him, commenting on her 'ability' in sexual terms which reduces her to a mere sexual functionary. The intent is clear: the serial killer asserts patriarchal dominance through the disavowal of the woman's active sexuality, forcing an act upon her in order to sublimate her sexuality in deference to his authority. This is a patriarchal sexual pathology founded on the need to subordinate women and punish them for their active sexuality as inherently destabilizing male supremacy. Women's consent and women's pleasure is anathema to patriarchy as it is enacted in the sexualized psychodrama of the rape-murder set piece as structuring trope within the serial killer genre. Rape-murder is the symbolic restoration of patriarchal power and privilege through the sexualized subordination of woman.

Costello introduces another level of discursive criticism in the second rape-murder set piece. Here, the female victim is introduced nude and about to shower—a means of establishing the female as simultaneously vulnerable and desirable. Forced into sex again, first fellatio and then anal rape as Reems expands his ritualistic repertoire, the victim allegorically represents patriarchy's traditional sublimated woman. While Reems goes through what has become routine, Costello develops the individuality of the victim. Indeed, the scene's potency—its interest as a dramatized sexually explicit rape fantasy—rests not in Reems's violence but in actress Laura Cannon's improvisations.

Cannon establishes this set-piece's subversive intent from the outset in her decision to sing the song "Some Day My Prince Will Come" while showering naked. Her song choice is a demonstration of the naive optimism which young women are socialized toward; for example, via the (heterosexual) romance fiction patriarchy markets to them—the dream of sublimation to a powerful man. With vicious irony, this ideal man promised to her by way of interpellation as patriarchal feminine, is indeed the epitome of patriarchal masculinity she next encounters: the serial killer. Cannon's subsequent performance as rape victim implies a woman for whom a sexuality in deference to the appeasement of a man is enforced upon her by patriarchal authority, hence Reems continuously makes reference to how much she likes it. Again, this does not endorse the patriarchal sexual pathology it depicts, but dramatizes and critically interacts with it for deconstructive purposes.

Cannon and Costello discussed her performance during the protracted rape scene as the camera would focus more on her; Reems by this point portraying an 'everyman'. Thus, as she is being raped by Reems, she cries out to another "please don't let him kill me," rather than addressing the killer. Again, in this she represents the ideal sublimated woman—when victimized her response is a virtual prayer, appealing to the authority that sublimates her (God as conceptualized within Christianity perhaps) in order to save her life. Yet, the irony for Costello is twofold: both the ideal man she longs for and the God she appeals to are cultural constructs which exist to reinforce the authority that demands her sublimation. She is a victim both in the sense that she has no consent in the sexual uses her body is put to and her ideological subservience to patriarchal authority (through theism: God "the father"). Significantly, the killer repeatedly says that the victim enjoys her own rape, so dramatizing the sexual socialization offered women by patriarchy—to be used at will by the male and to enjoy being used.

The victims in the third and final rape-murder set piece are of a different ilk altogether. A generation younger than both of the preceding victims, they represent the 'hippie chicks', the products of the sexual revolution. The killer, who does not do drugs, resents their open independence and, with typical robotic pathology, seeks to put them in their place. They are runaways who, in their 'lesbian' disobedience and defiance against the patriarchal femininity that defined the previous victim, present a threat to patriarchal authority as much as the first victim in her active sexual self-assertion. The crucial difference here is that the lesbians have no sexual need for a man and do not define their sexuality in relation to the phallus. Hence, as the killer tries to rape them they are not threatened and joke and giggle, catching him off-guard to the point where he commits suicide rather than live as a failed patriarch unable to follow through with the rape of the 'disobedient daughters'.

Thus, the killer's symbolic demise comes from his inability to subordinate a generation of young women who reject patriarchal indoctrination and resist, defy, and mock its sexual pathology. In the presence of the naked women who resist his objectification, he cannot rape and collapses into a heap. An edited montage of war victims is then intercut with the giggling defiance of the 'hippie chicks' before the killer shoots himself, symbolically putting a bullet in GI Joe's brain concealed beneath the American flag baseball cap. Here, the subversive gender allegory is clear: patriarchal pathology, as founded on the sexual sublimation of women, legitimates rape-murder as a reaction to the social progress of the sexual revolution which works to ultimately liberate women from their subordination. The film presents the paradox that an unadulterated, uncontained performance of masculinity will inevitably cause patriarchy to implode.

Significantly, Costello here again stages female nudity but this time without the orientating presence of the erect penis. The scene is thus dephallicized as the killer loses control of the gun and knife. Indeed, patriarchy in this final set piece is without its photorealist signifier of sexual authority—the 'cum shot'—and has no recourse but to self-destruct. It is implicit that patriarchal authority disintegrates if it fails to subordinate the gendered Other. The extinction of patriarchy begins with the removal (through women's sexual empowerment) of the authority to achieve orgasm through women's sexual sublimation: the ejaculating penis now functions as absent signifier, its power subverted in the killer's suicide and usurped by the objectified 'victims' it attempted to sublimate.

After a subsequent two decades of reactionary profiler-oriented mainstream serial killer cinema, post-9/11 the serial killer figure became emblematic of American national identity (Schmid 2005, 68). The likes of *Dahmer* (2002), *Ted Bundy* (2002), *Monster* (2003), *The Hillside Strangler* (2004), and *Night Stalker* (2007) saw an emphasis on the 'true-life' serial killer case study. Again, in total contrast to the traditional profiler-oriented narrative, these films jettisoned the previously all-too important figure of the profiler in detailed explorations of serial killer's performances of patriarchal masculinity and/or male sexuality. Of these, *Ted Bundy* set the allegorical frame of reference, one in which the serial killer was, as Caputi (1989, 449) had argued in the real-life case of Bundy the man, a martyr to patriarchy. Caputi (1989, 449) explains "we might further recognize Bundy as a martyr for the patriarchal state, one who, after getting caught, had to pay for his fervor, the purity of his misogyny, and his attendant celebrity with his life."

These films confronted the experiential reality of rape-murder as had *Forced Entry*, though by then Dworkin and her supporters had succeeded in denouncing 'pornography' to the point where these more mainstream films lacked any comparable sexual explicitness. Unlike profiler-oriented fiction, the paraphilia was dramatized within the rape-murder set piece, not intuited by the profiler. Forensic science informs serial killer cinema now in the aestheticization of rape-murder behavior rather than the previously mainstream procedural narrative. Although these films were not explicitly pornographic in the sense of *Forced Entry*, their structural emphasis on rape-murder as a set piece owed to the equation between patriarchy and sexual pathology delineated so well in that film in particular and in much violent pornography of the 1970s.

Many of the films were set in this era: indeed, the murderers in *The Hillside Strangler* (2004) drive past a theatre showing a double bill of *Deep Throat* (1972) and *The Devil in Miss Jones* (1973) and, after raping and killing a woman, one congratulates the other on finally becoming a real man, that is, a worthy patriarch. Indeed, ever since Ted Bundy's fabricated death-row confession to a Christian minister, James Dobson, implying that viewing pornography made him commit his sex crimes, popular cinema has allied serial killer behavior to a culture of pornography (Cameron 1990, 787; Barzilai 2004), just as the supposed (but unproven) causal connections between viewing pornography and committing rape are central to anti-porn censorship arguments (MacKinnon and Dworkin 1997; Dines 2010, 95). However, as *Forced Entry* demonstrated, the underlying analysis of patriarchy and sexual pathology was shared by 'pornography' and the serial killer film; their intersection making political speech of sexually explicit, violent iconography.

Of these post-9/11 films, director Ulli Lommel's *Night Stalker* (2007)—based on the case of satanic killer Richard Ramirez—offers the most direct companion piece to *Forced Entry*. Lommel, an associate of German New Wave figure Rainer Werner Fassbinder, first essayed the serial killer 'true' case study with *The Tenderness of Wolves* (1973) about Fritz Haarmann. Some 30 years later Lommel relocated to the United States to begin a series of post-9/11 serial killer case studies, including films on 'The Zodiac Killer', 'The BTK Killer', 'Son of Sam', and 'The Green River Killer' comprising a systematic reinterpretation of the genre. Of his works, all shot on inexpensive digital video and often dismissed as 'amateurish', *Night Stalker* owes the clearest debt to *Forced Entry* in that it continues the latter's bold critique of patriarchy—specifically the law of the father—and incarnations of aggressive male sexuality that it enables. Indeed, this would be the most contentious point to emerge in the case study series. For instance, in the first film on Ted Bundy, Matthew Bright's eponymous 2001 film, the killer boasts in his first rape-murder that, although he may be failing in his university studies and his interpersonal relationship, when with a victim, he is in complete control, a master and true man. The subsequent rape-murder set pieces clearly reveal Bundy's pathological need for sexual dominance and control as borne in his own perceived failure to live up to the level of patriarch demanded of men around him. By intended comparison, highway 'hooker' Aileen Wuornos in *Monster* (2003) takes to killing men whom she believes would rape her. This is her means of asserting her mastery over the patriarchal system that she feels contrives to keep her servicing it as a disposable sex worker, in time uncontrollably driven to kill her clients. *The Hillside Strangler* depicts two men so contemptuous of being humiliated by women that they can only reassert their masculinity by raping, torturing, and murdering them, proving to themselves and the world that they have 'balls'. These serial killer films present men who function as a synecdoche of patriarchal authority; the films dramatizing an equation between patriarchy and forceful intimidation first isolated in feminist theory by Kate Millet in 1970 (Caputi 1989, 438).

It is at the familial level that *Night Stalker* first targets cultural anxieties about masculinity. Beginning with the killer—a teenager wandering the streets of downtown Los Angeles—the film, through a series of flashbacks, reveals the killer's childhood experiences with the dominant male role model in his life, his uncle. This uncle is a Vietnam veteran, a drunk who tells atrocity stories to the young boy: he is in a line of descent from the Vietnam veteran/GI Joe as monster figure played by Reems in *Forced Entry*, and has a similar attitude to subordinating women. He, thus, once again, represents contemporary patriarchy, as was established in *Forced Entry*, as exemplified during the Vietnam War. In reaction to the sexual revolution, *Night Stalker* locates women as a demonized Other to be subordinated as an expression of patriarchy. The uncle considers women disposable creatures, little better than animals, which can be killed accordingly. To prove his misogynistic point in front of the boy, he takes out his pistol and shoots his wife, laughing all the while as blood spray covers the boy. If the family remains the site for the installment of patriarchal values and the learning of gender roles, *Night Stalker* embraces this principle to exaggerate the connection between floundering patriarchal relations and the chaos which erupts in the social.

The film flashes to contemporary Los Angeles where the handsome young man is picked up by two young women who take him to their place, ostensibly for sex. In voice-over narration he refers to them in sexually degrading terms (borrowed from his uncle) but admits that he as yet does not know what to do with them. Though they are clearly independent women, initiating sexual contact, he sees it as his failure to perform that indicates that he is not yet a 'man' able to subordinate women sexually—as is, allegorically, the sexual socialization all men receive under patriarchy. Subsequently, when falling back on such socialization, he hears the voice of his uncle saying that women can and should be killed. His sense of self, his masculine identity in reaction to women, is determined by his experience with his uncle. Within patriarchy, thus, he is a 'good son'; his actions as a killer merely the dutiful following of the 'law of the father'. After his first murder, in voice-over he says that he has finally become his uncle and feels a true power for the first time: through the murder of the despised Other to his patriarchal authority—the women—he constructs himself as patriarch.

Significantly, his first murder is not shown in overt sexual terms, but is more akin to a random shooting. Subsequent rape-murder set pieces are more sexually explicit, beginning with a nude victim in the shower, an allusion to the sublimated victim in *Forced Entry*. The killer grows in confidence with each new crime, his behavior clearly revealing the depths of sexual pathology driving the crimes, ever closer to necrophilia. The paradox here is that just as this killer's belief in nonrestraint alienates him from patriarchy's strict (and hypocritical) theist regimentation of sexual desire, the killer's unrestrained rape-murder of women exemplifies that same silencing of women that patriarchy requires to maintain power.

The killer's murders, as expressed through the stylized, aestheticized structuring of rape-murder set pieces, thus represent a journey of both self-discovery and self-assertion for the killer—such being dramatized in behavioral terms during the rape-murder set pieces. Thus, the closer to behavioral authenticity it gets, the more 'pornographic' each set piece in *Night Stalker* becomes in its visualization of victim–killer interaction. The serial murderer's crimes express at an individual level what is, for Lommel (as it was for Costello and is also for Bright), the underlying pathological ideology of patriarchy. However repressed and disguised it is, in carefully constructed facades of moral authority, it remains the male-supremacist law of the father. Indeed, stern authorial control by the father over the son has proven to be common among serial rapists (Burgess et al. 1988).

Pornography is deployed in such serial killer films as those referenced in this chapter for its depiction of sexualized (and phallicized) masculinity within a pathologically perverse and morally solipsistic patriarchy. The sexually explicit subordination of women is utilized within the serial killer film to foreground precisely this paradox. In films which so deconstruct sexually pathological, patriarchal authority, the role of rape-murder as the ultimate performance of male (hetero)sexuality is aestheticized in self-conscious, meta-cinematic allusion to pornography as a genre: both of them about pathology and patriarchal authority. Rape-murder is often the central set piece in the serial killer film. The genre's core dichotomies—its radical political critiques and its erotic ambiguity—are played out in this set piece, its pornographic allusions being sociopolitical tropes. Just as 'mainstream' films deploy the profiler to effect the restoration of patriarchal authority and the moral condemnation of the sexually abject serial killer, so too radical (read: pornographic) serial killer films abandon this figure and assert the serial killer as a functionary of a patriarchy hypocritical in its denouncement of such rape-murder as abject sexuality. A significant paradox also emerges in the transgressive embrace of sexually explicit imagery and the discourse of pornography in order to expose, attack, and subvert the power of patriarchy.

References

Barzilai, G. 2004. "Culture of Patriarchy in Law: Violence from Antiquity to Modernity." *Law and Society Review* 38(4): 867–84.

Berger, Ronald J., Patricia Searles, and Charles E. Cottle. 1991. *Feminism and Pornography*. New York: Praeger.

Buchbinder, David. 1991. "Pornography and the Male Homosocial Desire: The Case of the New Men's Studies." *Social Semiotics* 1(2): 51–68.

—. 1998. *Performance Anxieties: Re-producing Masculinity*. St. Leonards, NSW: Allen & Unwin.

—. 2012. *Studying Men and Masculinity*. Abingdon, UK, and New York: Routledge.

Bullock, Alan, Oliver Stallybrass, and Stephen Trombley. 1988. *The Fontana Dictionary of Modern Thought*. London: Fontana.

Burgess, Ann W., Robert R. Hazelwood, Frances E. Rokous, Carol R. Hartman, and Allen G. Burgess. 1988. "Serial Rapists and their Victims." *Annals of the New York Academy of Sciences* 528: 277–95.

Cameron, Deborah. 1990. "Discourses of Desire: Liberals, Feminists and the Politics of Pornography in the 1980s." *American Literary History* 2(4): 784–98.

Caputi, Jane. 1989. "The Sexual Politics of Murder." *Gender and Society* 3(4): 437–56.

Cettl, Robert. 2003. *Serial Killer Cinema: An Analytical Filmography*. Jefferson, NC: McFarland & Company, Inc.

Cheng, Cliff. 1999. "Marginalized Masculinities and Hegemonic Masculinity: An Introduction." *The Journal of Men's Studies* 7(3): 295–315.

Dines, Gail. 2010. *Pornland*. North Melbourne: Spinefex.

Dworkin, Andrea. 1981. *Pornography: Men Possessing Women*. London: The Women's Press.

Dworkin, Andrea, and Catherine A. MacKinnon. 1988. *Pornography and Civil Rights: A New Day for Women's Equality*. Minneapolis: Organizing Against Pornography.

Dyer, Richard. 1997. "Kill and Kill Again." *Sight and Sound* 7(9): 14–17.

Jameson, Fredric. 1983. *The Political Unconscious: Narrative as a Socially Symbolic Act*. London: Methuen.

Jefferson, Tony. 1994. "Theorising Masculine Subjectivity." In *Just Boys Doing Business?: Men, Masculinities and Crime*, edited by Tim Newburn and Elizabeth A. Stanko, 10–31. London: Routledge.

Jensen, Robert, and Gail Dines. 1998. "The Content of Mass-Marketed Pornography." In *Pornography: The Production and Consumption of Inequality*, edited by Gail Dines, Robert Jensen, and Ann Russo, 66–100. London and New York: Routledge.

Kappeler, Susanne. 1986. *The Pornography of Representation*. Oxford: Polity.

MacKinnon, Catherine. 2010. "Gender—The Future." *Constellations* 17(4): 504–11.

MacKinnon, Catherine, and Andrea Dworkin. 1997. *In Harm's Way: The Pornography Civil Rights Hearings*. Cambridge: Harvard University Press.

Messerschmidt, James W. "Men Victimizing Men: The Case of Lynching, 1865–1900." In *Masculinities and Violence*, edited by Lee H. Bowker, 125–51. Thousand Oaks, CA: Sage.

Reburn, Jennifer. 2012. "Watching Men: Masculinity and Surveillance in the American Serial Killer Film 1978–2008." Glasgow Theses Service, http://theses.gla.ac.uk/.

Schmid, David. 2005. "Serial Killing in America After 9/11." *Journal of American Culture* 28(1): 61–69.

Seidler, Victor J. 1989. *Rediscovering Masculinity: Reason, Language and Sexuality*. London and New York: Routledge.

Williams, Linda. 1989. *Hard Core: Power, Pleasure, and the "Frenzy of the Visible."* Berkeley: University of California Press.

Wolf, Barbara C., and Wendy A. Lavezzi. 2007. "Paths to Destruction: The Lives and Crimes of Two Serial Killers." *Journal of Forensic Sciences* 52(1): 199–203.

Wolfe, Alan. 1990. "Dirt and Democracy." *The New Republic*, February 19, 1990.

Filmography

CSI: Crime Scene Investigation. Television. Produced by Jerry Bruckheimer. Santa Monica, CA: CBS, 2000–.

Dahmer. DVD. Directed by David Jacobsen. 2002; Century City, CA: First Look Studios, 2005.

Deep Throat. VHS. Directed by Gerard Damiano. 1972; Herts, UK: Arrow, 1987.

The Devil in Miss Jones. DVD. Directed by Gerard Damiano. 1973; New York, NY: Media Blasters, 2006.

Forced Entry. DVD. Directed by Shaun Costello. 1973; Butler, NJ: After Hours Cinema, 2007.

The Hillside Strangler. DVD. Directed by Chuck Parello. 2004; Enfield, Middlesex: Prism Leisure Corporation, 2006.

Law and Order. Television. Produced by Dick Wolf and Joseph Stern. New York, NY: NBC, 1990–.

Monster. DVD. Directed by Patty Jenkins. 2003; Culver City, CA: Sony Pictures Home Entertainment, 2004.

Night Stalker. DVD. Directed by Ulli Lommel. 2007; Santa Monica, CA: Lionsgate Home Entertainment, 2009.

Ted Bundy. DVD. Directed by Matthew Bright. 2002; Century City, CA: First Look Studios, 2002.

The Silence of the Lambs. DVD. Directed by Jonathan Demme. 1991; Los Angeles, CA: Orion Pictures Corporation, 1997.

The Tenderness of Wolves. DVD. Directed by Ulli Lommel. 1973; Beverly Hills, CA: Anchor Bay Entertainment, 1999.

5

Defining Deviance: The Rearticulation of Aileen Wuornos in *Monster*

Kumarini Silva and Danielle Rousseau

Monsters cannot be announced. One cannot say: 'here are our monsters', without immediately turning the monsters into pets.

JACQUES DERRIDA, 1989, 80

Representations of criminality are staples of North American media. One only needs to take a cursory look at the numerous mutations of *Law and Order* (1990–), *CSI* (2000–), *NCIS* (2003–), and the popularity of sanctioned serial killer Dexter, to recognize that narratives of murder are of interest to the culture. According to Brian Jarvis (2007, 327), "serial killing . . . has become big business within the culture industry" and "The Internet Movie Database (imdb 2012) lists over 1000 films featuring serial killers and most of them have been made in the past 15 years." Clearly the old journalistic adage of 'if it bleeds, it leads' has now become part of popular media consumption. While a handful of these narratives offer representations of female serial killers (*Kill Bill* (2003/4), for example), many more media portrayals focus on male serial killers, with an implicit assumption that such violence and aggression is an inherent male trait. When female serial killers become media and public fodder, their purported rejection of conventional female traits—such as caring and compassion—are constructed as a 'masculine' performance that (re)presents their violence as a socially deviant anomaly located outside the discursive sensibilities of patriarchal femininity. Furthermore, within this reinscribed conflation of masculinity and violence on the 'deviant' female body, the female serial killer is redeployed as 'male like'. Perhaps the best example of this complicated restructuring is the much-lauded *Monster* (2003), directed by Patty Jenkins and starring Charlize Theron as convicted serial killer Aileen Wuornos. The critically acclaimed biopic garnered Theron an Academy Award, a Golden Globe, and a Screen Actor's Guild Award for Best Actress. It was also hailed as one of the most humane representations of Wuornos, who was executed for her crimes in 2002.

Acknowledging the popularity of *Monster*, the subject matter, and the approbation of Theron, this chapter approaches the film as at the intersection of several cogent issues in contemporary culture. *Monster* begs an analysis of feminine performance and a critique of the cultural ascription of violence and (masculine) gender through the seemingly unique story of a female offender. The film constructs a particular notion of counter-feminist masculine performance through Wuornos's sexual identity that seems to speak to social constructions of gender and sexual deviance. While *Monster*, as a popular crime film, defies common representations of female violence by moving it out of domestic spaces, it also demonstrates gendered biases present in criminology as well as popular media representation of serial crimes. Most often, in both practice and representation, the domestic/private space—a feminine space—rather than the public/masculine space becomes the locus of female violence. Indeed, as Kyra Pearson (2007, 259) writes, "[s]o saturated with domesticity is criminology's classification of female killers that Wuornos stumped serial killing expert Robert Ressler because she acted violently in a non-domestic space and with strangers." According to Ressler, "[w]hen there is violence involving women, it's usually in the home, with husbands and boyfriends. It's a close in, personal crime" (quoted in Pearson 2007, 259). Since Wuornos's crimes were neither at home nor involving emotionally intimate, socially sanctioned, relationships, her 'unconventional' violence—a systematically executed, non-feminine performance of aggression—is rearticulated in the film as a popularized version of psychopathy. Here we approach psychopathy as a construct that is used to discuss a personality-centered disorder commonly attributed to a particular subset of criminals. According to Hare (1998, 188):

> Psychopathy is a socially devastating disorder defined by a constellation of affective, interpersonal, and behavioral characteristics, including egocentricity; impulsivity; irresponsibility; shallow emotions; lack of empathy, guilt or remorse; pathological lying; manipulativeness; and the persistent violation of social norms and expectations.

As a construct, psychopathy is clinically supported and has been frequently examined in various conceptualizations, both historically and currently (Hare 1998; Hare et al. 2000). However, popular presentation of the 'psychopath' does not always coincide with a purely clinical contextualization. In suggesting the portrait of a psychopathic 'monster', the film overlooks many of the environmental factors that played a significant role in Wuornos's criminality, factors including abuse and trauma that often characterize a uniquely 'feminine' pathway into crime. Here we would suggest that the character of Wuornos can be seen to represent a masculinized 'monster' in an instance where gender and environmental explanations might prove less palatable (or entertaining) through a popular culture lens.

While Wuornos's crimes themselves are gruesome and shocking, the film utilizes far more than the acts of violence alone to contextualize Wuornos's character. Its approach to Wuornos as a tragic figure, whose violent life separated her from a viewing public (at least, in theory), is firmly grounded in her gendered identity. By pitting her against socially sanctioned gender performances both within—through Selby, Wuornos's girlfriend—and outside—through actor Charlize Theron—the film *Monster* (re)presents mediated social expectations for femininity. Because killing, especially serial killing, is seen as a male crime, Wuornos's crimes alone would have been fairly unconventional movie script material. But, here we contest that the actor playing the serial killer further complicates *Monster*'s representation of gender. The significance of iconic Hollywood beauty Charlize Theron performing as the 'first female serial killer' adds to, and extends, the monstrous nature of Aileen Wuornos. Theron's ability to transcend her 'natural' beauty to become a 'monster' reiterates Wuornos's marginality. For us, then, part of this discussion hinges on the convergence of celebrity representations of violent realities. The publicly lauded female star is able to *add* to the representation of deviance. Focusing on these issues, among a host that this film raises, allow us to conclude the chapter with a brief discussion of the relationship between popular representations and gendered accounts of female serial killers.

The portrayal of a gendered killer

She looked like a frightened animal. She was so terrified. Terror-ridden eyes, and so full of the rage of misunderstanding. You just get misunderstood and misunderstood and it builds and builds and causes such terrible violence. And yet I knew she'd killed seven people, the majority probably in cold blood. It was unforgettable.

PATTY JENKINS ON AILEEN WUORNOS (quoted in Braun 2004)

In January 2004 *Monster* was widely released to much critical acclaim, with 13 nominations and 16 awards, including a Best Actress 'Oscar' for Charlize Theron (imdb 2012). Because of its immense popularity, and the view into psychopathy it presented, *Monster* is significant beyond the artistic merits for which it was recognized. The film focuses on the life of convicted real-life killer Aileen Wuornos who, in 1989–90, killed seven men in the state of Florida, and was convicted and executed for six of those crimes in 2002. At the initial stages of her trial, Wuornos claimed that the men had either raped her or attempted to rape her, while hiring her for sex, and that all the killings were in self-defense. Later on, as the hearings continued, she also admitted that she would continue to kill under the same circumstances, fired her lawyers, and refused to appeal the execution. While the gritty and gruesome details of the actual case garnered much press, it was the film based on her life that attracted public attention.

The critical acclaim of and the large audience for a film dealing with the violent life of a convicted killer speaks to the ongoing fascination society has with crime. Certainly, the nature of the 'psychopath', and his or her apparent cunning capacity to manipulate and deceive, has intrigued people for decades. Although constituting a clinical term, psychopathy represents a construct familiar to many, and one with significant popular appeal. For example, one needs only to look to the allure of the psychopathic serial killers in the popular media. Here both actual criminal individuals, like Ted Bundy, and fictitious characters, such as Alex DeLarge in Kubrick's *A Clockwork Orange* (1971); Dr Hannibal Lecter in Jonathan Demme's *The Silence of the Lambs* (1991); or Dexter Morgan in the critically acclaimed television show *Dexter* (2006–), rise to an almost heroic status captivating audiences. Their representations saturate books, film, and television media, transcending the realms of forensic examination and becoming staples of popular culture. As Jarvis (2007, 327) notes, "a search for 'Jack the Ripper' uncovers 248 books, 24 DVDs, 15 links to popular music, a video game, and a 10' action figure. The Jack the Ripper video game invites players to solve the Whitechapel murders, but a large number of its competitors profit by encouraging 'recreational killing'."

The very characteristics that delineate the definition of a true psychopath also make for the ideal villain in popular crime film: the grandiose yet extremely charming 'bad *guy*' that audiences love to hate (or possibly hate to love). The charming 'rogue' killer, ala Hannibal Lecter and Dexter, evoke a kind of devotion and affection that speaks to a 'boys will be boys' culture that is normalized and naturalized in many cultures. Here, we are not saying that killing is accepted or that murder/cannibalism goes unpunished but, rather, the popularity and sympathetic abhorrence they evoke in audiences speak to a larger cultural acceptance of male deviance as 'normal, viewable and, indeed, profitable. For example, in 2003, the year that *Monster* premiered, the American Film Institute (AFI 2012) declared Dr Hannibal Lecter 'The #1 Villain' in their "100 years . . . 100 Heroes and Villains" rankings, and since its release the 'Hannibal Lecter' franchise has made close to half a billion dollars in domestic sales alone (Filmsite 2012).

Such a devotion to the male psychopath, and male criminality generally, within popular culture parallels the study of crime and the discipline of criminology, with much of the focus on male deviance. And, like many disciplines, it has simply ignored women's violence, failing to include women in research and discounting the value of understanding the female experience (Chesney-Lind 1989; Belknap 2007). The female offender was perceived as an anomaly, and if attention was given, it was generally in a fashion of application of male-developed and tested criminological theories to a female population. In such manner, popular media portrayal of female criminals appears to parallel extant criminological research and portrayal of women. In general, lead female characters are predominantly excluded from crime film, particularly in examination of the serial killer subgenres. Thus, one of the most unique aspects of *Monster* is that it focuses on a female serial killer (and potential psychopath) rather than the stereotypical abnormally violent male predator. As a female villain, the character of Wuornos takes a primary and solitary role in her deviance, contrary to the popular characterization of female criminality as passive or occurring in a co-defendant role. It is almost as if the film seeks a more feminist approach to criminality. Here a feminist approach suggests acknowledging the realities of individual experiences. However, a more open viewing of behavior may be difficult both for criminology and popular culture to rationalize fully, as these institutions are inherently gendered themselves. Ultimately, gender stereotypes and attempts to rectify violation of normative gender behavior are evident throughout the film, highlighting Wuornos's specific deviance. Her commissions of crime are not subservient to a male character that she simply accompanies in a stereotypically gendered relationship; however, as we discuss more fully later, this role of subservience *is* present through Wuornos's girlfriend, Selby (Christina Ricci).

Unlike the stereotypical male serial killer (for example, Ted Bundy), Wuornos's character lacks a sense of charisma, and can be seen to fail to elicit any significantly emotional response. In this sense, the film can be seen to fit the development of critical crime film—films which seem to lack traditional happy endings or specific character identification. As Rafter (2006, 230) suggests, critical crime films "tend to decenter criminality, interweaving it with larger patterns of daily life." Here Rafter points out that such films move away from the seemingly escapist nature of traditional crime films where viewers are offered a vicarious means of punishing evil, resisting authority, criticizing society, or observing the suffering of others from a safe vantage point. Critical crime films do not offer a glorified dichotomy of good versus evil or a cathartic experience of escapism. Realism enters that which is portrayed, and "instead of Hollywood's explosions, car chases, and knife-wielding serial killers, critical crime films offer something very like the grind of daily life" (Rafter 2006, 232). *Monster* appears to fit this critical classification in that it portrays the life of Wuornos in a seemingly ambivalent way. Wuornos's daily and criminal endeavors are presented, but in a manner that does not evoke either a truly empathic or repulsive response.

It is possible to conceptualize the critical crime film as an attempt for a more realistic integration of crime and everyday-life, in that these film's' 'real' life portrayal of 'daily grind' purports to reflect the way these acts of violence actually happen. Unlike the car explosions and long drawn-out knife fights that Rafter identifies as typical of Hollywood crime dramas, films like *Monster*, based on *bona fide* life events, present the acts of violence and deviance as circumstantial and, because of this, tragic and meaningless both for the victim and the perpetrator. As such, the typical Hollywood monstrous villain, including Hannibal Lecter, or slasher, like Jason from *Friday the 13th* (1980), is replaced with a more 'humanized' criminal actor. The focus on the life of an actual criminal/perpetrator leads the viewer away from the hyperbolized dichotomy of good versus evil to examine what innate characteristics of mental defects might lead a human being to deviancy.

This is not to suggest that the viewer is empathic with Wuornos's character. In fact, despite the (albeit limited) portrayal of Wuornos's authentic trauma history, victimization, and mental illness, the viewer is potentially less empathic and more ambivalent than in relation to a film such as *Sling Blade* (1996) (in which the antagonist is a mentally handicapped individual who has spent most of his life in a psychiatric hospital for the murder of his mother). For example, in response to a review of *Monster* by Stephen Holden (2003) in *The New York Times*, where Holden provides a sympathetic take on Wuornos, a reader/viewer ("LD" 2010) responds: "AW was a multiple killer, and we shouldn't sanctify her. Many have suffered similar terrible circumstances without resorting to murder, or crime, for that matter. No, her rape was abominable, but let's not cross the boundary between reasons and excuses." While this is one comment in many, it acts as a cogent articulation of the general sentiment toward Wuornos, as well as Theron's performance of her. While Wuornos's circumstances aroused some sympathy, it was generally understood that what made her monstrous was her response to her circumstances as a *gendered* being, to the extent that the title 'Monster' maybe more suggestive of *female* deviancy, and the violation of gender norms, rather than the criminal acts themselves.

Difficulty arises in conceptualizing the humanized nature of female criminality because of the role gender plays. To a degree, Wuornos must be transformed to a pathetic monster—the proverbial pet, that Derrida refers to in the epigraph, that needs to be (re)presented and contained within a particular narrative—because society does not know what to do with a woman exhibiting the traits of predatory and instrumental violence. She essentially becomes one side of, what David Buchbinder calls, a "fabulous monster." According to Buchbinder (1998, 3), the fabulous monster is always on show, both as a role model and as a warning. Fabulous monsters are simultaneously invitations to perform and follow the positive representations, and to be heeded as warnings of 'how not to be'. As such, Wuornos is presented in a characterization to which middle-class viewers ultimately cannot relate based on issues of gender and class, for she embodies multiple levels of deviance in being a woman, poor, in a same-sex relationship and, finally, a criminal (Figure 5.1).

Because of the fact that Wuornos does not abide by the gendered role society dictates for women, she must be defined as a monster, despite the clear presence of other potential explanatory factors including mental illness, victimization, and personality disorder—many of the characteristics that help explain gendered pathways into crime (for discussion of women's

FIGURE 5.1 *A "fabulous monster": Aileen Wuornos (Charlize Theron) in* Monster *(2003), MDP/New Market. The Kobal Collection.*

unique pathways into crime see Chesney-Lind 1989; Daly 1994; Owen 1998; Covington 2000; Bloom et al. 2003; Chesney-Lind and Pasko 2004; Covington and Bloom 2006; Belknap 2007). Wuornos faced a significant history of abuse, poor attachment, and even potentially a genetic proclivity for criminality. Throughout her life, she faced physical, sexual, and emotional abuse. Wuornos lacked appropriate attachments, both in childhood as well as in her adult relationships. She was estranged from her parents and raised by her grandparents, who she believed to be her parents; her grandfather was one of her many abusers. At 20, she married a man over 50 years her senior. Wuornos's biological father was a sex offender who committed suicide in prison (Arrigo and Griffin 2004). Her life was an interwoven pattern of trauma, abuse, substance abuse, delinquency, and aggression. However, the film does little to explore the potential explanatory power of these factors, instead presenting an ambiguous character of weak will and limited intellectual capacity.

Ultimately, as a female serial killer, Wuornos can be perceived as dualistically deviant; conforming neither to normative gender roles nor crime film's construction of an appropriate villain, thus demonstrating a disjuncture in the portrayal of women as criminal actors. This deviance is further illustrated by the film's portrait of sexuality and physical representations of gendered bodies, where masculine aggression becomes the conduit through which Wuornos channels her violence, and her affections (toward Selby). According to Chesney-Lind and Eliason (2006, 37), "masculinity, including willingness to employ dominance behaviors like direct aggression, has long been used to mark a woman as deviant and lesbian—so much so that traditionally, 'masculine' [when used in reference to a woman] is a code word for lesbian." In keeping with this expectation, Wuornos displays aggressive posturing and an uncouthness that seems to signify an essentialized and stereotypical masculine identity. Her relationship with Selby, who is more docile and feminine, magnifies these characteristics and presents them as 'evidence' of her deviance. Furthermore, Wuornos reverses a dominant serial killer narrative in popular culture: the 'sex worker who gets murdered'. In such narratives, the sex worker is a double-victim—of society and of sexual slavery. She is a character to be pitied because her circumstances have forced her to sell her last possession: her body. Where the murder victim is often a female sex worker and the perpetrator of the crime a male, Wuornos defies the conventional story by becoming both female sex worker and female/masculine murderer. Devoid of a broader context, where one may be able to see an emergent pattern of 'gender appropriate' criminal behavior resulting from abuse or neglect, Wuornos as sex worker turned killer reinforces her deviant gender performances as freakish, and an example of marginality.

Here we witness an example of how both traditional criminology and popular culture marginalize the female offender.

Throughout the film we see specific moments where Wuornos's gender performance and sexual identity become symbolic representations of Otherness. For example, when Wuornos commits her first murder and transitions to the 'monster', she changes, putting on the clothes of her male victim, driving his car and drinking his alcohol. By rejecting femininity, and systematically transforming into a 'strong' persona that demands acknowledgment, Wuornos assumes a violent masculine persona that positions the viewer to read her as rejecting 'proper' feminine behavior. This is compounded by the fact that the transition to 'monster' is abrupt, and reinforces a seemingly unstable female psyche; there is no grace or subtlety that one expects from a 'real' woman. The focus rests on the irrational and sudden nature of the transition, and does not account for either Wuornos's history of abuse or the deliberate and violent behavior Wuornos assumes. Wuornos's actions are portrayed as a violation of normative gender behavior, physically depicted as a dichotomous transition into the masculine: the victim has now become the perpetrator, and the transition from victim to abuser represents a metaphorical masculinization.

This dichotomy can be further identified in the portrayal of Wuornos's relationship with Selby. Here, the film attempts to force their relationship into the confines of heterosexuality. As with any simplistic representation of homosexuality vis-à-vis heterosexuality, Selby is simultaneously the passive female who demands care but is also performing her accepted class position as a middle-class woman. Selby's classed, feminine sensibilities—her need for stability, money, and a nice place to live—coupled with her physical appearance—she is attractive, slender, small in stature—is in sharp contrast to Wuornos, whose aggressive posturing and clothing is emphasized by her physical proportions. Even as Selby is presented as the 'good girl gone bad', she is also the demanding 'wife' who enables Wuornos's psychopathic behavior by forcing Wuornos to support her. She is the quintessential nagging wife. In spite of this, Selby arouses sympathy, however irrational and unreasonable her demands are under the conditions, because she is relatable (as a *woman*) in a way that her girlfriend is not. Selby is the daughter of a preacher, a man of God, who has sent her to relatives in Florida because she was caught kissing a girl—deviant in its own way, but neutralized and made more tolerable through Selby's class and relative docility.

Unlike Selby, since Wuornos is portrayed as no-good, 'white trash' from the onset of the film, her irrational and unstable behavior needs little explanation or context. While Wuornos is presented as knowing right from wrong, she is simultaneously helpless and defiant in the face of circumstance. And, unlike

Selby, or even a predatory male character in popular culture, Wuornos's moments of vulnerability and defiance have no redeeming qualities—such as physical beauty, feminine characteristics, intellect, or even regret—to which the viewer can relate. It is as if popular media does not know what to do with a female psychopath, and the viewer is left with no means to reconcile and make sense of such a person and representation. Because the representation positions the viewer ambivalently in relation to Wuornos, we can feel neither empathy nor true disgust. Instead, she is to be pitied, and as she "is hurried into the death chamber, we can see her not as a serial killer against whom to lob our hatreds, but as a pathetic woman in whom good is mixed with evil" (Rafter 2006, 224–5). The character Wuornos states in the film that she is ". . . not a bad person. I'm a real good person," but clearly the complexity of this statement—which goes beyond its surface good/bad binary and speaks to Wuornos's own convoluted understanding of her self—goes unexamined.

In examination of the character of Aileen Wuornos, both film and documentary accounts (for example, *The Selling of a Serial Killer* (1993) and *Aileen: Life and Death of a Serial Killer* (2003)) suggest the applicability of many of the characteristic traits of a clinical diagnosis of psychopathy. However, the film portrays a more instrumental nature to Wuornos's criminality, describing a woman targeting men as a means of avenging wrongs done to her in a lifestyle of sex work. Such portrayal suggests a woman who may in fact be a 'monster', a character to which the viewer would have difficulty relating, not even deserving the onlooker's empathic response. In the viewer's relationship to this character, there exists a distance and neutrality. The character in *Monster* represents an individual who has violated not only societal norms of appropriate behavior (through murder), but perhaps, even more significantly, violated norms of gender behavior through masculine performance and sexuality. Wuornos was neither contained nor 'proper', nor was she sexually reserved, as socially ingrained gender roles define a 'good' woman should be. But, in examining the actual person of Aileen Wuornos, we witness an individual who might more closely characterize exemplification of a gendered pathway into criminality. Here, Wuornos's trauma and significant abuse history as well as biologically driven genetic factors could be seen to theoretically explain entry into a life of deviance. However, the film minimizes the explanatory potential of these variables and is instead characterized by the marginalization of the character of Wuornos. Beyond the limited characterization of psychopathy, *Monster*, in many ways, fails to engage the complexities of the female offender. In popular culture, film is used to tell a story, and narrative conventions are employed to construct a *specific* social identity. On account of the form, we are only allowed a brief synopsis of a complex life, and the abbreviated tale that is told is one that is framed within common tropes of gender and sexual deviance, coupled with class struggles that speak to larger ideological lessons on propriety.

Beauty and the beast: Ideological lessons

She's a beauty who played a beast—and brought home a Best Actress Oscar for her effort.

OPRAH WINFREY, OF CHARLIZE THERON (Oprah 2005)

It wasn't about getting fat. It wasn't that she was fat. She was just [strong]. I was shocked to find out she was only five foot three. When I watch all that footage—she walks into the court and [she has a] presence. Everybody that we talked to at the Last Resort [the bar where Wuornos would go] used to say the same thing. When she came in, you knew she was in the bar.

CHARLIZE THERON, ON PLAYING AILEEN WUORNOS (AboutFilms 2004)

As part of Buchbinder's (1998, 3) explication of "fabulous monsters" he also reminds us that "*it is ideology's task to make itself invisible* in order that it continue undisturbed to sustain the existing class structure and the consequent power relations among social groups." Certainly, the representation of Selby as the 'nagging' wife, who stereotypically represents feminine desire for material goods that drive men (in this case, Wuornos) to attain them, reinforces the notion of a conventional classed gender ideology that can resonate with an audience. Through this, Wuornos's crime is then translated as doubly deviant: in addition to performing an 'unnatural' masculinity, she is also unable to understand the capitalist expectations of the 'male' provider. Unlike a 'real' man, who would work a job sanctioned by a capitalist state, Wuornos resorts to violent crime in an attempt to 'provide', exemplifying her inability to understand *true* masculinity, and reinforcing her failure as a 'man', a woman, and a responsible capitalist subject/citizen.

The (re)presentation of Wuornos as unable to understand 'simple' life lessons (male/female, work/money etc.) in the way of nonpsychotic, successfully interpellated, capitalist, gendered subjects is further complicated by the media spectacle that emphasized the convergences and divergences between the mediated Wuornos and the actor who played her. Charlize Theron's performance, as noted in the epigraph above, was widely and wildly acclaimed, mainly for its embodied transformation 'from beauty to beast'. In his review of the film, renowned film critic Roger Ebert (2004) noted that he was unaware of who the lead actress was when he walked into the film and did not recognize Theron until the credits rolled. He writes:

> I have already learned more than I wanted to about the techniques of disguise used . . . to transform an attractive 28-year-old into an ungainly street sex worker, snapping her cigarette butt into the shadows. . . . Watching the film, I had no sense of makeup technique; I was simply watching one of the most real people I had ever seen on the screen.

Ironically, Ebert seems to miss the point that the film purports to offer access to the life of a *real* person. While Ebert may not have recognized the actor, many audience members did.

Through such recognition Wuornos's monstrous nature becomes even more shocking because we know how antithetical Theron's own *real* appearance is to the character she is playing. Speaking to this, interviews with Theron, following her nomination and subsequent win of a slew of best actress awards, without exception, included a discussion of physical transformation. Many of the questions dealt with Theron's weight gain for the role, and the decision to use minimal prosthetics, instead relying on body language through aggressive movements to convey Wuornos. Such a transformation was lauded, on one hand, because of the incredulity that Theron could become as unattractive as the serial killer, and on the other, because Theron's own rise to stardom was a Cinderella story of sorts. At the age of 15, Theron witnessed her mother shoot and kill her alcoholic father when he threatened to kill them both. Theron arrived in LA after working as a model in Milan and London, having never finished high school, with $400 and a tattered suitcase. She stayed at an hourly rental hotel overlooking the Hollywood sign until a chance encounter at a bank introduced her to an agent (Oprah 2012). All of this Theron has shared numerous times in interviews; her 'rags-to-riches' story is a narrative of epic proportions that reinforces what is 'good' and 'true' and 'possible', even under challenging circumstances. Theron's success—her 'rags-to-riches' story—is a 'win' for capitalism, which, outside the frame of the film, is juxtaposed with Wuornos's 'failure'. Read outside the diegesis, Theron is the ideal female, capitalist subject: beautiful, hardworking despite hardship, heterosexual; all the things Wuornos is not.

The casting of Theron, then, emphasizes Wuornos as monster, especially within the terms of patriarchal capitalist ideology. Indeed, Theron's story reinforces the possible (but not probable, given the extreme nature of her circumstances) opportunities that Wuornos herself ignored or missed. In a sense, Theron is the fabulous monster that we *should* become. Such an ideological expectation is fairly common in the United States—'the land of opportunity'—where even Wuornos is interpellated to become a subject of the 'American dream'. In response to documentarian Nick Bloomfield asking her "Aileen . . . do you think if you hadn't had to leave your home and sleep in the cars it would have worked out differently?," Wuornos responds:

> If I could do my life all over again . . . and I came from a family that was supportive, we didn't have split sister/half sister and brother stuff and all of that, [if] it was all true blood, real blood and everything was financially stable and everybody was really tight I would have became more than likely an outstanding citizen of America who would have either been an archaeologist, a police officer, a fire department gal or an undercover worker for DEA or a . . . did I say archaeology? Or a missionary. (Quoted in Horeck 2007, 144)

Like Wuornos, in spite of the clear evidence that her life needed more than a home and proper sleeping quarters, we are encouraged to believe that changing some, relatively minor, aspects of her life, and following social convention, would have made her an 'outstanding citizen' rather than a serial killer.

Conclusion

The intent of this work was to interrogate the various gendered relationships both within and outside the film *Monster* that contribute to the ideological construction of gendered crime. By discussing the representation of Aileen Wuornos, alongside her relationship to her girlfriend, Selby, as well as mapping an ideological cartography that centralizes the significance of Charlize Theron playing Wuornos, we argue that there are multiple layers that make up the gendered 'lessons' within mediated representations of female serial killers. We are not saying that the popular film portrayal of Wuornos represents the sole realm in which gendered disparity exists. In fact, gendered bias exists throughout the criminal justice system and was evident in Wuornos's actual trial. For example, during trial, prosecutors downplayed the fact that Wuornos's victims were seeking to pay her for sex, instead portraying them as chivalrous men attempting to help a woman in distress. Further, both court actors and journalists made much of Wuornos's same-sex relationship, even though Selby was her first female partner (Miller 2004), because it reinforced Wuornos's masculine representation and, by extension, her 'deviance'. It may be that the masculinization of Wuornos's character and movement away from the characterization of a gendered pathway into crime becomes necessary for the general public to 'buy' the believability of the seriousness of her offenses and her portrait as a female serial killer.

We also want to note that not all women experience the criminal justice system in an equal manner, and that interpretations of 'good' and 'bad', under gendered propriety, are very much part of how justice is arbitrated: 'good' women are frequently granted leniency while nontraditional women are punished more harshly (see examples in Visher 1983; Albonetti 1998; Albonetti 2002). The gendered experience of the justice system is conditioned by a variety of factors including 'race', class, sexuality, and other formal and informal ties to social norms. Such factors lead us to conclude that there may have been a need to characterize Wuornos as an abnormal or 'deviant' female—outside her actual mental state and circumstances—to justify that a woman could in actuality commit heinous acts of crime. Such characterizations and interpretations transcend popular media, encompassing state-sanctioned institutions and influencing perspectives more generally. As with other gendered theories of crime, the 'evil woman' hypothesis arises from rigid constructions of gender norms and rules where severe punishments are imposed on females when illegal behavior or inherent characteristics contradict normative gender behavior.

What we have touched upon here are examples of how gendered stereotypes dictate norms and interpretative lenses, both institutionally and within the eye of popular media. Here we understand popular media as a directive force, inviting viewers to participate in a mediated text through particular ideological strategies that are translated through various nodes of consumer culture. For example, in her discussion of the representations and marketing of Wuornos, Tanya Horeck succinctly points to two such examples (Horeck 2007). First, she cites the inclusion of a theatrical release to Jenkin's *Monster*—a film "that burrows deep beneath the tabloid-sized headline stories to the abusive neglect, doomed romance and lost opportunities that plagued Aileen's life" (quoted in Horeck 2007, 141)—in the DVD set of Nick Broomfield's two documentaries on Wuornos, *The Selling of a Serial Killer* and *Aileen: Life and Death of a Serial Killer*. Second, she refers to Britain's Channel 4's (Spring 2005) double-billed screening of *Monster* followed by *Aileen: Life and Death of a Serial Killer* as evidence of both marketing and ideological synergy. Horeck (2007, 141–2) points out that a convergence between 'reality' and 'fiction' subtly leads the viewer to "interpret the documentary and the drama together" where such a merging reinforces each other. Such a bleeding between 'fiction' and 'reality' reinforces not only patriarchal capitalist notions of gendered identity, but also ultimately shapes and informs public opinion of what might constitute a female psychopath.

References

AboutFilms. 2004. "Interviews: Charlize Theron." Accessed December 26, 2012. www.aboutfilm.com/features/monster/interviews.htm.

AFI. 2012. "AFI's 100 years . . . 100 Heroes and 100 Villains." Accessed December 26, 2012. www.afi.com/100years/handv.aspx.

Albonetti, Celesta A. 1998. "The Role of Gender and Departures in the Sentencing of Defendants Convicted of a White-Collar Offense Under the Federal Sentencing Guidelines." In *Sociology of Crime, Law and Deviance Vol 1*, edited by Jeffery T. Ulmer, 3–48. Greenwich, CT: JAI.

—. 2002. "The Joint Conditioning Effect of Defendant's Gender and Ethnicity on Length of Imprisonment Under the Federal Sentencing Guidelines for Drug Trafficking/Manufacturing Offenders." *The Journal of Gender, Race & Justice* 6: 39–60.

Arrigo, Bruce A., and Ayanna Griffin. 2004. "Serial Murder and the Case of Aileen Wuornos: Attachment Theory, Psychopathy, and Predatory Aggression." *Behavioral Sciences and the Law* 22(3): 375–93.

Belknap, Joanne. 2007. *The Invisible Woman: Gender, Crime, and Justice*. Belmont, CA: Thomson Wadsworth Publishing Company.

Bloom, Barbara, Barbara Owen, Jill Rosenbaum, and Elizabeth Piper Deschenes. 2003. "Focusing on Girls and Young Women: A Gendered Perspective on Female Delinquency." *Women & Criminal Justice* 14(2–3): 117–36.

Braun, Liz. 2004. "Inside the Monster." *Canoe—Jam! Movies*, January 15. Accessed December 26, 2012. http://jam.canoe.ca/Movies/Artists/J/Jenkins_Patty/2004/01/15/759374.html.

Buchbinder, David. 1998. *Performing Anxieties: Re-Producing Masculinity*. St. Leonards, NSW: Allen & Unwin.

Chesney-Lind, Meda. 1989. "Girl's Crime and Woman's Place: Toward a Feminist Model of Female Delinquency." *Crime and Delinquency* 35(1): 5–29.

Chesney-Lind, Meda, and Michele Eliason. 2006. "From Invisible to Incorrigible: The Demonization of Marginalized Women and Girls." *Crime Media Culture* 2(1): 29–47.

Chesney-Lind, Meda, and Lisa Pasko. 2004. *The Female Offender: Girls, Women, and Crime*. Thousand Oaks, CA: Sage.

Covington, Stephanie S. 2000. "Helping Women Recover: Creating Gender-Specific Treatment for Substance-Abusing Women and Girls in Community Correctional Settings." In *Assessment to Assistance: Programs for Women in Community Corrections*, edited by Maeve W. McMahon. Lanham, MD: American Correctional Association, 171–233.

Covington, Stephanie S., and Barbara E. Bloom. 2006. "Gender Responsive Treatment and Services in Correctional Settings." In *Inside and Out: Women, Prison, and Therapy*, edited by Elaine Leeder, 9–33. Binghamton, NY: The Haworth Press.

Daly, Kathleen. 1994. *Gender, Crime, and Punishment: Is Justice Gender-Blind, or are Men and Women Offenders Treated Differently by Courts?* New Haven: Yale University Press.

Derrida, Jacques. 1989. "Some Statements, etc." In *The States of Theory*, edited by David Carroll. New York: Columbia University Press.

Ebert, Roger. 2004. "*Monster* (Film Review)." *Chicago Sun Times*, January 1. Accessed December 26, 2012. http://rogerebert.suntimes.com/apps/pbcs.dll/article?AID=/20040101/REVIEWS/40310032/1023.

Filmsite. 2012. "All-Time Top Film Franchises." Accessed December 26, 2012. www.filmsite.org/series-boxoffice.html.

Hare, Robert D. 1998. "Psychopaths and Their Nature: Implications for the Mental Health and Criminal Justice Systems." In *Psychopathy: Antisocial, Criminal and Violent Behavior*, edited by Theodore Millon, Erik Simonsen, Morten Birket-Smith, and Roger D. Davis, 188–212. New York: The Guilford Press.

Hare, Robert D., Danny Clark, Martin Grann, and David Thornton. 2000. "Psychopathy and Predictive Validity of the PCL-R: An International Perspective." *Behavioral Sciences and the Law* 18: 623–45.

Holden, Stephen. 2003. "A Murderous Journey to Self-Destruction (Film Review)." *The New York Times*, December 24. Accessed December 26, 2012. www.nytimes.com/2003/12/24/movies/film-review-a-murderous-journey-to-self-destruction.html.

Horeck, Tanya. 2007. "From Documentary to Drama: Capturing Aileen Wuornos." *Screen* 48(2): 141–59.

Jarvis, Brian. 2007. "Monsters Inc.: Serial Killers and Consumer Culture." *Crime Media Culture* 3: 326–44.

"LD." 2010. "For Cryin' Out Loud!" Readers' Reviews, March 23. http://movies.nytimes.com/movie/287615/Monster/overview.

Miller, V. 2004. "'The Last Vestige of Institutional Sexism'? Paternalism, Equal Rights, and the Death Penalty in Twentieth and Twenty-First Century Sunbelt America: The Case for Florida." *Journal of American Studies* 38(3): 391–424.

Oprah. 2005. "Oprah Talks to Charlize Theron." Accessed December 26, 2012. www.oprah.com/omagazine/Oprah-Interviews-Charlize-Theron.

Owen, Barbara. 1998. *In the Mix: Struggle and Survival in a Women's Prison.* Albany: State University of New York Press.

Pearson, Kyra. 2007. "The Trouble with Aileen Wuornos, Feminism's 'First Serial Killer'." *Communication and Critical/Cultural Studies* 4(3): 256–75.

Rafter, Nicole. 2006. *Shots in the Mirror: Crime Films and Society.* New York: Oxford University Press.

Visher, Christy A. 1983. "Gender, Police Arrest Decisions, and Notions of Chivalry." *Criminology* 21(1): 5–28.

Filmography

Aileen: Life and Death of a Serial Killer. DVD. Directed by Nick Broomfield and Joan Churchill. 2003; Culver City, CA: Columbia TriStar, 2004.

Aileen Wuornos: The Selling of a Serial Killer. Documentary. Directed by Nicholas Broomfield. 1993; La Vergne, TN: Dej (Ingram), 2004.

A Clockwork Orange. DVD. Directed by Stanley Kubrick. 1971; Burbank, CA: Warner Home Video, 2007.

Dexter. Television. Produced by Showtime Networks. 2006. New York, NY: Showtime, 2006–.

Friday the 13th. DVD. Directed by Sean S. Cunningham. 1980; Hollywood, CA: Paramount Home Entertainment, 1999.

Monster. DVD. Directed by Patty Jenkins. 2003; Culver City, CA: Sony Pictures Home Entertainment, 2004.

Sling Blade. DVD. Directed by Billy Bob Thornton. 1996; Santa Monica, CA: Miramax, 2011.

The Silence of the Lambs. DVD. Directed by Jonathan Demme. 1991; Los Angeles, CA: Orion Pictures Corporation, 1997.

6

"LOOK AT ME": Serial Killing, Whiteness, and (In)visibility in the *Saw* Series

Mark Bernard

On October 20, 2008, the reality show *Scream Queens* premiered on the American cable network VH1. In typical reality-TV fashion, the program pitted ten aspiring actresses against each other, and the prize was a role in the upcoming film *Saw VI* (2009) as one of the Jigsaw killer's victims. This prize would have been highly coveted; the *Saw* series, which at this point consisted of four films—*Saw* (2004), *Saw II* (2005), *Saw III* (2006), and *Saw IV* (2007)—had grossed a combined total of around half a billion dollars in worldwide box office. The next film in the series, *Saw V* (2008), was slated for release in the United States on October 24, 2008, just days after the premiere of *Scream Queens*.

In some ways, *Saw* was an unlikely franchise, given its dark and violent subject matter. The films chronicle the exploits of John Kramer, aka the Jigsaw killer (Tobin Bell), a serial killer mastermind who sets intricate, deadly traps for his prey. As horrible and dangerous as Jigsaw's traps are, however, he always constructs them so that it is possible for his victims to escape and survive if they are willing to do something terrible to themselves or others. Moreover, Jigsaw's traps are usually intended to teach his victims to appreciate their lives or some other grandiose, existential lesson, provided that they survive the ordeal. Another storyline in the films is Jigsaw's search for a successor, someone to continue his work after his imminent passing; he is diagnosed with terminal cancer before the plot of the first film begins. In fact, this fatal diagnosis is initially inferred to be the inciting moment for his killing spree: since his life has been taken from him, he will teach others to appreciate theirs.

Out of the ten actresses on *Scream Queens* vying for the chance to portray a Jigsaw victim in *Saw VI*, one ultimately emerged victorious: Tanedra Howard, a 28-year-old actress from Inglewood, California. Howard's win was surprising for a few reasons, not the least of which was her 'race'. Columnist Zettler Clay (2009) described Howard as the 'underdog', noting that as the only African American actress in competition, she represented a "demographic that doesn't show up in abundance in the horror genre." Similarly, Howard was heralded by Clay Cane (2009), author of *What the Flick*, BET.com's movie blog, as the "First Black Scream Queen" in the title of an interview Cane conducted with Howard to coincide with the release of *Saw VI*.

While these commentators were surprised by Howard's win, those paying close attention to the *Saw* series should not have been surprised at all. In fact, that the one African American cast member of *Scream Queens* was picked to play Jigsaw's victim makes perfect sense given the series's problematic racial politics, which only become apparent once one is able to look past the films' Rube Goldberg traps, Grand Guignol gore, and labyrinthine plot twists. In his incisive critique of the *Saw* films and their reactionary politics, Christopher Sharrett (2009, 32) decries the films and their "intellectual bankruptcy and retrograde politics." According to Sharrett, the *Saw* series leads viewers to identify with Jigsaw, a "disgruntled, middle-class white male professional" (Sharrett 2009, 35) who, feeling powerless, strikes out against those whom he feels are unworthy and unappreciative of their lives. In doing so, the films encourage viewers to overlook that most of Jigsaw's victims are, in fact, 'non-whites' who have not squandered opportunities, but who have been born with considerable societal disadvantages (Figure 6.1).

While Sharrett broaches the matter of Jigsaw's 'whiteness' in relation to the conservative ideology informing the *Saw* films, he focuses more on the films' gender politics and how the series fits into the conservative politics of other contemporary horror films. In this chapter, I consider Jigsaw's whiteness in detail. Jigsaw strikes out against his victims and society because he feels invisible, unseen, and therefore unappreciated. However, this feeling of invisibility is actually a privilege afforded him by his whiteness that he misinterprets as weakness. Perceiving his invisibility as a curse rather than as power, Jigsaw makes himself seen by victimizing others, evincing a particular animus toward those people who do not have the privilege of being 'unseen': non-whites, women, and the poor.

The *Saw* films posit the figure of the serial killer as a disgruntled 'white' male who sick of being ignored in favor of 'special interest' groups, such as

FIGURE 6.1 *Death to the 'visible underdog': Tanedra Howard—the "First Black Scream Queen"—in* Saw VI (2009), Twisted Pictures. The Kobal Collection.

non-whites, women, and the poor, attacks these groups in a grisly fashion. In this way, the films can be seen as an illustration of the connection between whiteness and death that Richard Dyer (1997) observes in his highly influential book *White*. According to Dyer (1997, 210), "The idea of whites as both themselves dead and as bringers of death is commonly hinted at in horror film and literature." Further, Dyer (1997, 210) claims that horror provides a "cultural space that makes bearable for whites the exploration of the association of whiteness and death." However, as I argue here, these films do more than encourage whites to think over "the association of whiteness and death"; instead, these films unabashedly celebrate the marriage of whiteness and death in the figure of Jigsaw. In doing so, they often encourage spectator identification with Jigsaw, thus constructing the ideal viewer position as a victimized white male.

Whiteness, serial killing, and invisibility

In his critique of the *Saw* films, Sharrett (2009, 33) remarks that the franchise "owes more than a little" to *Se7en* (1995), a serial killer drama that had been a cinematic success almost a decade before the release of the first *Saw* film. Like *Se7en*, the *Saw* films feature a moralistically motivated killer. *Se7en*'s Jonathan Doe (Kevin Spacey) feels that he is a messenger from God dispensing divine justice on a fallen world, while Jigsaw's goal is to teach those whom he feels have wasted their life to appreciate it. Both killers construct elaborate traps for their victims that sometimes lead victims to harm themselves or others. Other similarities are the *film noir*-influenced *mise-en-scène* and tone of the films: both *Se7en* and the *Saw* films take place in anonymous cities filled with dirt, grime, and crime, and both are relentlessly bleak in their outlook. Although Jonathan Doe claims he is doing God's work, his cycle of murders based on the seven deadly sins only assures trauma and damnation, especially for Detective Mills (Brad Pitt) and his doomed wife (Gwyneth Paltrow). Similarly, most of Jigsaw's traps end the lives of their victims rather than redeem them. Even those select few who survive his traps are not made happier by their survival. For instance, Amanda Young (Shawnee Smith), a victim of the 'reverse bear trap' helmet in the first film, survives her ordeal and even gets promoted to the position of Jigsaw's accomplice, but her promotion only causes her more tribulation.

In his passing reference to *Se7en*, Sharrett also mentions Richard Dyer's (1999) in-depth analysis of *Se7en*, published as a monograph by the British Film Institute. This reference is fitting because Dyer's comments on Fincher's film, particularly those pertaining to serial killing and whiteness, provide a useful framework for analyzing the *Saw* films. In his monograph, Dyer devotes a chapter, entitled "Seriality," to discussing the figure of the serial killer in popular culture and cinema. From the outset of his analysis, Dyer (1999, 37) remarks: "Actual serial killing is a statistically unimportant phenomenon. In the USA, much less than 1 per cent of all murders are serial murders, and murder accounts for less than 1 per cent of all causes of death." Serial killer cinema, then, is surely not to be taken as inherently concerned with any real or imminent threat to human life; it is apparent that the danger of being murdered by a serial killer is statistically improbable (much less being murdered by a serial killer with the time, resources, and engineering skills that the Jigsaw killer has). However, in recognizing that serial killer narratives remain prevalent, it is useful to read them as offering a commentary on broader cultural issues.

Dyer (1999) convincingly argues that serial killer narratives often represent social anxieties relating to whiteness. According to Dyer (1999, 38), characters like *Se7en*'s Jonathan Doe reflect the statistical facts that "serial killing remains an ostensibly white male phenomenon" and that these serial killers generally "prey specifically on women or socially inferior men (young, black, gay)." While serial killer films tend not to explicitly address issues of race and gender privilege, Dyer (1999, 40) feels that, nevertheless, viewing the films can "inadvertently flush out something more often shoved under the carpet, that serial killing is a white thing." Dyer (1999, 45) explains that many filmic serial killers, like Doe, occupy a "position of power in everyday life in contemporary society . . . of notional invisibility, seeing but unseen, unmarked by particularities of class, race, or gender, a position that is mostly nearly and readily occupied by white men."

However, the anxiety of whiteness stems from how serial killers in Hollywood films often believe their invisibility and anonymity do not bestow upon them power or advantage, but interpret their invisibility or ordinariness as weakness. For instance, Jame Gumb (Ted Levine) in *The Silence of the Lambs* (1991) kills because he desires a body marked by (sexual) difference, as opposed to his 'ordinary' white male body. Another cinematic serial killer, Patrick Bateman (Christian Bale) in Mary Harron's satirical adaptation of *American Psycho* (2000), is similarly motivated; as Daniel Mudie Cunningham (2009, 42) observes, Bateman sees himself as lacking "social or cultural importance" and is spurred into serial killing by being "disenchanted with being perceived as ordinary, invisible and . . . a dork." As a result, these white men often attempt to make themselves seen and craft a visible identity for themselves through their murderous actions. As these killers go about the business of serial murder, their desire for mastery over the world is often executed methodically, thus making them what Dyer (1999, 46) calls the "amused, superior, cold geniuses of death, the apotheosis of what has been historically a white masculine ideal." This achievement leads, however, to an irony central to the character of the serial killer. Even though the serial killer often sees himself (masculine pronoun intended) existing outside of mainstream society, the serial killer, in doling out his brand of 'justice' or 'judgment', ends up replicating the values of mainstream society. As Dyer (1999, 47) explains it, "far from being against or outside society, as embodied in the law, [serial killers] in fact over-identify with it."

Several of the characteristics of both real-life and cinematic serial killers that Dyer (1999) lays out in his taxonomy of Se7en's Jonathan Doe apply to an even greater degree to John Kramer, the Jigsaw killer. Like the typical serial killer described by Dyer (1999, 37–8), Jigsaw is a white male. Additionally, it is revealed later in the series that before he began his murderous career, he was an upper middle-class engineer and urban planner, a job that places him even further into the province of privilege along with his whiteness and maleness. Jigsaw's job and its connection to real estate have specific racial implications. Following the work of George Lipsitz (2006), Steve Garner (2007, 16) observes that "racialised residential segregation" is common in "cities across the USA." This segregation is the result of urban planners like Jigsaw who "impinged disproportionately on areas where minorities live" (Garner 2007, 17–18), forcing non-whites into neighborhoods with a "heightened probability of crime, poorer-performing schools, etc., thus limiting their life chances" (Garner 2007, 18). Significantly, Jigsaw leaves out these details of his own culpability when inflicting his brand of punishment upon the people who faced societal disadvantages from their very birth due to actions taken by those urban planners like himself.

The only factor that sets Jigsaw apart from the average white, middle-aged, middle-class male is his illness. One of the catalysts for Jigsaw's crime spree is learning that he has terminal, inoperable cancer. However, Jigsaw's illness, his one marker of difference, causes him to be even more invisible. For instance, one of Jigsaw's primary victims in the first film is Dr Lawrence Gordon (Cary Elwes), who wakes up in a dingy bathroom with his foot shackled to a metal pipe. Jigsaw always leaves a microcassette and a player with instructions for his victims. When Gordon plays his tape, he learns that in order to escape and save the lives of his wife and daughter—whom, Jigsaw feels, Gordon does not appreciate because he is tempted to have an affair with another woman—he must use a hacksaw to saw through his foot. After this, he must crawl over to a gun located in the middle of the room and use that gun to kill another man, Adam (Leigh Whannell), being held captive in the room. Gordon must perform this grisly task before his allotted time runs out.

Through flashbacks, the film shows Gordon nonchalantly and unaffectedly going about his life as a doctor. In a key scene, he describes the condition of a cancer patient in his ward to a group of medical students while an orderly, Zep (Michael Emerson), toils outside the door. In a brief but telling exchange,

Gordon repeatedly speaks coldly and clinically about the patient, and Zep interrupts him:

GORDON: Okay. This patient has an inoperable frontal lobe tumor extended across the midline. Started as colon cancer. The patient has come in for a standard checkup by which we are able to monitor the rate at which his condition is declining. The patient had . . .

ZEP: (interrupting) His name is John, Dr Gordon. He's a very interesting person.

GORDON: (condescendingly) Thank you for that information, Zep. (To the students) As you can see, our orderlies form very special bonds with the patients. Continuing on . . .

Initially, it seems that this scene is intended to illustrate Gordon's callous nature and to establish tension between him and Zep. Later scenes show Zep holding Gordon's family hostage and suggest Zep is the Jigsaw killer. However, it is not until the film flashes back to this scene for a second time that the truly important information comes to the fore: the Jigsaw killer is the cancer patient who is dehumanized by Gordon's clinical language, and ignored and unseen by other characters in the film, save Zep. The film's form reinforces this idea. During this scene, only one brief shot, lasting about a second, of Jigsaw in his hospital bed is inserted into the shot-reverse-shot pattern of Gordon and Zep's exchange. The matter of Jigsaw's whiteness is also enhanced by the *mise-en-scène*; his pale body almost seems to disappear into his white hospital gown and the drab sheets on his bed.

However, this invisibility is also a privilege lent to him by his white, 'normative' body. Indeed, John/Jigsaw's invisibility places him at a great advantage throughout the first *Saw* film. None of his victims ever see him—during the time when they are trapped and tested, Jigsaw always delivers his instructions via microcassette or by speaking through a puppet that is broadcast on a television screen—and this invisibility allows him great mobility. In fact, Jigsaw's invisibility enables him to deceive the people hunting him into thinking that Zep is the Jigsaw killer. While these people are concerned with catching and stopping Zep, who has been forced by Jigsaw to hold Gordon's family hostage, Jigsaw's plans are able to unfold unimpeded. It is also worth noting that in forcing Zep into his mechanisms by poisoning him and offering an antidote only if he takes Gordon's family hostage, Jigsaw shows his hatred and disgust for those with societal disadvantages. Why should he punish Zep, a working-class man who, by all indications, had been friendly with Jigsaw during his hospital stay and had formed a "special bond" with him?

Further, one of the film's final twists is that Jigsaw has been in the dingy bathroom in which Gordon and Adam have been shackled the entire time. When they first regain consciousness, one of the first things they notice is a (presumably) dead body in the floor between them. The person appears to have committed suicide, but it turns that the dead body is Jigsaw, playing possum. Dramatically, in the film's final moments, he rises, removes some of this make-up, and shuts the door on a screaming Adam. There is no strategic reason for Jigsaw to lie on the floor in the same room with his intended victims, other than to emphasize his invisibility and that people never notice him until it is too late.

Mikel Koven (2009, 402) remarks that the "saw" referred to in the film's title most obviously refers to the saw that Gordon must use to saw through his foot to escape, but the title is also a play upon "the act of 'seeing' itself." He writes:

> Throughout the film is a strong game element, playing with sight and what is hidden from sight. The final revelation, of where the killer has been hiding the whole time, can be dismissed as a narrative trick, but given these "sight oriented" themes of the film and the rules of the game [director James] Wan and [screenwriter Leigh] Whannell invite us to play, it is the most logical of all the trumps they could have played. What we don't see has been right in front of our eyes the whole time.

Koven's comments are apt, but it is crucial to remember the importance of race in these concepts of seeing, visibility, and invisibility. Only a figure like Jigsaw who is 'unmarked' by race, possessing what Dyer calls "notional invisibility," can get away with hiding in plain sight.

Jigsaw's victims: An animus against non-whites

Regardless of the tremendous advantages afforded him by his invisibility, Jigsaw's ire still continues to be raised not, as he constantly claims, by people not appreciating their lives but, rather, by his feeling of invisibility, of not being noticed. Jigsaw's anxiety over not being seen continues even after he becomes famous as a notorious serial killer and criminal mastermind. In *Saw III*, Jigsaw, who is, by this point, extremely sick, instructs Amanda, his once-victim now-accomplice, to kidnap Dr Lynn Denlon (Bahar Soomekh) and to bring her to his hideout to force her to perform brain surgery on him to extend his life. When Amanda delivers the doctor, Denlon and Jigsaw have an extremely telling exchange. Jigsaw mentions that he was once a patient at her hospital and asks if she remembers him, insinuating that she has ignored him like everybody else. When he asks how long he has left, Denlon gives him a technical answer, which prompts him to ask her: "Why are you speaking to me in that graduate school medical jargon?" When Denlon drops her head in confusion, he screams: "LOOK AT ME!" She complies, and satisfied, Jigsaw remarks, "Now you look at me." This scene stands as an illustrative example of the social anxiety of being white, the fear of not being noticed.

He proceeds to explain that Denlon is being tested because, among other reasons, she is "dead inside" and has had "every possible advantage in life, but [has chose] not to advance." If she fails to keep Jigsaw alive for an allotted time, a deadly device around her neck will explode. Even though the audience is never given an extensive look into Denlon's background, there are two problems with Jigsaw's claims that Denlon has had "every possible advantage in life." First, Denlon is a woman in a world in which women still make less money than men and are regularly passed over for promotion in favor of men. Secondly, she is non-white, the character being played by an Iranian American actress, in a culture and society in which white is still privileged. Thus, the viewer can infer that by becoming a doctor, Denlon has overcome several societal disadvantages. Jigsaw constantly admonishes his victims that they did not work hard enough to achieve and make something of their lives. However, his victimization of Denlon illustrates that even achieving personal goals is not enough, as Jigsaw is always changing the rules. As Garner (2007, 14) notes, whiteness has the "power to invent and change the rules and transgress them with impunity; and the power to define the Other, and to kill him or her with impunity. The arbitrary imposition of life and death is one end of the spectrum of power relations that whiteness enacts."

Although the *Saw* films never explicitly address Jigsaw's whiteness, it is constantly underscored by pitting him in opposition to non-white characters. In this way, the *Saw* films again have a significant thematic element in common with David Fincher's *Se7en*. Dyer (1999) writes that while the narrative of *Se7en* does not make much of Jonathan Doe's whiteness, it becomes important in light of the casting of Morgan Freeman as Detective Somerset, Doe's ultimate adversary, and "by a number of other, in intention race neutral decisions" (39). These include casting iconic blaxploitation star Richard Roundtree, best known as the title character from *Shaft* (1971), in a key supporting role as the city's District Attorney and using music from blaxploitation film *Trouble Man* (1972) on the film's soundtrack.

In a similar manner, Jigsaw's whiteness becomes more pronounced when considered in opposition to his enemies. Although two of Jigsaw's most notable adversaries, Detective Eric Matthews (Donnie Wahlberg) and FBI agent Peter Strahm (Scott Patterson), are white men, a notable number of his foes and victims are from minority groups. For instance, in the first film, Jigsaw is doggedly pursued by Detective David Tapp (Danny Glover), an African American, and Detective Steven Sing (Ken Leung), a Chinese American. Even though Jigsaw ultimately evades these men and causes their deaths, they both prove themselves to be capable police officers. Detectives Tapp and Sing have corollaries in the characters of Xavier (Franky G) and Jonas (Glenn Plummer) in *Saw II*. In this sequel, Jigsaw captures a group of ex-convicts in a house full of elaborate and grisly traps. While the victims are relatively varied in terms of gender, race, and age, the two "leaders" of the group, as described by producer Gregg Hoffmann on a "making-of" documentary included on the film's DVD, are Xavier and Jonas, an Hispanic and an African American. Thus, the first two films in the series indicate that Jigsaw targets non-whites on both sides of the law. Also, as Jane Gaines (1994, 182) argues, there are "[r]acial hierarchies" to the gaze, with the white male gaze being superior and subordinating any gaze from a non-white character. Accordingly, Jigsaw's white male gaze, via a seemingly endless amount of hidden cameras housed in hidden labyrinthine lairs, always trumps those of his victims.

Another non-white character who challenges Jigsaw and is mercilessly punished for it is Officer Rigg (Lyriq Bent), an African American police officer who assists with key investigations into the Jigsaw murders in *Saw II* and *Saw III* and is subjected to a multilayered trap in *Saw IV*. The fact that Rigg is a capable and dedicated police officer is made apparent in the trap that Jigsaw arranges for him: Jigsaw reveals to Rigg that he is holding his friend Eric Matthews captive and that Rigg has "but 90 minutes" to run through a gamut of tests, gather clues, and find Matthews. However, Rigg does not realize that Jigsaw's tests were meant to teach him that he has been working *too* diligently at this job and that he needs to save Matthews *after* the 90 minutes have run out rather than saving him before the clock counts down. After all, it is one of the privileges of being white to arbitrarily change or break the rules and/or impose new ones. Rigg's failure to understand the purpose of his test—which was made very unclear by Jigsaw's vague and ambiguous language—leads to his death and Matthews's.

Rigg is not the only non-white character who suffers at Jigsaw's hand for performing a job too proficiently. In *Saw IV*, the FBI is called in to stop Jigsaw's reign of terror, and they send Agent Peter Strahm and his partner, Agent Perez (Athena Karkanis), an Hispanic character. Agent Strahm proves himself to be the more hotheaded and inept of the two. He badgers Jigsaw's ex-wife, Jill Tuck (Betsy Russell), for her alleged involvement in the murders, and while he makes the correct conclusion that Jigsaw has another accomplice besides Amanda Young, he incorrectly identifies Jigsaw's second accomplice as Art Blank (Justin Louis). Conversely, Agent Perez competently performs her job.

Like with Dr Denlon, there is little information given about her background, but being a non-white woman suggests that she has overcome several obstacles set in her path by white patriarchy.

Predictably, Jigsaw plants a particularly nasty trap for this accomplished non-white woman. As she and Strahm investigate a school where a Jigsaw murder took place, they find one of Jigsaw's dolls with a tape player in its hand. On the tape, Jigsaw welcomes her to "a world she has long studied" and cryptically warns her that her next move is "critical." After that, a whisper emanates from the doll, and when Perez leans forward in an attempt to hear it, the puppet's face explodes, shooting spikes into her face and throat. She is rushed to the hospital and is not seen again until *Saw VI*, when she reemerges to investigate and eventually expose Detective Mark Hoffman (Costas Mandylor), a police officer who has been secretly working as Jigsaw's accomplice. Unfortunately, her discovery gets her murdered by Hoffman, and again, she is punished for doing her job too well.

If Jigsaw's intention is to teach people lessons and to make ungrateful people appreciate their lives, the trap left for Perez—not to mention her eventual fate—makes little thematic sense. This incident, along with others in the series that involve the arbitrary punishment of non-white characters, suggests that race is a larger factor in the Jigsaw murders than it first appears and that white anxiety is Jigsaw's most significant motivation. Jigsaw's frustration is based upon being invisible and unseen, which he perceives as a weakness, not a privilege. In reference to Ralph Ellison's "invisible man," Garner (2007, 21) explains that non-whites are "invisible only as human being[s]: [they are] visible as a representation of fear, crime, sex and danger conjured from the centuries of white violence and terror visited upon non-whites: a distorting mirror in which the dominant see themselves deformed."

Thus, Jigsaw strikes out and shatters this "mirror" in which he anxiously cannot see his own whiteness. He enacts vengeance against those bodies that are visible through racial and gender difference and strives to make them invisible through death or mutilation. If, as Dyer (1999, 40) claims, the casting of noted African American actors to play capable, compassionate, and intelligent characters in *Se7en* "inadvertently flush[es] out something more often shoved under the carpet, that serial killing is a white thing," the monstrousness of whiteness is on full display in the *Saw* films. If the films offered an indictment of this monstrousness, they would perhaps be worth celebrating. However, as Sharrett (2009, 33) notes, a major stumbling block for the *Saw* films is "the filmmakers are far too smitten by the idea that Jigsaw might 'have something' to his morality." Thus, the serial killer is mobilized in these films to give furious voice to those whites who bemoan their 'disappearance' in the wake of affirmative action and the election of

Barack Obama as President of the United States. When watching the seven *Saw* films, which often come across as a hymn to white vigilante violence against non-whites, it is difficult to not be reminded of the inflammatory and xenophobic rhetoric of the Tea Party Patriots.

Whiteness, serial killing, and the law: The case of Mark Hoffman

To be fair, Jigsaw does not only target non-whites with his traps and mechanisms. The seven *Saw* films boast a large body count, and admittedly these victims are from a wide variety of social strata. Jigsaw's targets range from the white and privileged (like the aforementioned Dr Gordon and Art Blank, his lawyer) to non-white upper middle-class characters (Dr Denlon and Officer Rigg) and various members of the working class from a variety of genders and ethnic backgrounds (the group of victims captured and placed in a trap-filled house in *Saw II* include African American and Hispanic characters). Regardless, it is difficult not to consider his actions and his murders in the context of his whiteness for a multitude of reasons, not the least of which include his anxiety over the invisibility that his whiteness and privilege afford him and his opposition to, and particular malice against, non-whites. Two other aspects of the films that foreground how Jigsaw's murderous motives are grounded in whiteness are the politics behind his reason for killing and his choices of accomplices and how their respective 'careers' unfold.

The narratives of the first three *Saw* films insinuate that the sole motive behind Jigsaw's reign of terror is his discovery that he has terminal cancer and not long to live. However, *Saw IV* shows that Jigsaw's murderous spree has much different, more problematic, origins. The fourth film reveals in flashback that Jill Tuck, Jigsaw's wife, was a doctor who ran an inner-city clinic for the underprivileged, a duty that she continued to fulfil even as she was pregnant with their first child. However, a drug-addicted patient named Cecil (Billy Otis) attempts to break into the clinic one night to get methadone and, in the process, slams Jill between a door and a wall, causing her to miscarry. Afterward, a scene reveals Jill in her hospital bed with John sitting by her bedside. Referring to her patients at the clinic, Jill despairs, "All I wanted to do was help them." John coldly replies, "You can't help them. They have to help themselves." Thus Jigsaw insinuates that social programs for the underprivileged and the disadvantaged, whether it be in terms of race, class, or gender, are all doomed to failure and that the solution is to put these people in situations where the only two possible outcomes are death or learning to "help themselves" or, to use the rhetoric of rugged individualism, 'pull themselves up by their own bootstraps' even when considerable societal disadvantages have been placed in their path.

Shortly after Jill's miscarriage, Jigsaw enacts his twisted version of social programming on Cecil, kidnapping him and devising his first trap. Cecil is bolted to a chair, and in order to get free, he must press his face through a rack of knives and press a release button with his forehead, an action that will horribly mutilate his face. Even when he completes the task and gets free, there is no hope for Cecil (as it is for most of the underprivileged). In a blind rage, he attacks Jigsaw, but Jigsaw easily sidesteps Cecil, who has been blinded by the blood gushing from his face wounds, causing him to rush into a pit of barbwire. The more Cecil struggles, the more he becomes ensnared while Jigsaw methodically looks on, taking notes with a pencil and notepad.

In this regard, Jigsaw truly embodies Dyer's (1999, 47) observation that serial killers in cinema often seem like they are the antithesis of "the law," but ironically "over-identify" with it. In other words, serial killers rarely offer any opposition to the dominant status quo because their actions resemble the oppressive law of dominant society taken to a twisted, but chillingly logical, extreme. In his analysis of *Se7en*, Dyer (1999) discusses Jonathan Doe's admiration for Detective Mills, one of his pursuers, and this admiration eventually leads Doe to attempt to 'become' Mills and 'lead his life' with his wife Tracy during the 'Envy' crime. While *Se7en* explores the surprising kinship between the serial killer and the law in ways that uncover the connections between whiteness and vigilante justice, Jigsaw's kinship with the law is disturbingly harmonious.

One of the most significant examples of Jigsaw's place being with the law rather than outside it is his partnership with Detective Mark Hoffman. Jigsaw is such an effective criminal mastermind, able to devise and build elaborate traps and execute complex plans, because he has three accomplices: Amanda Young, Mark Hoffman, and Dr Lawrence Gordon (after his trap depicted in the first film converts him to Jigsaw's philosophies and cause). In the second film, it is revealed that Jigsaw is working with Amanda, but Jigsaw's partnership with Hoffman is not revealed until the fourth film. Significantly, Hoffman is one of the few white characters on the police force who is trying to catch the murderer, so it makes sense that Jigsaw and Hoffman would gravitate toward each other. Another similarity between these two men is that their whiteness makes them invisible. Like Jigsaw in the first film, who 'hides in plain sight' at the heart of his trap, Hoffman appears to be a victim in the trap from which Rigg attempts to save Matthews. The invisibility that their whiteness grants them allows them to hide out in the open without fear of being noticed.

Hoffman also shares Jigsaw's desire to enact the law to its most grotesque extremes. In *Saw V*, it is revealed that Hoffman's sister was murdered by a man named Seth Baxter (Joris Jarsky), who was sentenced to life in prison, but released after only five years because of a technicality. After Baxter's release, Hoffman kidnaps him and places him in a Jigsaw-esqe trap. In the trap, Baxter is stretched out on a slab as a razor-sharp pendulum slowly descends, swinging, above him. To stop the pendulum from slicing him in half at his waist, Baxter must destroy his hands, the instruments that have destroyed others, in small hydraulic presses. Baxter is able to carry out the destruction of his hands, but the pendulum does not stop and eventually descends to slice him in half. Hoffman then makes the scene of the crime look like a Jigsaw murder.

Jigsaw eventually hunts down Hoffman, kidnaps him, and takes him back to one of his lairs. There, Jigsaw lectures Hoffman about the error of his murderous ways, but offers him a chance of 'redemption' by becoming his accomplice. Jigsaw's partnership with Hoffman explicitly demonstrates the cinematic serial killer's paradoxical affinity with the law and social order. In this case, serial killer and cop work to achieve the same end: a fascistic circumvention of due process and the individual's rights in a war against the disenfranchised, underprivileged, and anybody whom they feel does not meet their moral standard.

However, things do not work out with Hoffman. After Jigsaw's death, Hoffman carries out Jigsaw's final plans, but also begins killing people for selfish reasons. For instance, he murders Agents Strahm, Perez, and Erikson (Mark Rolston) to protect his double identity. Jigsaw, foreseeing Hoffman's renegade activities, appeals from beyond the grave (via videotaped messages left behind with his will) to Jill Tuck and Dr Gordon to stop Hoffman. Ultimately, Hoffman's rampage, which is eventually ended by Dr Gordon in the final film, *Saw 3D: The Final Chapter* (2010), brings to mind Robin Wood's (2003, 150) claim that, in American popular film, "democratic capitalism" is forever threatened by its potential to become fascism. In other words, Hoffman is the offspring of Jigsaw's white vigilante worldview who shows just how monstrous Jigsaw is underneath all his glib moralizing. Thus, it makes sense that Jigsaw would be willing to put his beloved ex-wife in danger to stop Hoffman since the corrupt police officer foregrounds the lies of Jigsaw's philosophy.

Fall from whiteness: The case of Amanda Young

Things also do not work out with Jigsaw's first accomplice, Amanda Young, but for different reasons. The fact that Jigsaw has a female accomplice who helps perpetrate many of his crimes may seem, at first, to undermine the claims made here about the connections between serial killers and privileges afforded by whiteness and maleness. However, the ways in which Amanda's story unfolds do not undermine these connections, but only serve to strengthen them because Amanda is a failure at being a serial killer and at being a 'successful' Jigsaw accomplice. Moreover, her failure is directly tied to how her body is marked by 'difference'; her femaleness does not afford her the same invisibility and disconnectedness that makes Jigsaw a successful serial killer. Apparently, serial killing is not only a white thing, but also a 'guy thing'.

Amanda is introduced in the first film as the victim of one of Jigsaw's most memorable traps: the 'reverse bear trap' helmet. In *Saw*, the story of Amanda's trap is revealed in flashback as she recounts the story to Detective Tapp. In her flashback, she wakes up in the 'reverse bear trap' helmet, and on a video screen, Jigsaw, through his puppet, explains that since she has spent much of her life as a drug addict, he does not feel that she properly appreciates her life. Thus, her trap is meant to teach her to appreciate her life by being forced to fight for it. She is given a brief amount of time to dig out the key from the stomach of an unconscious person locked in the room with her and unlock the helmet before her time runs out and the helmet rips her head open. As her story ends and the film returns to the police station, Tapp confronts Amanda about her troubled history as a drug addict, to which Amanda tearfully replies, "He . . . helped . . . me," a response that shocks Tapp and Dr Gordon, who is looking on from another room.

Amanda returns in *Saw II*, as the ending of this sequel reveals that since she passed her Jigsaw test, she has been helping Jigsaw as his accomplice. However, it becomes apparent that Amanda will not be as effective as Jigsaw because her anger makes her unable to become the 'ideal' serial killer, that is, the emotionally detached and intelligent white male. Amanda cannot achieve this ideal because of her emotional troubles, and in secret she cuts herself, an affront to her white skin that should bring her happiness. After she begins constructing traps that are impossible to survive, Jigsaw tests her in *Saw III*. He commands Amanda to kidnap Denlon and bring her to their hideout both to perform improvised brain surgery on him and to put Amanda's ability to overcome her anger to the test.

After Denlon temporarily saves Jigsaw's life, he shows her a great deal of affection in Amanda's presence to make Amanda jealous. In one instance, as Jigsaw is kind to Denlon and treats Amanda harshly, Amanda storms out of the room, and Jigsaw explains that "[Amanda's] emotion is . . . her weakness," an observation that shows Amanda falling short of the cold detachment that is the hallmark of the white male serial killer. At the film's conclusion, Denlon actually passes her test and keeps Jigsaw alive for the prescribed amount of time, but by this point, Amanda is in hysterics because of the emotional abuse she has endured. With tears in her eyes and a trembling voice, she holds a gun on the doctor and threatens to kill her even though she passed her test. When Jigsaw tells her that she should not harm Denlon because their fates are connected in his game, Amanda angrily accuses him of hypocrisy, claiming that his games do not work: "[N]obody fucking changes. Nobody is reborn. It's all bullshit. It's all a fucking lie. And I'm just a pawn in your stupid games."

Unbeknownst to Amanda, Jigsaw has arranged for Denlon's estranged husband, Jeff (Angus Macfadyen), who has just undergone his own series of Jigsaw tests and has been given a loaded handgun, to emerge through a door in the room Jigsaw, Amanda, and Denlon are standing. Amanda finally loses her temper, hangs her head in shame, and shoots Denlon in the back just as her husband enters the room. Reacting, Jeff shoots Amanda in the throat, and as she falls to the ground, gasping for breath and blood gushing from her throat, Jigsaw reveals his plan to her, that all of this has been a test to see if she could control her emotions. In short, Amanda's anger, which stems from her legitimate status as victim, causes her to become too involved in her interactions and keeps her from being the ideal serial killer. A flashback in *Saw VI* reveals that Amanda does not kill Dr Denlon just because of her anger. Instead, Hoffman, without Jigsaw's knowledge, slips Amanda a note beforehand, telling her that Denlon knows that she was present the night Cecil broke into Jill Tuck's clinic and accidentally caused Jill Tuck to miscarry. Hoffman assures Amanda that Denlon will share this information with Jigsaw and that, as a result, Jigsaw would blame Amanda for the death of his unborn son.

This incident illustrates the impossibility of Amanda becoming the perfect, detached, white, male, middle-class serial killer. Through Amanda's character, another type of white anxiety is introduced: the fear of not being 'white enough'. Amanda is emblematic of Cunningham's (2009, 49) claims "that privileged whiteness is increasingly being represented as an identity that can no longer claim access to privilege simply on the grounds of race." Disqualified by her gender and class, she is cast out of whiteness and into the substrata of 'white trash', which is represented in popular culture as "poor, dirty, drunken, criminally minded, and sexually perverse" (Newitz and Wray 1997, 1). Instead of having the privilege of invisibility afforded to the white, male, middle-class serial killer, Amanda must inhabit a body marked by the ravages of drug addiction, self-mutilation, and criminalization forced upon her by patriarchal white law. In this way, Amanda is the perfect symbol for an era of intense economic recession in which many previously comfortable members of the middle class have watched helplessly as their class markers (homes, jobs, etc.) slip away, thus making her another example of how the figure of the serial killer obtains cultural resonance in the *Saw* series.

Material and cultural effects of race and representation

Race is never explicitly mentioned in the *Saw* films until the final one. Four members of a skinhead gang—Evan (Chester Bennington), Jake (Benjamin Clost), Dan (Dru Viergever), and Kara (Gabby West, who was, incidentally, the winner of the second season of *Scream Queens*)—find themselves in an elaborate trap. Evan has been strapped into the driver's seat of an automobile sitting on jacks inside of an abandoned garage, his shirtless back glued to the seat. Jake is chained to the wall directly in front of the car, and Dan's wrists and jaw are chained to the back of the car. Beneath one of the car's rear wheels, Kara is bound with barbwire. Jigsaw/Hoffman's taped message informs them that they "are all racists" who have "intimidated others based on their physical differences." The message also explains that Evan will have to tear himself away from the seat, ripping off the skin of his back, to reach a lever sticking through the broken windshield. If he does not reach the lever in 30 seconds, the jacks beneath the by-then-fully-revved car will fall away, dismembering and killing them all.

Predictably, Evan does not reach the lever in time, and he and all his friends are gruesomely killed as the car speeds through the wall of the garage and into some wreckage outside. So, all these 'racists' have been duly punished for their crimes in an elaborate set-up that seems to reverse the racist bent of Jigsaw's other crimes. However (and also predictably), any chance that Hoffman/Jigsaw has become racially self-aware and is now punishing racists, instead of non-whites, is undermined by a revelation that comes later in the film; Hoffman sets this trap to distract the police while he sneaks into a police safe house where Jill Tuck checked in seeking protection against Hoffman. While the police are distracted, Hoffman is able to infiltrate the safe house and murder Jill with the 'reverse bear trap' helmet. Thus, any gesture toward punishing race-hate is mere smokescreen to throw off the audience. The series keeps its disturbing attitudes about race subordinated to stomach-churning gore and mind-numbing plot twists.

Tanedra Howard, the *Scream Queens* winner who was awarded a part in *Saw VI*, puts forth what could be the only positive spin on the abundance of victims who are non-whites in the *Saw* films. In an interview, Howard praises the *Saw* films for their diverse casting: "Sometimes in a lot of horror films you don't see other races. . . . For *Saw*, there is always different people so each race can connect. Like, 'Oh, I see me on the screen—this is cool'" (Cane 2009). While Howard undeniably has a point about the material circumstances of *Saw*'s casting—at least non-white actors are getting consistent work from the series—it is nevertheless unfortunate that the roles are mostly limited to playing the victim of a white maniac for whom the audience is encouraged to cheer as the figure of the serial killer is utilized in this series as a vehicle of white frustration, anxiety, and vigilantism. While short-term material circumstances for non-white actors may be positive, long-term cultural circumstances could be less so.

References

Cane, Clay. 2009. "First Black Scream Queen: Tanedra Howard." What the Flick, October 22. Accessed November 26, 2011. http://blogs.bet.com/celebrities/what-the-flick/first-black-scream-queen-tanedra-howard.

Clay, Zettler. 2009. "Tanedra Howard: A Dream Deferred No More." *Clutch Magazine*, January 15. Accessed November 26, 2011. www.clutchmagonline.com/2009/01/tanedra-howard-a-dream-deferred-no-more.

Cunningham, Daniel Mudie. 2009. "Patrick Bateman as 'Average White Male' in *American Psycho*." In *Pimps, Wimps, Studs, Thugs and Gentlemen: Essays on Media Images of Masculinity*, edited by Elwood Watson, 40–50. Jefferson, NC: McFarland & Company, Inc.

Dyer, Richard. 1997. *White*. New York: Routledge.

—. 1999. *Seven*. London: BFI Publishing.

Gaines, Jane. 1994. "White Privilege and Looking Relations: Race and Gender in Feminist Film Theory." In *Multiple Voices in Feminist Film Criticism*, edited by Diane Carson, Linda Dittmar, and Janice Welsch, 176–90. Minneapolis: University of Minnesota Press.

Garner, Steve. 2007. *Whiteness*. New York: Routledge.

Koven, Mikel. 2009. *"Saw."* In *101 Horror Movies You Must See Before You Die*, edited by Steven Jay Schneider, 402. Hauppauge, NY: Barron's.

Lipsitz, George. 2006. *The Possessive Investment in Whiteness: How White People Profit from Identity Politics*. Philadelphia: Temple University Press.

Newitz, Annalee, and Matt Wray. 1997. "Introduction." In *White Trash: Race and Class in America*, edited by Annalee Newitz and Matt Wray. Durham: Duke University Press.

Sharrett, Christopher. 2009. "The Problem of *Saw*: 'Torture Porn' and the Conservatism of Contemporary Horror Films." *Cineaste* 35(1): 32–7.

Wood, Robin. 2003. *Hollywood from Vietnam to Reagan . . . and Beyond*. New York: Columbia University Press.

Filmography

American Psycho. DVD. Directed by Mary Harron. 2000; Santa Monica, CA: Lionsgate Home Entertainment, 2005.

Behind the Scenes. Saw II. DVD. Director unknown. 2006; Santa Monica, CA: Lionsgate Home Entertainment, 2006.

Saw. DVD. Directed by James Wan. 2004; Santa Monica, CA: Lionsgate Home Entertainment, 2005.

Saw II. DVD. Directed by Darren Lynn Bousman. 2005; Santa Monica, CA: Lionsgate Home Entertainment, 2006.

Saw III. DVD. Directed by Darren Lynn Bousman. 2006; Santa Monica, CA: Lionsgate Home Entertainment, 2007.

Saw IV. DVD. Directed by Darren Lynn Bousman. 2007; Santa Monica, CA: Lionsgate Home Entertainment, 2008.

Saw V. DVD. Directed by David Hackl. 2008; Santa Monica, CA: Lionsgate Home Entertainment, 2009.

Saw VI. DVD. Directed by Kevin Greutert. 2009; Santa Monica, CA: Lionsgate Home Entertainment, 2010.

Saw 3D: The Final Chapter. DVD. Directed by Kevin Greutert. 2010; Santa Monica, CA: Lionsgate Home Entertainment, 2011.

Se7en. DVD. Directed by David Fincher. 1995; Los Angeles, CA: New Line Home Entertainment, 2000.

Shaft. DVD. Directed by Gordon Parks. 1971; Burbank, CA; Warner Home Video, 2000.

The Silence of the Lambs. DVD. Directed by Jonathan Demme. 1991; Beverly Hills, CA: MGM Home Entertainment, 2001.

Trouble Man. DVD. Directed by Ivan Dixon. 1972; Los Angeles, CA: 20th Century Fox Home Entertainment, 2006.

7

Shopping and Slaying, Fucking and Flaying: Serial Consumption in *American Psycho*

Christina Lee

In the words of the old saying, every society gets the kind of criminal it deserves.

ROBERT F. KENNEDY, 1965, 47

onvicted serial killer Jeffrey Dahmer once stated: "My consuming lust was to experience their bodies. I viewed them as objects, as strangers" (quoted in Egger 2003, 195). Between 1978 and 1991, Dahmer murdered 17 people (all males) in the states of Ohio and Wisconsin. Often committing rape and necrophilia, he would dismember the victims and store body parts before allegedly feeding on them. While he "confessed to eating part of one of his victim's arm muscles" and a human heart, according to Richard Tithecott (1997, 66) the emphasis upon anthropophagy was dubious and spoke more to the workings of sensationalist tabloids than to the evidence.[1] Nonetheless, cannibalism became, and endures as, a crucial component of the Dahmer mythos. Intense media attention surrounding his trial further signaled a form of cultural cannibalism. An estimated 450 journalists covered the trial in July 1991, and in the years following his conviction in 1992 there was a slew of media productions based on Dahmer's crimes that included movies, documentaries, novels, and comic books (Vronsky 2004, 19). Dahmer was offered up for ritualized consumption in various cultural representations that were perversely enthralling and repelling. His body count included a growing, captive audience even after he had died.

While the concept of serial murder can be considered a product of modernity, the postmodern condition has allowed the serial killer to flourish as the contemporary icon/superstar.[2] As Jon Stratton (1996, 95–6) argues, the shift to a society of spectacle has resulted in the aestheticization of serial killing. In the simulatory social (or the hyperreal), the moral has been replaced by the aesthetic as "the privileged mode of judgement." The exploits, and subsequent exploitation, of the serial killer represents the extremity of postmodernity and late capitalism whereby virtually everything, from information to relationships, can be reduced to a monetary value (Miles 1998, 16). Violence is big business, and 'making a killing' from tragic narratives has become *de rigueur* in popular media. The cultural construction of the serial killer as yet another fetish commodity legitimates, even naturalizes, our lurid attraction by concealing the audience's role in the production of this figure. The origin of the term 'serial killer', coined by FBI profiler Robert Ressler in the late 1970s, is a reminder of its conceptualization within a consumerist discourse. The nomenclature was influenced by the serial adventures Ressler viewed at the movies as a youth. He aligned the episodic nature of *The Phantom* series with the mentality of serial killers (Ressler and Shachtman 1992). Just as cliff-hangers would lure audiences back to the cinema, the "very act of [serial] killing leaves the murderer hanging, because it isn't as perfect as his fantasy . . . his mind jumps ahead to how he can kill more nearly perfectly the next time; there's an improvement continuum" (Ressler and Shachtman 1992, 33). As the audience craves satisfaction through continuous consumption, so too does the serial killer. Both have a hunger with an inherent violence.

There is a thriving industry capitalizing on the lives and transgressions of factual and fictional serial killers. Alongside depictions of popular culture anti-heroes such as Dexter Morgan and Hannibal Lecter, there can be found a more diffused attraction to actual killings and the macabre. They comprise part of what Mark Seltzer (1998, 253) terms "wound culture," that is, shared excitations "of the torn and opened body, the torn and exposed individual, as public spectacle." Carnage as entertainment is nothing new. The gladiatorial challenges of the Roman Empire and public executions of Elizabethan England attest to early exhibitions of sanctioned corporeal violation. However, Seltzer's (1998, 265) concept is specific to postmodernity in that "the subject of wound culture is not merely subject to recurrence but to the recurrence of recurrence itself." Technology facilitates mimesis and allows the re-playing and re-experiencing of a collective trauma. We need only recall the looped footage of hijacked planes penetrating the Twin Towers in 2001 and our compulsion to watch suffering and broken bodies.

One of the by-products of wound culture is the murderabilia trade in which backseat spectatorship of serial murder is elevated to the overt fetishizing and procurement of artifacts. A google search of "murderabilia" produces a cornucopia of items available to build a true crime collection. On the website Supernaught.com for instance, the enthusiast can purchase a note handwritten and addressed to a Florida Death Row inmate by Ted Bundy, original Pogo the Clown artwork by John Wayne Gacy, an unfinished bag of *Chips Ahoy!* chocolate cookies once owned by Charles Manson, and plate fragments collected from the site where Ed Gein's farmhouse of horrors once stood (includes a photograph of the building). Your very own piece of homicide history is only a credit card and mouse-click away. The sale of murderabilia constitutes a small component of a vast serial killer industry that has, since the late 1970s/early 1980s, "become a defining feature of American popular culture" (Schmid 2004, n.p.). While murderabilia operates outside of the mainstream and is generally regarded as unethical and unsavoury, the relationship between serial murder and its consumption in manifest forms is pervasive and unavoidable.[3] For example, speculations of Jeffrey Dahmer's story being sold to Hollywood when he was still alive prompted the family members of his victims to sue for any money he might have received. After his murder in 1994 while in prison, they (unsuccessfully) attempted to auction his possessions. The proposed register of over 300 items included prosaic objects such as Dahmer's toothbrush, and instruments used directly in the killings such as the hammer and saw used for dismemberment, the refrigerator for storing human hearts and a 55-gallon vat for decomposing bodies.

> The victims' families recognized the value of certain ordinary objects that were turned into sacred relics through Dahmer's rituals and his televised trial. They wanted to possess the remains from his crimes in exchange for the body parts of their loved ones that Dahmer had fetishized. These surrogate objects would then be offered to other consumers. (Pizzato 1999, 91)

The motives of the family members were to reclaim a sense of control over their tragedies by implementing Dahmer's personal effects. However, their actions inadvertently participated in the prior fetishization of those props by the killer himself and reinforced "the consumption of his cannibal drama by a mass audience" (Pizzato 1999, 91). Human afflictions do not exist outside of a consumerist discourse.

The Dahmer case draws an obvious analogy between serial killing and the act of consuming (bodies as objects). This relationship is captured in Bret Easton Ellis's novel *American Psycho* (1991) and Mary Harron's film adaptation in 2000. The protagonist Patrick Bateman's insatiable appetite extends to his cataloguing of people before slaying and, in some cases, eating them. The narrative proposes a limit case where there are no more limits; where the lines separating reason from irrationality, actuality from constructed narrative, consumer from the consumed, and subject from object have been problematically ruptured. In discussing the novel and film adaptation, this chapter considers the serial killer as a monstrous cultural artifact whose thrill to kill is not isolated. The compulsion to consume/possess implicates an audience whose fascination with gruesome spectacle exemplifies the basic economic principle that the market will strive to meet ever-increasing demand; revealing a mask of sanity that has, to borrow from Bateman, begun to slip. When we have consumed all there is around us, what else is left to feed on but ourselves? The mordant depiction of the serial killer in *American Psycho* is informed by, and a response to, a postmodern culture of rampant consumerism where capitalism and the aestheticization of the self has reached its frightening, logical endpoint.

Murders and acquisitions: Serial killing, serial consumption

> The history of capitalism can be told as a monster story from beginning to end. (Newitz 2006, 12)

American Psycho is an indicting representation of the sociocultural milieu of the late 1980s and early 1990s in the United States of America. This historical juncture was marked by the excesses of Reaganomics and the dominance of a ruthless corporate culture (Dickenson 2006, 15). Shaped by the ideology of individualism, conservatism, and aggressive economic and social policies espoused by the Reagan administration (and similarly the Thatcher government in the United Kingdom), the 1980s in particular has become synonymous with solipsistic materialism—the pursuit of happiness translated to the pursuit of hyper-consumerism. In the United States, the unrelenting quest for personal wealth and self-interest took precedence over critical national and international issues that included the increasing disparity between the rich and poor, the ravaging effects of the AIDS epidemic (and the government's delayed response to the situation), the widespread infiltration of narcotics into the country and the overflow in prisons (Cannon 2000, 1187). The thinly veiled hostility toward social democracy and civil liberties was evidence of a cut-throat culture in which Darwin's 'survival of the fittest' was deemed not only inevitable but beneficial (MacKinnon 1992, 31). The government's antiwelfarist position was signaled by actions such as tax reforms, cuts to non-military programs (including Medicaid, public housing, food stamps, and school lunch subsidies), and its zealous support for traditionalist values. These had significant material and ideological implications for the country's most disadvantaged and discriminated citizens (primarily women, the working class, African Americans, and homosexuals) (Krieger 1987, 188, 195). In his State of the Union address in 1982, Ronald Reagan's declaration that his administration was beginning to mobilize the private sector and would not "duplicate wasteful and discredited Government programs" was indicative of new national priorities which polarized its subjects (quoted in Linden 2004, n.p.). 'Moral' citizens were the heroic entrepreneurs while 'slacker' citizens were the human 'waste' that leeched from the system.

In *American Psycho*, Patrick Bateman functions as a severe caricature exposing the underlying ideology of the New Right stripped of its sugar-coated spin and sloganeering. A militantly conservative and *laissez-faire* mentality finds its staunchest supporter in the unapologetic Bateman who makes the admission that he has all the characteristics of a human being "but not a single, clear identifiable emotion, except for greed and disgust." It is perhaps no coincidence that his initial victims in the novel (homosexuals, the homeless, and immigrants) include those identified in Reagan's policies as impeding the nation's path to prosperity. The assault upon the welfare system translates into Bateman's attack on those he deems society's parasitic dregs who are undeserving of the right to live. The protagonist's inalienable sense of entitlement and self-importance is a crude rendering of the rhetoric of good versus evil, premised on individual responsibility and the supposedly common sense notion of morality, that conflates industry and entrepreneurship (progress and productivity) with the capacity for goodness.

Just as Reagan broadly applied "this understanding of the nature and meaning of human life to issues as wide-ranging as work and welfare, crime and punishment, the family, and relations with the Soviet Union" (Busch 2001, 12), Bateman's propensity for outrage and sneering aversion toward that which he considers sinful is expansive. In the film when he chastises a homeless man named Al for his poverty before murdering the drifter, Bateman's own generalized feelings of injustice and his inability to recognize that the personal is political are illustrated. His initial façade of humanitarianism ("You want some, uh, money? Some food?") quickly devolves into condescension ("Why don't you get a job? . . . You got a negative attitude. That's what's stopping you") and then abuse ("You know how bad you smell? You reek of shit. . . . I don't think I have anything in common with you"). In Bateman's mind, gutting and maiming the vagabond is justifiable punishment. It fulfills his need to rid the streets of undesirables. Those who are not useful in society—human refuse—are extirpated. Bateman is the self-aggrandizing Moneyed Avenger with the unquestioned authority of upward social mobility and wealth.

In relation to the serial killer, Anthony King (2006, 109, 122) makes the argument that this figure presents an apposite study of the postmodern self that is constituted by the temporary euphoria of commodified consumption. *American Psycho* exemplifies this assertion, functioning as a satirical commentary on the homology between serial murder and unchecked capitalism. It is significant that Bret Easton Ellis includes an extract from Fyodor Dostoyevsky's *Notes from the Underground* as an epigraph to the novel; a reminder of the connection between the fictional and factual realms. While Dostoyevsky (1992 [1918], 1) confirms the imaginary nature of the narrator/protagonist of *Notes from the Underground*, he adds that "such persons as the writer of these notes not only may, but positively must, exist in our society, when we consider the circumstances in the midst of which our society is formed."[4] Dostoyevsky's and Ellis's anti-heroes are 'Underground Men'; social figures who are products of their environments. They are the manifestations of our deepest cultural anxieties. The character of Patrick Bateman echoes the narrator/protagonist of Dostoyevsky's novella who indulges his bitter contempt for society. Both are hypocrites whose elevated positions (intellectually, morally, or as part of the social elite) are predicated on the suffering of others. As with Dostoyevsky's protagonist, Bateman devolves rapidly to a state of what appears illogical reasoning and uncontrollability. However, the hyperbolic prose and increasingly erratic behavior of the individuals are symptomatic of their contextual 'rotten to the core' societies that have created these abominable character types.

Bateman epitomizes a hedonistic culture whose lust for money and power was so brilliantly conveyed in Gordon Gekko's infamous maxim: "Greed is good." He is the serial killer as "gothic projection of the commodifying fury of late capitalism" (Jarvis 2007, 343). Bateman works on Wall Street and holds the position of Vice President at the investment firm Pierce & Pierce. He lives in a luxurious Upper West Side apartment, dates a Manhattan socialite, and is Hollywood-attractive. Patrick Bateman is also a psychopath. He avers: "There is an idea of a Patrick Bateman. Some kind of abstraction, but there is no real me. Only an entity. Something illusory . . . I simply am not there." His multiple murders reify the notion that serial killing cannot be divorced from general forms of seriality and irrational fixation, "[t]he collecting of things and representations, persons and person-things like bodies" (Seltzer 1998,

64). The protagonist's accumulation of victims become souvenirs alongside his accumulation of consumer products. Bateman's serial consumerism and serial killing are (failed) attempts to satiate his compulsion for repetition (Seltzer 1998, 65).

In the opening credits of the film, the inseparability of the commodification of violence and the violence of commodification is blatantly established (Jarvis 2007, 328). Over a white background, an ominous soundtrack plays. Red droplets begin to fall from the top of the frame, accompanied by a subdued *Psycho*-like discordant violin. As the music transitions to a knowingly playful classical score, it becomes apparent that the droplets are the decorative *jus* on a plate. Images of a knife chopping through a slab of meat and shots of people eating in an upscale restaurant are interspersed throughout the credits to emphasize the seductive and unsettling act of devouring. Gastronomic pleasure requires a ritual of violence before and during the act of consumption, that is, in its preparation (killing, eviscerating, crushing, severing) and its ingestion (mastication, tearing, gorging, and so on). This violent process is civilized through the use of fine cutlery, etiquette, and language that transforms living organism into 'food' (captured in one waiter's announcement: "For entrées this evening, I have swordfish meatloaf with onion marmalade, rare roasted partridge breast in raspberry coulis with a sorrel timbale and grilled free-range rabbit with herbed French fries"). What is made clear is the tenuous line separating unacceptable destruction from acceptable consumption.

In *American Psycho*, as everything has a price everything can therefore be acquired, expended, and discarded. The narrative evokes all possible meanings of the word 'consume'—to purchase (possess), to eat, and to destroy—to articulate "a confused consumerism that has run out of control and exceeded all boundaries" (Annesley 1998, 16). Even when Bateman is sporadically aware of the intolerability of his heinous actions, this is superseded by his unconstrained lust. His casual approach to human abuse presents a limit case of commodity fetishism that no longer recognizes the process of production, merely the act of consumption. He can only conceptualize of things in their finished form, that is, the money form of a commodity. If, as Karl Marx (1957 [1930], 49) asserts, man "begins by an examination of the finished product, the extent result of the evolutionary process," then Ellis's protagonist represents a (d)evolution in which *only* the finished product matters. This complete detachment is evident from Bateman's dehumanization of sex workers. He objectifies these women by renaming them (in one scene in the film, he says: "You're Christie. You're to respond only to Christie," "Christie, get down on your knees," "Christie, look at the camera") and positions them as props in his reconstructed sadistic, pornographic fantasies. After fucking and flaying

FIGURE 7.1 *"Greed is good": Patrick Bateman's ménage à trois in* American Psycho *(2000), Lionsgate. The Kobal Collection.*

them, he gnaws on several of their bodies and uses their skulls as bowls (in the novel), unperturbed by the fact that these were living human beings not long before (Figure 7.1).

The dissociation of social relations of labor from finished product is also conveyed through the indulgent, leisure-driven lifestyles led by Bateman and his associates. There appears to be little or no labor involved in the acquisition of their wealth. Bateman spends his days in the office listening to his Walkman, doing crossword puzzles, and browsing through entertainment magazines. Status symbols, including job titles, "never refer to the effort that it took to attain them or to the activities that they involve" (Robinson 2006, 27). The signifier has become detached from its sign, leading to a loss of reference. For instance, Bateman's murder of Al (the vagrant) and his mutt shows his inability to distinguish between the adrenalin rush of slaying and shopping, murder and a McHappy meal. In the novel, he comments:

Afterwards, two blocks west, I felt heady, ravenous, pumped up, as if I'd just worked out and endorphins are flooding my nervous system, or just embraced that first line of cocaine, inhaled the first puff of a fine cigar, sipped that first glass of Cristal. I'm starving and need something to eat, but I don't want to stop by Nell's, though I'm within walking distance and Indochine seems an unlikely place for a celebratory drink. So I decide to go somewhere Al would go, the McDonald's in Union Square. (Ellis 1991, 132)

Hyper-consumerism is substituted for fulfilment, leading to a perversion of (in)human responses. Bateman's most genuine moments of expression do not occur in the heat of his ferocious attacks. Rather, they are in direct response to the status that certain symbols accord and their exchange value. In the film, such moments are captured in Bateman's voice-overs when trying to secure an enviable table at an exclusive restaurant ("I'm on the verge of tears by the time we arrive at Espace, since I'm positive we won't have a table"); in relation to the fatuous details of his colleague's business card ("Look at that subtle off-white coloring. The tasteful thickness of it. Oh my God. It even has a watermark"); and when he deduces that his dead rival's domicile trumps his own ("There is a moment of sheer panic when I realize that Paul's apartment overlooks the park and is obviously more expensive than mine").

Careful detailing in the *mise-en-scène* and setting descriptions in *American Psycho* recreate a late 1980s America characterized by wanton consumption. Characters dine in haute cuisine restaurants, slavishly wear only fashion labels, spend countless conversations discussing luxury goods and trading restaurant reviews, and indulge in drink, drugs, and sex. Bateman's conspicuous consumption is mirrored in his meticulous accounts. Shortly after the film's exposition, we are shown a montage sequence of the protagonist going through his morning ritual involving rigorous exercise and an extensive grooming regime. Overlaid with his voice-over, the scene establishes the narrative's major theme of inexhaustible, meaningless consumption. Bateman states:

In the morning, if my face is a little puffy, I'll put on an icepack while doing my stomach crunches. I can do a thousand now. After I remove the icepack, I use a deep pore cleanser lotion. In the shower, I use a water-activated gel cleanser. Then a honey-almond body scrub. And on the face, an exfoliating gel scrub. Then I apply an herb mint facial masque which I leave on for ten minutes while I prepare the rest of my routine. I always use an aftershave lotion with little or no alcohol, because alcohol dries your face out and makes you look older. Then moisturiser, then an anti-aging eye balm, followed by a final moisturising protective lotion.

Bateman's obsessive detailing and listing are the only means he has for defining himself. It is a case of "I buy, therefore I am," even though he admits that beyond the illusion, beyond the idea of a Patrick Bateman, there is a void (which shall be discussed in greater detail in the following section). In the novel, this cataloguing is accentuated by the tedious citation of brandnames and items that include not only beauty products, clothing, household items, and gourmet food, but also people as 'concepts'. For instance, Bateman incessantly name-drops celebrities such as Bono and Tom Cruise. Yet none of the encounters with these individuals is a meaningful exchange, and they become symbols of what the protagonist aspires to but does not possess—fame, individuality, and visibility.

In his sharp designer suits, Bateman projects the image of yuppie success. However, it is a thin veneer concealing his overwhelming sense of invisibility, emptiness, and dissatisfaction. His sense of self (or lack of) is wholly dependent upon his capacity to serially possess and consume objects, including people. But just as there is nothing behind the façade of Patrick Bateman, there is nothing meaningful beyond the product. Bateman's intimate knowledge of 'things' does not amount to a richness of cultural capital, but a portrait of mechanical consumption (Kauffman 1998, 247). The litany of details signify a glut of over-burdened style that, in its excess, is transformed into the banal. *American Psycho* is a hyper-representation of a society in which the public defines itself as a market, and its citizens as consumers (Kauffman 1998, 244). Bateman is the embodiment of a desire marked by an aesthetics of nothingness in which the act of consuming becomes in and of itself the necessity, that is, consumption for consumption's sake.

Fine young cannibal: Consuming the self

A Richard Marx CD plays on the stereo, a bag from Zabar's loaded with sourdough onion bagels and spices sits on the kitchen table while I grind bone and fat and flesh into patties . . . I just remind myself that this thing, this girl, this meat, is nothing, is shit. (Ellis 1991, 345)

At one point in the film, Patrick Bateman's *ménage à trois* with two women climaxes with his eating one of them while she is still alive (he emerges from beneath the bedsheets with a blood-smeared face) and butchering the other with a chainsaw. In this scene, his slaughterhouse is uncovered. There are human heads preserved in the refrigerator and naked female bodies strung up in the cupboard like animal carcasses in an abattoir. In this moment, the serial killer's cannibalistic impulse as a form of savage serial consumption is actualized. If indeed "the mode of organization of the relation to the body reflects the mode of organization of the relation to things and of social relations" (Baudrillard 1998, 129), *American Psycho* proposes a culture where human relations have been commodified to the point that the body is reduced purely to capital and fetish (consumer object).

Bateman as cannibal conflates the unbridled consumerism in a late capitalist society with the voracious appetition of the serial killer. Just as Bateman's sadistic compulsions are without bounds, late capitalism is marked by its limitless devouring and destruction of resources and the subsequent mass production of detritus. Brian Jarvis (2007, 329) claims that this consuming involves:

> . . . pollution, waste and the ravaging of non-renewable resources, bio-diversity and endangered species; the slaughter of animals for food, clothing and medicine; countless acts of violence against the consumer's body that range from spectacular accidents to slow tortures and poisonings. . . . At the international level, consumer capitalism depends heavily on a "new slavery" for millions in the developing world who are incarcerated in dangerous factories and sweatshops and subjected to the repetitive violence of Fordist production.

Capitalism's "invisible imprint of violence" enables us to consume without guilt or conscience (Renner 2002, 53). This is represented in *American Psycho* by Bateman's indiscriminate switching from copious lists of luxury items to step-by-step graphic accounts of barbarism that include rape, torture, necrophilia, and mutilation. Reaching a crisis point in consumerism, people and inanimate objects become interchangeable and indiscernible. Despite his undeniably deplorable acts, Bateman is himself the product of a pervasive culture of use and abuse. For instance, while we may advocate against continued environmental degradation by big industry, memories of razed forests and exploited third-world farmers are easily forgotten at the mere scent and savoured first taste of single origin coffee beans blended into a skinny latte. For the average consumer, the smooth finish lingers. The images of violence involved in its production, however, do not.

The enduring and potent link between capitalism and cannibalism finds its origins in the colonial narratives of the New World and its menagerie of exotic and frightening Others. While earlier reports of anthropophagy still remain highly contested, these stories persist because they serve an ideological purpose in (post)colonial/capitalist ventures.[5] Peoples whose alleged abject appetite signified primitiveness and deviancy were rendered subhuman, thereby legitimating their 'civilizing' (domination) through the disciplines of physical labor, sanctioned punishment, and re-education (Lefebvre 2005, 46). Cannibalism as a catch-all phrase of barbarism "was used to reinforce the boundary between civilization and savagery, as a screen for colonial violence at a historical moment when European powers were spreading their influence all over the globe" (Parasecoli 2008, 58). Exploitation of bodies was justified as a necessity for progress and expansion into new colonies, intertwining discourses of industriousness with discourses of morality and virtue (which seems to have been reappropriated in the 1980s as discussed earlier in the chapter). The concept of the cannibal was integral in establishing the "appetite relations" between capital and labor, and constructing a binary between positive (proper) and negative (improper) appetite (Bartolovich 1998, 214). Richard Tithecott (1997, 66) wryly notes that "[e]ating people, it would seem, is not necessarily wrong. It depends on who's doing the eating and who's being eaten." While consumption of human labor is acceptable, consumption of human flesh is not. The former qualifies as healthy, while the latter is desire without discipline.

In *American Psycho*, the line separating taboo from acceptable practice is dissolved. While Bateman's initial inventory of victims is a line-up of society's impoverished and disempowered, his cannibalistic turn begins to target those within his own socioeconomic circle. The spirit of the free-market and entrepreneurial 'killer instinct' finds its sublimated form in *American Psycho* in which the capitalist's conquest, like the cannibal's, is "justified by the law of the jungle: eat or be eaten" (Kilgour 1998, 243). Table manners need not apply. Previously, the cannibalistic instinct was figured in terms of production as captured in Marx's (1957 [1930], 232) oft-cited passage: "Capital is dead labour, and, like a vampire, can only keep itself alive by sucking the blood of living labour. The more blood it sucks, the more vigorously does it live." However, there has been a shift in emphasis from capitalist production toward the anthropophagic nature of mass consumption. In other words, "viewing people primarily as purchasers of fast food burgers and toiletries rather than producers of these items" (Bartolovich 1998, 235). Furthermore, the consumer feeds not only on its own kind but also its own self. Late capitalism has segued into what Crystal Bartolovich (1998, 204) refers to as the "cultural logic of late cannibalism." The repetitive consumption of representations of men and women as body-objects, particularly in fashion and advertising, reifies the cannibalistic/serial killer impulse into a familiar pattern of desire, creation, and mutilation. External images become projections of a more desirable self (Lefebvre 2005, 51–2). In *American Psycho*, Jean Baudrillard's (1998, 135) assertion that "[t]he individual has to take himself as object, as the finest of objects, as the most precious exchange material" is taken literally. Bateman's physical assaults on others and his own self find their equivalent in our own subjection to voluntary violence and the dissection of bodies into parts/things. Self-exploitation is naturalized through the rigors of exercise, starvation via strict diet, painting the skin with toxic chemicals, wounding through cosmetic surgery, and enduring impractical accoutrements that deform and inflict pain (stilettos, corsets, and so on). Violence merges with discipline, and pain with the pleasures of ideal representation. The vigor of late capitalism has turned people into resources for production *and* consumption.

American Psycho makes the heavy-handed point that the socially desirable attributes of competitiveness and success have contributed to a nihilistic aesthetics of nothingness. Within a late capitalist society, the packaged self is a coalescence of personal identity and consumer identity (Loudermilk 2003, 88, 90). Investment in the artifice of surfaces becomes paramount, but ultimately presents a shift toward hollow consumption (or to use a food-related analogy, 'empty calories'). For Bateman, flaying several of his victims merely confirms that beneath the skin/surface there is "meat, is nothing, is shit." This nothingness is reinforced in his empty rhetoric (Cunningham 2009, 45). During a dinner scene, Bateman vapidly espouses the importance of ending apartheid, terrorism, world hunger, and the nuclear arms race, providing welfare for the homeless, opposing racism, promoting gender equality and civil rights, encouraging a return to traditional moral values, and most importantly promoting "general social concern and less materialism in young people." These are, of course, all politically correct sound-bytes that the protagonist does not ascribe to but is able to mechanically parrot. His nonexistent moral conscience is irrelevant.[6] What matters is his ability to perform and triumph over his opponents (the other dinner guests).

Bateman's "blocked needs" cannot be satiated because his need is the very act of consuming (Ellis 1991, 338). René Girard (2005 [1972], 155) argues that one's intense desire is the unattainable fantasy, predicated on the desire for "*being*, something he himself lacks and which some other person seems to possess." If we are to apply this to *American Psycho* and consumer culture in general, we can posit that the drive for the ideal life (and body) keeps the individual in a perpetual state of dissatisfaction or starvation. We gorge on popular representations that circulate in the mass media. Yet these images hold the ideal self at a distance, reinforcing our lack based on what others possess. Hence the glut of, and gluttony for, tabloid magazines, celebrity-based television programs, and gossip columns about the rich and (in)famous. Despite his escalating body count, Bateman is ironically the ultimate (fashion) victim in the narrative. Shackled to trends and fads, he is "as generic as the mass-produced consumables he uses, items sold on an empty promise of individuality, authenticity, and exclusivity" (Cunningham 2009, 43). Just as he does not distinguish people from objects, so too is he indistinguishable from others. As with several other characters, the protagonist is continually mistaken for someone else (even by his own lawyer when he attempts to confess his crimes at the film's conclusion). If anything, Bateman's serial sameness to those around him is his (un)defining feature.[7] Even his diabolical acts are plagiarized versions of the 'accomplishments' of real-life serial killers, such as Ed Gein and Ted Bundy, who he refers to during conversations. Their notoriety, fame, and popularity elude Bateman and reiterate his failure. At one point in the novel, Bateman describes three vaginas stored in his gym locker and nonchalantly remarks: "There's a barrette clipped to one of them, a blue ribbon from Hermès tied around my favorite" (Ellis 1991, 370). However, he is not the first to have committed such grotesquely comical disfigurement. Gein tied a red ribbon through one of the vulva he kept in a shoebox (Vronsky 2004, 187). Any semblance of shocking originality by Bateman is exposed as an imitation.

The mimetic nature of Bateman's personality is mirrored in the narrative's style. Bateman speaks in the language of mediated representation. James Annesley (1998, 7) writes that blank fiction (which *American Psycho* may be categorized as) "does not just depict its own period, it speaks in the commodified language of its own period." Littered throughout the novel are Bateman's descriptions directly poached from the lexicon of cinematography and advertising. He speaks of pans, dissolves, smash cuts, jump zooms, scenes playing in slow motion, and so on. The character is a "cut-up (like his victims) of commodity signs" (Jarvis 2007, 334). This is demonstrated in the film via clichéd scenarios that overtly borrow from well-known genres, such as the slasher film and pornographic movie. For example, in one scene we see Bateman working out while *The Texas Chainsaw Massacre* (1974) plays in the background on his television. Later on, the protagonist re-enacts his own version of this classic horror story when he pursues, and exterminates, a prostitute with a gleaming chainsaw. The intentional hackneyed shots cutting between the hysterical victim (a wayward, blonde female), the dismembered body parts she uncovers and Bateman's crazed expressions, as well as the noir lighting and gothic corridors and staircase, fulfill the format of the archetypal slasher film. *American Psycho*'s incorporation/ingestion of *The Texas Chainsaw Massacre* transforms the American enterprise of meatpacking—or "mergers and acquisitions" in this case—into "murders and executions" (Robinson 2006, 28). Furthermore, it reveals a blurring between the protagonist's actuality and narrative fantasies, and the merging of subject with object.[8] As the leading star in his own horror story, Bateman has become a character/trope/object for *our* viewing pleasure.

Coda

Convicted serial killer Edmund Kemper once apologized to his interviewer: "I'm sorry to sound so cold about this but what I needed to have was a particular experience with a person, and to possess them in the way I wanted to; I had to evict them from their human bodies" (quoted in Ressler and Shachtman 1992, 97). While his depraved delectation may invite disgust, Kemper's dehumanization of the victims is perhaps less detached from our own consumerist practices and yearnings than we would like to believe. Beneath the patina of civilized consumption lies an incessant, cannibalistic hunger. The mediation and framing of contemporary acts of serial killing through commodity consumption implicates the audience/market, making us concurrently victims and perpetrators (King 2006, 117). The thrill and terror of consuming (violence) does not belong to the serial killer alone.

In the character of Patrick Bateman, we find a nightmarish manifestation of our greatest aspirations. His vacuous attractiveness masks a brutality intrinsic to mass consumption. The figuration of the serial killer (and late capitalist) as cannibal holds sway over the public imagination not only because of its deplorability, but also because we—as the audience—have helped create it and participated in its fetishization. As James Annesley (1998, 13) writes, "[i]n the terms laid down by Ellis, Patrick Bateman's murders are crimes for which an increasingly commercial and materialistic society must take ultimate responsibility." The serial killer is a social functionary; a cautionary dark reflection of specific cultural and historical contexts. As Robert F. Kennedy (1965, 47) once stated, "every society gets the kind of criminal it deserves." In times of famine or feast there will always be desire. And where there is desire, the market will strive to meet demand. I am reminded of David Schmid's (2004, n.p.) question: "When the logic of consumerism dominates, is anyone truly innocent, or are there just varying degrees of guilt, of implication?" As I write the final words of this chapter, I need not look too far for the answer. The collectible Patrick Bateman action figurine stares at me with his dead, plastic eyes from inside his boxed home, and I switch off John Cale's mischievously morbid soundtrack to *American Psycho*. All are inspirations for/from the monster (within).

Notes

1 In court on January 30, 1992, Lieutenant Dennis Murphy provided details of Dahmer's attempt to consume one of his victims: "[Dahmer] indicated that

he had filleted his [victim's] heart and kept it in a freezer and he also kept his bicep. He indicated that he had eaten the thigh muscle of this subject but it was so tough he could hardly chew it. He then purchased a meat tenderiser and used it on the bicep" (quoted in "Jeffrey Dahmer: Monster Within," 1996).

2   In modernity, the rise of the metropolis produced a teeming mass of anonymous individuals (victims reduced to innumerable unidentifiable figures; perpetrators as spectres in a crowd), new technologies and modes of communication facilitated widespread reporting of illegal activities, and transformations in the relationship between individuals and the state resulted in new understandings and definitions of criminality.

3   In May 2001, eBay banned the sale of murderabilia after mounting pressure and criticism by the mainstream public (Schmid 2004, n.p.).

4   This quote is taken from a republication of the novella as it appeared in *White Nights and Other Stories* by the Macmillan Company (1918). It therefore contains minor differences to the extract in Ellis's novel.

5   See William Arens (1998).

6   This reinforces the earlier argument made by Jon Stratton (1996, 93) that the social has been transformed into a simulatory social, that is, a spectacularized social "where the moral has been translated into the aesthetic" and in which "we are all becoming anomic."

7   See Daniel Cunningham (2009).

8   This blurring is brought to the foreground in the novel when Bateman is pursued by police after shooting dead a street busker. There is an abrupt shift from first- to third-person point of view, indicating his loss of perspective and subjectivity. He experiences the event like a scene from a movie. Fantasy ruptures his reality: "racing blindly down Greenwich I lose control entirely, the cab swerves into a Korean deli . . . the cab rolling over fruit stands, smashing through a wall of glass, the body of a cashier thudding across the hood, Patrick tries to put the cab in reverse but nothing happens" (Ellis 1991, 349).

References

Annesley, James. 1998. *Blank Fictions: Consumerism, Culture and the Contemporary American Novel*. London: Pluto Press.

Arens, William. 1998. "Rethinking Anthropophagy." In *Cannibalism and the Colonial World*, edited by Francis Barker, Peter Hulme, and Margaret Iversen, 39–62. Cambridge: Cambridge University Press.

Bartolovich, Crystal. 1998. "Consumerism, or the Cultural Logic of Late Cannibalism." In *Cannibalism and the Colonial World*, edited by Francis Barker, Peter Hulme, and Margaret Iversen, 204–37. Cambridge: Cambridge University Press.

Baudrillard, Jean. 1998. *The Consumer Society: Myths and Structures*. London: Sage Publications.

Busch, Andrew. 2001. *Ronald Reagan and the Politics of Freedom*. Lanham, MD: Rowman and Littlefield Publishers.

Cannon, Carl. 2000. "The '80s vs. the '90s." *National Journal* 32(16): 1186–94.

Cunningham, Daniel Mudie. 2009. "Patrick Bateman as 'Average White Male' in *American Psycho*." In *Pimps, Wimps, Studs, Thugs and Gentlemen: Essays on Media Images of Masculinity*, edited by Elwood Watson, 40–50. Jefferson, NC, and London: McFarland & Company, Inc.

Dickenson, Ben. 2006. *Hollywood's New Radicalism: War, Globalisation and the Movies from Reagan to George W. Bush*. London and New York: I.B. Tauris.

Dostoyevsky, Fyodor. 1992 [1918]. *Notes from the Underground*. New York: Dover Publications, Inc.

Egger, Steven. 2003. *The Need to Kill: Inside the World of the Serial Killer*. Upper Saddle River, NJ: Prentice Hall.

Ellis, Bret Easton. 1991. *American Psycho*. New York: Picador.

Girard, René. 2005 [1972]. *Violence and the Sacred*. Translated by Patrick Gregory. London and New York: Continuum.

Jarvis, Brian. 2007. "Monsters Inc.: Serial Killers and Consumer Culture." *Crime Media Culture* 3(3): 326–44.

Kauffman, Linda. 1998. *Bad Girls and Sick Boys: Fantasies in Contemporary Art and Culture*. Berkeley: University of California Press.

Kennedy, Robert F. 1965. *The Pursuit of Justice*, edited by Theodore J. Lowi. London: Hamish Hamilton.

Kilgour, Maggie. 1998. "The Function of Cannibalism at the Present Time." In *Cannibalism and the Colonial World*, edited by Francis Barker, Peter Hulme, and Margaret Iversen, 238–59. Cambridge: Cambridge University Press.

King, Anthony. 2006. "Serial Killing and the Postmodern Self." *History of the Human Sciences* 19(3): 109–25.

Krieger, Joel. 1987. "Social Policy in the Age of Reagan and Thatcher." *The Socialist Register* 23: 177–98.

Lefebvre, Martin. 2005. "Conspicuous Consumption: The Figure of the Serial Killer as Cannibal in the Age of Capitalism." *Theory, Culture and Society* 22(3): 43–62.

Linden, James. 2004. *State of the Union Addresses of Ronald Reagan*. Project Gutenberg EBook. Accessed December 27, 2012. www.gutenberg.org/cache/epub/5046/pg5046.html.utf8/.

Loudermilk, A. 2003. "Eating 'Dawn' in the Dark: Zombie Desire and Commodified Identity in George A. Romero's 'Dawn of the Dead'." *Journal of Consumer Culture* 3(1): 83–108.

MacKinnon, Kenneth. 1992. *The Politics of Popular Representation: Reagan, Thatcher, AIDS, and the Movies*. Rutherford, NJ: Fairleigh Dickinson University Press.

Marx, Karl. 1957 [1930]. *Capital: Volume 1*. Translated from the 4th German edition by Eden and Cedar Paul. London: Dent.

Miles, Steven. 1998. *Consumerism: As a Way of Life*. London: Sage Publications.

Newitz, Annalee. 2006. *Pretend We're Dead: Capitalist Monsters in American Pop Culture*. Durham and London: Duke University Press.

Parasecoli, Fabio. 2008. *Bite Me: Food in Popular Culture*. Oxford and New York: Berg.

Pizzato, Mark. 1999. "Jeffrey Dahmer and Media Cannibalism: The Lure and Failure of Sacrifice." In *Mythologies of Violence in Postmodern Media*, edited by Christopher Sharrett, 85–118. Detroit: Wayne State University Press.

Renner, Michael. 2002. *The Anatomy of Resource Wars*. Washington, DC: Worldwatch Institute.

Ressler, Robert, and Tom Shachtman. 1992. *Whoever Fights Monsters: My Twenty Years Tracking Serial Killers for the FBI*. New York: St. Martin's Press.

Robinson, David. 2006. "The Unattainable Narrative: Identity, Consumerism and the Slasher Film in Mary Harron's *American Psycho*." *CineAction* 68: 26–35.

Schmid, David. 2004. "Murderabilia: Consuming Fame." *Media/Culture Journal* 7(5). Accessed December 27, 2012. http://journal.media-culture.org.au/0411/10-schmid.php.

Seltzer, Mark. 1998. *Serial Killers: Death and Life in America's Wound Culture*. New York: Routledge.

Stratton, Jon. 1996. "Serial Killing and the Transformation of the Social." *Theory, Culture and Society* 13(1): 77–98.

Supernaught. 2012. "Supernaught.com: True Crime Memorabilia and Gallery." Accessed December 28, 2012. www.supernaught.com.

Tithecott, Richard. 1997. *Of Men and Monsters: Jeffrey Dahmer and the Construction of the Serial Killer*. Madison: The University of Wisconsin Press.

Vronsky, Peter. 2004. *Serial Killers: The Method and Madness of Monsters*. New York: Berkley Books.

Filmography

American Psycho. DVD. Directed by Mary Harron. 2000; Santa Monica, CA: Lionsgate Home Entertainment, 2005.

"Jeffrey Dahmer: Monster Within." *Biography*. DVD. Produced by Christine Schuler. 1996; New York, NY: A&E Television Networks, 2009.

The Texas Chainsaw Massacre. DVD. Directed by Tobe Hooper. 1974; Universal City, CA: Universal Studios Home Entertainment, 2003.

8

'Slash Production': Objectifying the Serial "Kiler" in Euro-Cult Cinema Fan Production

Oliver Carter

Introduction

Since the mid-1990s I have been a fan of the *giallo*, a cycle of films particularly popular in Italy during the late 1960s and 1970s. A typical *giallo* film narrative will feature a crazed black-gloved serial killer murdering beautiful women in varying exaggerated fashions. In the early 1990s British and American horror film fans learnt about the *giallo* in fan publications such as *Giallo Pages* and *European Trash Cinema* which created interest and paved the way to forming a Euro-Cult fan culture centred around the *giallo* film. Euro-Cult cinema itself is a fan determined category; not only do fans discuss the films in online communities but also actively produce texts for distribution among the fan network. In early 2003 it came to my attention that a film called *Fantom Kiler* (1998) had been released on DVD; promotional materials for the film labeling it as a "stylish East European *giallo*." Its production shrouded in mystery, *Fantom Kiler* gained notoriety within the online Euro-Cult fan community. Apparently made in Poland, though most of the spoken dialogue is a mixture of both Polish and Russian, the film follows a masked serial killer who stalks and murders a number of scantily clad women. Filmed on video tape, suffering from constant changes of aspect ratio and having numerous subtitle spelling errors, the low-budget origins of the film are apparent. On viewing the film for the first time I did not find it pleasurable, primarily because of its amateurish appearance, the highly sexualized depiction of serial murder, and bawdy comic interludes. I found it to be similar in content to the large body of extremely low-budget 'shot-on-video' horror films that are produced by fans of horror and are specifically aimed at the horror fan community. These productions blend near hardcore pornography, gratuitous nudity, poor acting, and graphic scenes of serial murder into a near 90 minutes of running time. But, as a scholar of Euro-Cult cinema, I found it especially interesting as a contemporary interpretation/tribute to the *giallo* film. Through a close examination of the narrative and production of the *Fantom Kiler* film series, this chapter explores the politics of 'slash production'; a form of fan production that gives specific attention to serial murder and reproduces the serial killer as a fan object.

Following the release of the first instalment of the series, rumors began to circulate within online message boards regarding the mysterious production history of the *Fantom Kiler*. Who was Roman Nowicki, the credited director of the film? Were the production company Teraz Films responsible for any other films? Information emerged stating that 'Roman Nowicki' was a pseudonym for a British horror fanzine producer who played an important role in developing Euro-Cult cinema fandom in the United Kingdom. Clues to the British origins of the film could be found throughout the film; one particularly attentive viewer identifying the English locales used. As further details surfaced more *Fantom Kiler* films were released. To date, there have been four films in the *Fantom Kiler* series, with each sequel closely matching the theme of the earlier entries: scantily clad women being murdered in varying sexually aggressive ways by a masked serial killer. Yet each of these sequels becomes increasingly sexually explicit in their representation of serial murder.

Drawing on an interview conducted with 'Roman Nowicki', I will begin by defining the *giallo* film, demonstrating how serial murder is often a common element in the narrative of many *gialli*. Secondly, I will define the term 'slash production' and examine how it can be understood as an extension of slash fan fiction, but which focuses on fan reinterpretations of serial murder. Finally, the production, distribution, and consumption of the *Fantom Kiler* series will be analyzed in order to understand how it can be considered an example of 'slash production'. Conclusions will be drawn on how this specific example of fan film making is an extreme expression of fan passion for horror cinema but also has an important economic dimension; a way for fans to make an income from the texts that they have produced. In this sense, they are blurring the boundaries between amateur and professional media production. Additionally, the *Fantom Kiler* series also raises questions about policy and the regulation of production of such films in the United Kingdom. The *Fantom Kiler* series, through its intertextual relationship with *giallo*, further illustrates the contemporary fascination with the serial killer and allows for a new consideration of the ways this cultural figure is appropriated by fan cultures for pleasure *and* profit.

The *giallo*

Serial murder is a common plot device in the narrative of many *gialli*. The *giallo* film was based on pulp crime novels that were popular in Italy during the Second World War. They were often Italian translations of English books, authored by Agatha Christie, Edgar Wallace, and Sir Arthur Conan Doyle, published by a Milan-based company, Mondadori (Koven 2006, 2). These novels had distinctive yellow front covers, hence the Italian term *giallo* which translates into English as 'yellow'. They proved to be a welcome distraction to a country embroiled in fascism, and their popularity would influence a number of Italian film-makers and scriptwriters. Though there is a certain amount of conjecture as to what is the first *giallo* film, many scholars, such as Adrian Luther Smith (1999, 45), consider it to be Mario Bava's *La ragazza che sapeva troppo/The Girl Who Knew Too Much* (1963):

> Although there had been a number of Italian murder mysteries, Bava's *La ragazza che sapeva troppo* is generally regarded as the first thriller which typifies the term giallo as it uses plot elements from the popular crime novels with yellow covers and combines these with touches of horror.

Inspired by the Agatha Christie novel *The A.B.C. Murders*, *La ragazza che sapeva troppo* tells of a young woman who travels to Italy to visit her sick Aunt. While there, she witnesses a murder that is committed by a serial killer and discovers that he is murdering his victims in alphabetical order. The Italian police do not believe her, as the body of the murdered woman cannot be found. This film introduced a number of conventions that have been employed in the narratives of many *gialli* that followed its release: a foreigner who becomes a witness to a murder; the amateur sleuth; serial murder; incompetent Italian police; and a complex narrative structure. For many fans it is these generic elements that come to mind when attempting to define the *giallo*.

However, the *giallo* has a different meaning to Italian film audiences. Gary Needham (2003) suggests that the Italian understanding of genre is different to the British and American interpretation of genre. Italians use the word *filone*, which can refer to both a genre and a cycle of films. For example, in Italy, the label of *giallo* will be applied to any film that is considered a thriller regardless of its country of origin. Outside of Italy, many fans see the *giallo* as a distinct subgenre belonging to the category of horror film. I would argue that this interpretation is rather problematic as many of the films labelled as *gialli* by non-Italians fall outside of the 'typical' conventions. Though murder is a key ingredient of all *gialli*, serial murder is not common to all *gialli*. There are a number of films labeled as *gialli* that focus on embezzlement, such as *Il dolce corpo di Deborah/The Sweet Body of Deborah* (1968), *Paranoia* (1970), and *Il posto ideale per uccidere/Dirty Pictures* (1971), and others that are concerned with a woman's descent into madness such as *Le orme/The Footprints* (1975) and *Il profumo della signora in nero/The Perfume of the Lady in Black* (1974). Therefore, attempting to apply the concept of genre to the *giallo* is somewhat problematic, sharing similarities with debates surrounding film *noir* (Silver 1999). With this in mind, I will be referring to the *giallo* as a cycle or a movement of film that has an identifiable style, as opposed to a cohesive film genre, that is defined, in part, by a particular set of narrative and character elements.

The serial killer is a common entity in American and British culture. Mikel J. Koven (2006, 97) notes that while serial killing and serial murder does exist in Italy it is so uncommon that there is no actual equivalent Italian word for the term; it is considered very much an American phenomena. Koven (2006, 97) points to the term '*il mostro*' (the monster) as the one commonly used by Italians, such as in the infamous '*Il mostro di Firenze*' (The Monster of Florence) murders, when referring to serial murder. The lack of an Italian word for 'serial killer' is surprising considering the large number of *gialli* that focus on serial murder. The film of particular importance here is Mario Bava's *Sei donne per l'assassino/Blood and Black Lace* (1964), arguably the most influential film in the *giallo* canon and a stylistic influence on the *Fantom Kiler* film series.

Luther Smith (1999, 11–12) believes that *Sei donne per l'assassino* "encapsulates the very essence of what most people define as *giallo* cinema." This film focuses on a series of murders committed by a masked killer who is trying to recover a diary that contains scandalous information. The killer is dressed head-to-toe in black; black overcoat, black leather gloves, and black Trilby hat. The faceless gauze mask hides the identity of the killer, a distinctive generic iconography that has become ever present in the American stalk and slash subgenre, such as the mask worn by Michael Myers in the *Halloween* film series (1978–98). The film contains a number of notable murder set pieces where victims are stalked and ultimately murdered in lurid ways. For example, one female victim is tortured and then has her face scalded on a hot stove while another has a spiked glove thrust into her face. Though the scenes are not shown in graphic detail, they set a standard for a number of *gialli* that would be released after this film. Many future *gialli* would have particularly graphic murder sequences, where attractive women, often in varying states of undress, would be stalked and eventually murdered in horrific ways. This has led to many *gialli,* particularly the work of Dario Argento (Hope 2005), being labeled as a misogynistic due to the graphic representations of female murder in his films. As highlighted by Leon Hunt, many murder sequences found in *gialli* are highly sexualized, demonstrating "hostility to the female body" (Hunt 2005). Crotch stabbings feature in a number of *gialli*, such as *L'assassino ha riservato nove poltrone/The Killer Reserved Nine Seats* (1974) and *Giallo a Venezia/Thrilling in Venice* (1979), and murder weapons are commonly fetishized; the camera paying attention to the phallic quality of knives (Guins 1996). In an oft-cited quote, Argento has said that he prefers to see women murdered on screen than men: "I like women, especially beautiful ones . . . if they have a good face and figure, I would much prefer to watch them being murdered than an ugly girl or man" (quoted in Clover 1992, 42). In a macabre spin on the director cameo, popularized by Hitchcock, Argento is known for wearing the black gloves and assuming the role of the serial killer during many of the murder sequences in his films (Mendik 2000).

Though *gialli* were low-budgeted B movies they have a particular visual style that conflicts with their "low-budget" origins (Bondanella 2003, 419). Bava would draw on his skills as a cinematographer to employ unusual lighting techniques and use primary color filters in his films in order to "forge unforgettable images of visual poetry and narrative potency" (Jones 1997, 58). One of the murder sequences in *Sei donne per l'assassino* is shot using a variety of color filters, adding an artistic, fantastical element to the brutal murder. Argento is also renowned for his unique visual style that will often place viewers in the killer's gaze or position audiences in the shoes of the investigator. Raiford Guins (1996, 148) has suggested that Argento will often punish the viewer, as well as aesthetically please them, with his use of creative camera angles and setups. Like Bava, Argento also is known for his use of primary colors in his films, particularly the color red. Even some of the lesser-known and lower-budgeted *gialli* will have similar creative touches in their use of camera angles and color. Many *gialli*, but especially those directed by Argento, explicitly reference psychoanalytic ideas in their narratives. In *Profondo Rosso/Deep Red* (1975), for example, Freud's primal scene is used to explain the motivations of the film's serial murderer. This might explain why the majority of academic enquiry into the *giallo* has focused on psychoanalytical readings of the work of *giallo* auteurs such as Argento and Lucio Fulci (Mendik 1996, 1998, 2001; Gallant 2000). Having identified that serial killing is a key element of many *gialli* and that murder is represented in a particularly graphic, sexualized manner, I want to consider how fan communities might and do engage with these narratives of serial killing. To this end, I will examine in detail the production of the *Fantom Kiler* series as a form of 'slash production'. But, first, we must define the term.

From 'slash fiction' to 'slash production'

For my purposes, slash production can been defined as a form of amateur fan-produced film, or other fan-produced text, that is primarily concerned with serial murder and scenes of extreme violence. I wish to use the term as an extension of 'slash fiction', though it is significantly different in terms of its topic and concerns. According to Henry Jenkins (1992, 186), slash fiction is a form of fan writing that "refers to the convention of employing a stroke or slash to signify a same-sex relationship between two characters and specifies a genre of fan stories positing homoerotic affairs between series protagonists." Well-established examples of slash fiction are the homoerotic relationship between Spock and Kirk from the *Star Trek* television series (Penley 1992), Xena and Gabrielle in *Xena: Warrior Princess* (Caudill 2003) and, more recently, the characters in the *Harry Potter* series (Rowling 1997–2007) have been the subject of many online slash writings (Willis 2006). A large amount of academic enquiry has been devoted to such examples of homoerotic slash fiction.

Slash fan fiction, whether it is written or visual, offers alternative interpretations to the sanctioned, legitimate storylines and character relationships offered by scriptwriters. The difficulties in defining slash fiction are highlighted by Cheryl Harris and Alison Alexander (1998) who identify not only the sexually explicit and politically conscious nature of the genre but also see it as both complex and developing. For example, online searches for fan fiction will not only find homoerotic (re)imaginings involving popular television and film characters, it will also locate fan writings that can offer extreme sexual or violent reinterpretations of popular media. However, unlike typical homoerotic slash fiction, highly sexual or violent slash appears to lack a strategic political dimension; it is merely a deviant reinterpretation of a popular media text. An extreme example from a rather innocuous sector is a fan-written script for the Australian soap opera *Neighbours* that can be found online. This script focuses on the kidnap and subsequent sexual torture of a character from the show, providing a graphic detailed breakdown of the scene. Though potentially disturbing it provides an example of the diversity of slash fiction and how fan audiences can produce new meanings, no matter how deviant, from the media they consume. It also highlights how the ease of online publishing allows for a greater proliferation of slash fiction and makes it accessible to a wider audience. Previously confined to fanzines only obtained through grassroots fan networks, slash fiction can now be easily located through a simple Google search or on sites such as fanfiction.net. By looking at the wealth of categories on fanfiction.net, one can see both the variety and sheer abundance of fan-written material that offers all sorts of fan interpretations of popular media.

Camille Bacon-Smith (1992) believes that slash-fiction contains a number of subgenres. In the "genre of pain," she notes that slash fiction can be violent, focusing on both pain and suffering (1992, 55). This not only shows the diversity of slash fiction, but also how extreme the content of fan production can be. Therefore, I present 'slash production' as a subgenre of slash fiction; a subgenre that offers fan interpretations of serial murder through varying forms, such as fan film production. The term employs the literal interpretation of the word slash (to cut in a violent manner) and is primarily found within horror fan practices. Anyone familiar with the specialist fan publications devoted to horror films, particularly those originating from the 1990s, such as the US publications *Fangoria* and *Deep Red*, will have noticed that they gave a significant amount of attention to violent murder and the amount of gore contained in horror films. One can see that this association is clearly evident in the titles of these publications; *Fangoria* containing the syllable 'gor(e)' and *Deep Red* producing connotations of blood and sharing its name with the coincidental international release of Dario Argento's *giallo Profondo Rosso/Deep Red*. Guins (2005, 24) has noted how fan writings on Italian horror films, such as *gialli*, in the pre-DVD age would be viewed as "gore objects." These fan publications would place specific attention on the serial killer as part of their fascination with blood and gore. In Britain, horror film fan publications would have a similar focus, but adopt a more bawdy style of writing that is not too dissimilar to the tone of *The Benny Hill Show* television series or the *Carry On* films. They would also give a large amount of coverage to film and video censorship (Kimber 2002). The British fanzine *Is it Uncut?* is one of many that explores the censorship of horror films and identifies the most uncut version available on DVD or VHS. This suggests that fan publications can be important mechanisms in shaping the reception of horror films.

Linda Badley's (2009) research into horror cinema and video culture makes mention of the American underground horror scene and the fan-produced horror films that circulate among that community. Badley (2009, 51) suggests "underground horror appeals to people who want something 'real', raw or extreme." She refers to these as direct to video films (DTV); films primarily produced by and for the horror community. As the term DTV is somewhat limited, due to it being applied to any film that does not receive a theatrical release, I suggest that it is better to understand them as amateur-produced horror films made by fans who have professional aspirations. I use the term 'amateur' to reflect their low production values, such as the use of consumer video production equipment and unknown casts. Low-budget, amateur-produced horror films were a feature of the American VHS boom of the 1980s where a consumer demand for product created a market for horror films, especially those from the 'stalk and slash' subgenre. Badley (2009, 51) suggests that this movement of film-making shares some similarities with the DIY punk ethos of the 1970s and 1980s. The availability of video camcorders and home editing equipment meant that anyone with access to the technology could produce a homemade film. Kerekes and Slater (1995, 167) identify early examples of this form of fan production that were distributed in the United States in the mid-1980s. For example, they establish that in films such as *The New York Centerfold Massacre* (1985), "nothing happens but the torture of girls." Before the ubiquitous capacity of the internet was available these films were distributed through mail order, fan networks, and conventions but they have now become more noticeable in the internet age where fan word-of-mouth has allowed them to find a larger international audience.

There have been a number of recent amateur-produced horror films that have offered extreme representations of serial murder; these can be seen as examples of slash production. Films that are comparable to the *Fantom Kiler* series are *Murder Set Pieces* (2004), which tells of a fashion photographer who is also a serial killer who tortures and murders women in his basement; the *August Underground* series of films (2001–7) that follow serial killers who film each other committing murders to produce snuff films; and *Scrapbook* (2000), in which a serial killer tortures a woman for the duration of the film's running time. While even more extreme in their representation of serial murder than the *Fantom Kiler* series, they have found niche audiences. This is largely due to their graphic interpretations of serial murder, coverage given in fanzines, and online reviews that have awarded attention to their strong content. Alongside these films there has also been a recent spate of low-budget films that have paid attention to the crimes of infamous serial murderers such as Ed Kemper, 'The Coed Killer' (*Kemper* (2008)), and Ted Bundy (*Bundy: A Legacy of Evil* (2009)). One online reviewer ("The Foywonder" 2008, 2009) has labeled these films as "serial killer fan fiction" due to the way in which the narratives of the films deviate from the case files. I also include these under the rubric of slash production as they reproduce the serial killer as a fan object. These low-budget, digitally shot films are aimed at those with an interest in true crime and, more specifically, the serial killer. Having small budgets, slash production has been filmed using digital production techniques because of its affordability. The relatively low cost of digital camcorders and availability of digital editing software makes this an accessible pursuit for fans who are willing to devote the time required to make a movie. Despite having low-budget origins, slash producers attempt to mirror professional production practices. For instance, special effects and make-up are an integral part in making the murder set piece—a drawn-out sequence devoted to the stalking, torture, and murder of a female—as realistic as possible. This might involve the use of props, prosthetics, and fake blood. It is these murder sequences that are awarded the most attention; much like pornography, the acting and storyline are of less importance.

Because of the relaxed laws for producing and distributing amateur-produced films in the United States, slash production tends to be primarily an American phenomenon. When distinguishing the differences between American and British film classification, the British Board of Film Classification (BBFC) website highlights that classification in the United States is an entirely voluntary process that film-makers do not have to go through and, unlike in the United Kingdom, there is no specific classification process for videotape (SBBFC 2012). Therefore any film can be distributed in the United States providing that it does not breach copyright or obscenity laws. As 'slash production' contains extreme representations of serial murder they may not be available in countries that have strict film censorship policies, and can only be obtained via specialist online retailers or purchased at specialist horror conventions. Unlike in the United States, tighter regulatory laws in the United Kingdom and the need for certification by the BBFC discourages slash production in the United Kingdom. Submitting a film to the BBFC for classification incurs a considerable fee. A 90-minute English-language film costs approximately £730 plus VAT to be certified by the BBFC. In addition there is the risk of having your film censored or, more likely, rejected. For instance, the film *Murder Set Pieces*, which I identified earlier as being an example of slash production, was rejected by the BBFC for DVD release because the Board had:

> . . . serious concerns about the portrayal of violence, most especially when the violence is sexual or sexualised, but also when depictions portray or encourage: callousness towards victims, aggressive attitudes, or taking pleasure in pain or humiliation. (BBFC 2008)

Unlike in the United States, where it is possible to bypass the Motion Picture Association of America (MPAA) and release a film without a rating, distribution of unclassified material in the United Kingdom can result in a fine or a prison sentence. Therefore both the production and trading of slash production in the United Kingdom is very much an underground activity. Fans who wish to view slash production will either have to import DVDs from outside of the United Kingdom, and risk potential seizures from customs, or download it from a file-sharing website.

As a contextual examination of *Fantom Kiler* demonstrates, there is also an important economic dimension to the making of slash production. One possible explanation for slash production is that it gives fans an outlet to express both their passion and knowledge of horror films to the fan community, drawing on already established textual features as a form of homage. However, the amount of investment, in both time and money that goes into producing a film cannot be ignored. Will Brooker (2002, 175) has suggested that fan films are often produced to be "calling cards," acting as potential "springboards" to a professional career in film-making. This is also emphasized by Clive Young (2008, 134) in *Homemade Hollywood*. Using the example of Dan Poole's fan film *The Green Goblin's Last Stand* (1992) and an interview conducted with the director, Young discusses how Poole attempted to use the film as a calling card, sending copies to director James Cameron and Spider Man co-creator Stan Lee. There is, however, a greater economic incentive to slash production. The existence of slash production from the 1980s onwards suggests that the serial killer is a marketable cultural product. Both Ian Conrich (2003, 158–9) and David Schmid (2005) have made mention of the "murderabilia" industry, which Conrich (2003, 158) has defined as the "marketplace for serial killer-related products, which fetishize a murderer or allow for a particular private association." This not only highlights the fandom that surrounds the serial killer but also emphasizes how they are entertainment figures and have achieved celebrity status. The fictional serial killers of many horror films also demonstrate the existence of this market. Schmid (2005, 108) uses the examples of fictional serial murderers Freddy Krueger, Jason Voorhees, and Michael Myers who have featured in slasher film franchises as evidence of the "celebrity of the filmic serial killer" and how they have become stars of "extremely profitable" movie series. Therefore, the slash producer is not driven purely by homage; it is a potential profit-making activity that exploits an established market. The conditions for slash production, such as the low budgets, lack of named talent, small crews, inexpensive equipment, and independent distribution, further highlight how it is possible to make money from producing films that make the serial killer, and serial murder, the primary focus. The following case study of *Fantom Kiler* highlights this economic dimension of slash production.

Reimagining the serial 'kiler'

An exploration of the production, distribution, and consumption of the *Fantom Kiler* series reveals the ways in which it can be read as a form of slash production. The majority of information contained here was sourced from a semi-structured interview I conducted in December 2009 with 'Roman Nowicki'; the named director of the *Fantom Kiler* series. Speaking to the creator of these texts allowed for a greater understanding of their production and distribution context. Using information obtained from online fan discussions I approached Nowicki and was surprised to find how forthcoming he was about his involvement in the production of the films. I would like to indicate that this chapter does not intend to be an exposé of the true identity of the director, and because of the potential legal ramifications of producing and distributing such films in the United Kingdom, his identity and production company name will not be used. When referring to the director I will use his pseudonym, Roman Nowicki.

First, in order to understand the context in which *Fantom Kiler* operates as slash production it is important to take into account Nowicki's background as a producer of Euro-Cult-inspired fan-produced texts. Not initially a fan of horror cinema, Nowicki came to have an interest in the genre through owning a video recorder and renting VHS tapes. Even though the *Fantom Kiler* is renowned for its graphic representation of sexual serial murder, Nowicki ironically notes that he found films like *Conan the Barbarian* (1982) and *Creepshow* (1982) to be "a bit strong" in terms of their violent content. As his interest in horror cinema grew, he began to import photocopied fanzines from America, such as *The Gore Gazette*, as horror fanzines were uncommon in United Kingdom at that time. Finding himself unemployed and claiming jobseekers allowance, he was encouraged to enter the Enterprise Allowance Scheme and become self-employed. By entering this Conservative government-supported scheme, claimants were able to receive £40 a week to assist the development of a business. Using knowledge he had gained from earlier employment, he started a printing company with an intention of producing publications devoted to horror cinema. Unwilling to put the word 'horror' in the company named because of the negative connotations the genre had in 1980s Britain, mostly due to the ongoing moral panic surrounding 'video nasties', he decided to give the company a vague title so as not to draw unnecessary attention. His company released a number of amateur-produced publications purely aimed at the growing UK horror fanbase, focusing mainly on Euro-Cult cinema, the most popular example being the fanzine *Delirium*. The iconography of the serial killer is evident in many images found in these fanzines, reproducing images taken from Euro-Cult films that often feature the murder act.

Secondly, the positive response to the fanzines from the fan community led to Nowicki establishing a festival that would feature Euro-Cult directors and personalities such as Paul Naschy, Jean Rollin, and Jess Franco. Rare films were screened, fans could purchase memorabilia such as fan publications and films, and they had the opportunity to meet their idols in person. The company made a profit, mainly through the sales of the publications, and this allowed Nowicki to employ two people to assist in the running of the company. By the late 1990s, fan-produced publications had little resemblance to the traditional photocopied fanzines that had circulated among the community. The growth of home computers and basic desktop publishing software had allowed for fanzines to become "prozines" because of their more professional appearance (Kimber 2002). While the unique style of fan writing remained the same, the presentation was now akin to a professionally produced magazine. Prozines are often bound, use high-quality paper and have full color front covers and color inserts. Now having access to a large mailing list of around 2,500 reliable customers, Nowicki perceived that there was a market for a modern day interpretation of the *giallo* that could be targeted purely at the Euro-Cult fan community. This sequence of events led to *Fantom Kiler* going into development.

As the central figure within the vast majority of *gialli* is the serial killer it was inevitable that the antagonist within the *Fantom Kiler* series was going to be a serial murderer. The original working title for the first *Fantom Kiler* film was *A Town Called Hate*. Nowicki's initial idea for the film's narrative was to have a town occupied by misogynistic males; one of these male occupants possesses so much hatred toward women that it leads him to murder. This film's title was rejected on the basis that it might lead people to believe that it was a Western film rather than a *giallo*. The initial inspiration for *Fantom Kiler* was *fumetti* rather than *giallo*. *Fumetti*, also known as *fumetti neri*, are Italian comic books aimed at an adult audience. Their violent storylines and anti-heroes, such as the Diabolik character who would be popularized in Mario Bava's *Danger: Diabolik* (1968), would become influential to those directors commonly associated with Italian cult film (Paul 2002). Nowicki explained that it was the "outrageousness" of the *fumetti* that had inspired him and that no film he had seen matched the general "craziness" of the *fumetti*. He also pointed out that when setting out to make the film, he did not intend for it to be a *giallo*. However, the idea of making a modern-day film inspired by the *giallo* was appealing as there was growing fan demand for *gialli* to be released on VHS and DVD. Nowicki's awareness of this significant fan-based market surrounding Euro-Cult came from him being part of this community.

The first *Fantom Kiler* film was produced in 1998. Nowicki self-financed the films and estimates that the budget for the first *Fantom Kiler* film was "anywhere between £2,000 and £3,000." It was filmed using a Sony VX1000 digital video camera, a popular camera that was used by both professionals and semi-professionals in the late 1990s. The major difficulty encountered was the editing of the film, taking "well over a year to complete." Not only did Nowicki find software and hardware for editing expensive, it also took a long period of time to familiarize himself with the Ulead Media Studio Pro software. The difficulties encountered can be seen in the final edit of the film where the aspect ratio changes on a number of occasions, again reminding the viewer of the amateur origins of the film and signifying *Fantom Kiler* as slash production. The storyline, albeit rather thin, focuses on a series of murders that are being committed in a small, Polish village. It transpires that the men share such a hatred of the attractive women of the village that the hate manifests itself into an energy which results in the creation of the Fantom Kiler. The director maintains that the film is not about a masked serial murderer, but instead is a comment on misogyny and how religion can create repressed individuals. Defending his film, Nowicki believes that it has "more storyline" than the original *Friday the 13th* (1980) and cites the influence of psychoanalysis to explain the killer's motivations, particularly the drive of the id and the repressed sexuality of the villagers. Despite these high claims it is hard to see past the fact that this film devotes the majority of its running time to scenes of women being stalked by the Fantom Kiler and murdered in varying sexually violent ways.

Many of the prolonged murder set pieces will feature a woman, conventionally attractive with an oiled body and silicon-enhanced breasts, walking through foggy woodland. Contact with the branches of trees and barbed wire help to remove her clothes so that she is completely naked. The Fantom Kiler appears and informs the woman of her forthcoming 'punishment', in one scene uttering the following dialogue (please note that the spelling mistakes are intentional and are found in the actual subtitles):

> It's not safe to be in the woods after dark especially dressed only in a pair of hi-heels, you might catch a cold or something. You have such a pretty body, it would be a shame if something happened to it wouldn't it? Soft flesh . . . so delicate . . . what could be the worst thing that could happen to it? I wonder if you could even begin to image can you? Is that why you are here? To be punished? Do you feel the need to be punished? Why else would you be here? Defenseless and naked, you're a lady of expensive tastes, only the best is good for you: the best furs . . . the best jewellery but where are they now? Do you miss them? Has the lust for fine things

been replaced by a more basic lust? A lust for excitement, forbidden sexual desire? You've never felt this way before . . . my steele blade caressing your tender skin creating the ultimate sensation . . . the ultimate . . . orgasm . . . and death.

Rather than instil fear, this dialogue appears to arouse the woman and the killer finally vaginally assaults the female victim with a phallic replacement, either a knife or broom handle. In between these murder sequences we have scenes that feature inept police and two misogynistic janitors who offer nothing more than a crude commentary and serve as potential suspects for the murders. It is also worth pointing out that much of the humor offered by these two characters bears many similarities to the jovial misogyny contained in the fanzines previously produced by Nowicki and common within the British horror fan community. Jenkins (1992, 228) recognizes that many producers of fan videos have often had experience in producing fanzines, and that it is no coincidence that the content of the fan-produced texts share many similarities.

As with *gialli,* it would be easy to label *Fantom Kiler* as misogynistic due to the sexual 'punishment' of the female victims. Nowicki intentionally chose a "special look of girl" for the role. The women used are not actresses, but glamor models with heavy make-up, many having surgically enhanced breasts. None of the actors or actresses used in the production are professionals, many being friends or family of the director. While the film may not be as gory as the slash production I identified earlier, it is the textual specifics of these representations of serial murder and sexual violence that have the potential to disturb viewers; here sexual violence toward women is presented as an exciting spectacle. Defending these scenes, Nowicki states that because of their excess they border on the ridiculous, believing therefore they should be seen more as black comedy. Nowicki claims that his intention was that the murder sequences should be regarded as fantastical set pieces and be as "unrealistic" as possible. Nowicki might be suggesting that his films are an antidote to other slash production such as the *Murder Set Pieces* series of films, which are too violent for his liking. Nonetheless, fans of *Fantom Kiler* contacted him asking for more rather than less gore in his future productions. It is also quite easy to notice the similarities *Fantom Kiler* shares with pornography: the models are reminiscent of porn stars because of their artificial bodies, extended murder set pieces replace sex scenes, the act of penile penetration is replaced by phallic objects such as knives and wooden spoons, and the ensuing 'money shot' is the death of the victim. All of this is intercut with narrative 'filler'. While the first *Fantom Kiler* film does not involve genital sex, the acts of vaginal penetration with phallic objects and much of the spread-legged female nudity moves this beyond the category of softcore. In *Fantom Kiler* the serial killer is being portrayed as an excessively sexualized figure. The victims are seduced before they are murdered, sharing many similarities with the common cinematic representation of Dracula; an antagonist that is feared but also desired. In the ensuing sequels, the eroticization of the Fantom Kiler progressively presents the character as a rapist, as well as a sexual sadist, as the content moves further toward hardcore pornography.

The appearance of the titular character, the Fantom Kiler, shares many similarities to the masked serial killer of Mario Bava's *Blood and Black Lace*. They are both adorned in black trilby hats, long black coats, black gloves, and a faceless gauze mask. Surprisingly, given that this is a fan-based production, Nowicki claimed that the similarity was entirely unintentional. This would appear to suggest that the 'look' of the masked serial killer, as pioneered by Bava, has become so embedded within the iconography of the horror genre that it has become a recurrent stylistic trope for film-makers. There are a number of other stylistic touches present in the film that are reminiscent of many *gialli*. According to Nowicki, the gels and color filters used in the lighting were intentionally employed to resemble the lighting used by Bava and Argento and to add to the overall fantastical nature of the film. The opening close-up of an eye is yet another nod to Italian cult cinema; the eye, and particularly the destruction of the eye, has been identified as playing an "important role in Argento films" (Guins 1996, 146). These intertextual references to the *giallo* are seemingly employed to position fans to contextually read the generic signifiers—the black-garbed serial murderer, the close-up of the eye, and the use of lighting—to invoke fan pleasure.

The village setting of the film and its marketing would lead one to believe that it was produced in Poland when it was, in fact, filmed in a warehouse in London that belonged to Nowicki. His links to Poland enabled him to film some exterior shots there in order to add to the 'authenticity' of the film's supposed location. Friends helped to construct the woodland sets and the warehouse offices were used for several scenes. Such detail went into hiding the true location of filming that the cars shown in some of the exterior shots had their British license plates covered with Polish license plates. Originally shot in English, the film was dubbed into a combination of Polish and Russian during post-production, and English subtitles, containing intentional spelling errors, were added. Presumably this was done in order to create the myth that the film was produced in Poland rather than the United Kingdom. Much of the fan debate surrounding the *Fantom Kiler* series has been centred on trying to uncover who was responsible for their production and why a pseudonym was required. Speculation in online communities such as AV Maniacs, the Cult

Movie Forums, and IMDB forums results in a range of possibilities to explain the shroud of secrecy around the production. These can be summarized in three points:

- an effort on the part of the director to maintain artistic distance from the film,
- that the producer was not happy with the finished product, or
- a marketing ploy to incite rumor and attract attention.

According to Nowicki the actual explanation is very different. The name Roman Nowicki was chosen as it is a common Polish name. He believed that if he had attached his real name to the film many people would instantly think that it was a poor quality film regardless of the effort that he had put into the production. He also believed that there were a number of people in the community who would have been happy to see him get in legal trouble for producing and distributing a film that had not been certified by the BBFC. Regardless of Nowicki's genuine reasons, the debate about the film's origins in the Euro-Cult cinema fan community did help to create awareness of the film.

In another effort to make anonymous the film's production background, the film was produced and distributed under the Teraz Films label; again purposely created to support the supposed Polish origins of the film. *Fantom Kiler* received a lot of coverage in one of the fanzines produced by Nowicki—even featuring a self-conducted 'interview' with himself —on his company's website and in the catalogue distributed to the people on his mailing list. The director also produced the cover art and blurb for the DVD and VHS release, maintaining the DIY production ethos of the film. The film was available for purchase on VHS and DVD formats through the director's website and other online retailers specializing in the sale of cult horror films. It could also be found for sale at some fan conventions. The popularity of the film led to the making of three sequels: *Fantom Kiler 2* (1999), *Fantom Kiler 3* (2003), and *Fantom Kiler 4* (2008), which followed the identical formula of the first film yet becoming more sexually graphic; moving further toward hardcore pornography. The same production processes were utilized until the fourth instalment of the series where higher quality camera equipment was used.

The popularity of the films has led to Nowicki ceasing to produce fanzines; film-making is now his primary pursuit. Nowicki suggested that the reason for his sole devotion to film production is that DVDs are both cheaper and easier to distribute than magazines, requiring less packaging and having less chance of superficial damage. Also, the content that would make up a fanzine can now easily be sourced online at no cost, meaning a declining demand for printed publications. This is evidenced on the director's website where DVDs have replaced fan publications as the main items for sale. This illustrates that there is an economic incentive to this form of fan production. The *Fantom Kiler* series stands out from the numerous other fan films that are in existence, such as *The Lord of the Rings* (2001) fan film *Born of Hope* (2009), which are produced purely as homages and are intended for distribution online. Nowicki instead produced his films as a way to take advantage of the renewed attention the *giallo* was gaining thanks to the DVD revolution and to offer his many mailing list members something new to purchase. With the number of films Nowicki has now made, it would be safe to assume that there is both a market for them and also some form of financial reward. This is about the exploitation of a market rather than purely being an expression of fandom.

Conclusion

Slash production, defined as a subgenre of slash fiction, offers extreme representations of serial murder and objectifies the serial killer. These texts are motivated by (and toward) the presentation of spectacular, eroticized murder set pieces, often at the expense of narrative coherence. In opposition to fan films produced in other genres, slash production has a greater economic incentive. These are not mere expressions of fandom but are commodities that are intended to be sold to a fan community on DVD through both online and offline outlets. The *Fantom Kiler* films, as an example of slash production, unlike the majority of amateur fan-produced horror films, are produced in the United Kingdom (and not in the United States) by a key figure in the development of Euro-Cult cinema fandom. The *Fantom Kiler* series draws inspiration from the *giallo*, referencing both its style and general conventions, but they are interpreted in such a manner that extends the core pleasures found in *gialli* to extreme levels. Here the serial killer is presented to us as a highly sexualized figure who is both feared and desired by his victims. Stills featured on the DVD covers for each of the *Fantom Kiler* films further emphasizes how the scenes of sexualized serial murder are the main selling point for the films. Nowicki created a myth that the film was made in Poland, as a way to detract attention from its British origins. This helped to attract attention to the film from the Euro-Cult cinema fan community who were eager to uncover its true origins. It could also be seen as way to circumvent the regulations imposed by the BBFC on the distribution of unclassified material in the United Kingdom which stifles slash production and, to a larger extent, a thriving amateur film industry.

There is an interesting coda to the *Fantom Kiler* story. A fan of the *Fantom Kiler* series who worked for a well-established European pornography company contacted Nowicki and asked if he would be interested in producing hardcore pornographic versions of the *Fantom Kiler* series. The *Fantom Kiler* became the *Fantom Seducer* (2005) in two full-length pornographic features. The films follow the same themes found in the *Fantom Kiler* series and continue to show the sexual degradation of women, merging the genres of pornography and horror. Nowicki explained that the sexual violence had to be toned down, as there were limitations on what could be performed. This is just one example of the ways in which fan production can become commodified, moving from the amateur to the professional. The relationship with the company was short lived as Nowicki found the experience of working for the pornography company difficult due to a number of constraints that were placed upon him, both political and economic. Rather than work under these conditions, he decided to return to slash production. Nowicki continues to make films that reinterpret Euro-Cult cinema and objectify the serial killer as a highly sexualized figure.

Acknowledgments

The author would like to extend his gratitude toward the person known as Roman Nowicki and thank him for being so forthcoming in discussing the *Fantom Kiler* film series.

References

AV Maniacs. 2012. Accessed December 27, 2012. www.avmaniacs.com.
Bacon-Smith, Camille. 1992. *Enterprising Women: Television Fandom and the Creation of Popular Myth*. Philadelphia: University of Pennsylvania Press.
Badley, Linda. 2009. "Bringing it All Back Home: Horror Cinema and Video Culture." In *Horror Zone*, edited by Ian Conrich, 45–63. London: I.B. Tauris.
BBFC. 2011. "Murder Set Pieces." Last modified June 6, 2011. www.bbfc.co.uk/website/Classified.nsf/0/C459C3DC24C72664802573FC005EB482.

Bondanella, Peter. 2003. *Italian Cinema: From Neorealism to the Present.* London: Continuum.

Brooker, Will. 2002. *Alice's Adventures: Lewis Carroll in Popular Culture.* London: Continuum.

Caudill, Helen. 2003. "Tall, Dark and Dangerous: Xena, the Quest and the Wielding of Sexual Violence in Xena On-Line Fan Fiction." In *Athena's Daughters: Television's New Women Warriors*, edited by Frances H. Early and Kathleen Kennedy, 27–39. Syracuse: Syracuse University Press.

Christie, Agatha. 1936. *The A.B.C. Murders.* London, UK: Collins Crime Club.

Clover, Carol. 1992. *Men, Women and Chainsaws.* Princeton: Princeton University Press.

Conrich, Ian Mass. 2003. "Media/Mass Murder: Serial Killer Cinema and the Modern Violated Body." In *Criminal Visions: Media Representations of Crime and Justice,* edited by Paul Mason, 156–74. Devon: Willan Publishing.

Cult Movie Forums. 2012. Accessed December 27, 2012. www.cultmovieforums.com.

Deep Red. 1987–2002. Edited by Chas Balun. Hollywood, CA. www.zombiebloodbath.com/chas2.html.

Delirium. 1993–1997. Publication details unavailable.

European Trash Cinema. 1988–98. Edited by Craig Ledbetter. Spring, TX. www.eurotrashcinema.com.

Fangoria. 1979–. Edited by Chris Alexander. New York, NY. www.fangoria.com.

"The Foywonder." 2008. "*Kemper* (DVD)." Dread Central, December 5. Accessed December 22, 2012. www.dreadcentral.com/reviews/kemper-dvd.

—. 2009. "*Bundy: A Legacy of Evil* (DVD)." Dread Central, June 11. Accessed December 22, 2012. www.dreadcentral.com/reviews/bundy-a-legacy-evil-2009.

Gallant, Chris. 2000. *Art of Darkness: The Cinema of Dario Argento.* Surrey: FAB Press.

Giallo Pages. 1993–9. Edited by John Martin.

The Gore Gazette. 1981–91. Written, edited, and published by Rick Sullivan. Butler, NJ. www.j4hi.com.

Guins, Raiford. 2005. "Blood and Black Gloves on Shiny Discs." In *Horror International*, edited by Steven J. Schneider and Tony Williams, 15–32. Detroit: Wayne State University Press.

Guins, Ray. 1996. "Tortured Looks: Dario Argento and Visual Displeasure." In *Necronomicon Book One: The Journal of Horror and Erotic Cinema*, edited by Andy Black, 141–53. London: Creation.

Harris, Cheryl, and Alison Alexander. *Theorizing Fandom: Fans, Subculture and Identity.* Cresskill, NJ: Hampton Press, 1998.

Hope, William. 2005. *Italian Cinema: New Directions.* Oxford: Peter Lang.

Hunt, Leon. 2005. "A Sadistic Night at the Opera—Notes on the Italian Horror Film." In *The Horror Reader,* edited by Ken Gelder, 324–35. London: Routledge.

IMDB. 2012. Accessed December 27, 2012. www.imdb.com.

Is it Uncut? 1995–2012. London, UK: Midnight Media. www.midnight-media.net/id6.html.

Jenkins, Henry. 1992. *Textual Poachers: Television Fans and Participatory Culture*. London: Routledge.

Jones, Alan. 1997. *Nekrofile: Cinema of the Extreme*. Northamptonshire: Midnight Media.

Kerekes, David, and David Slater. *Killing for Culture*. London: Creation.

Kimber, Shaun. 2002. "Genre Fandom and Underground Film Culture in Britain." *Headpress: The Journal of Sex, Religion and Death* 18: 96–9.

Koven, Mikel J. 2006. *La Dolce Morte: Vernacular Cinema and the Italian Giallo Film*. Oxford: Scarecrow.

Luther-Smith, Adrian. 1999. *Blood and Black Lace: The Definitive Guide to Italian Sex and Horror Movies*. Cornwall: Stray Cat Publishing.

Mendik, Xavier. 1996. "Detection and Transgression: The Investigative Drive of the Giallo." In *Necronomicon: The Journal of Horror and Erotic Cinema, Book One*, edited by Andy Black, 35–54. London: Creation.

—. 1998. "From the Monstrous Mother to the 'Third Sex': Female Abjection in the Films of Dario Argento." In *Necronomicon: The Journal of Horror and Erotic Cinema, Book Two*, edited by Andy Black, 110–33. London: Creation, 1998.

—. 2000. "A (Repeated) Time to Die: The Investigation of Primal Trauma in the Films of Dario Argento." In *Crime Scenes: Detective Narratives in European Culture since 1945*, edited by Anne Mullen and Emer O'Beirne, 25–36. Amsterdam: Rodopi Press.

—. 2001. *Tenebré/Tenebrae*. London: Flicks Books.

Needham, Gary. 2003. "Playing with Genre: An Introduction to the Italian Giallo." In *Fear without Frontiers*, edited by Steven J. Schnieder, 134–44. Surrey: FAB Press.

Nowicki, Roman. Interview by Oliver Carter.

Paul, Louis. 2002. *Italian Horror Film Directors*. London: McFarland & Company, Inc.

Penley, Constance. 1992. "Feminism and Psychoanalysis and the Study of Popular Culture." In *Cultural Studies,* edited by Lawrence Grossberg, Cary Nelson, and Paula Triechler, 479–500. London: Routledge.

Rowling, J. K. 1997–2007. *Harry Potter Series*. London: Bloomsbury.

SBBFC. 2012. "Same Difference? A Comparison of the British and American Film and DVD Rating Systems." Accessed December 27, 2012. www.sbbfc.co.uk/mpaacomparison.

Schmid, David. 2005. *Natural Born Celebrities: Serial Killers in American Culture*. London: The University of Chicago Press.

Silver, Alain. 1999. *The Noir Style*. London: Aurum Press Ltd.

Willis, Ika. 2006. "Keeping Promises to Queer Children: Making Space (for Mary Sue) at Hogwarts." In *Fan Fiction and Fan Communities in the Age of the Internet: New Essays*, edited by Karen Hellekson and Kristina Busse, 153–70. London: McFarland & Company, Inc.

Young, Clive. 2008. *Homemade Hollywood*. London: Continuum.

Filmography

August Underground. DVD. Directed by Fred Vogel. 2001–7; Pittsburgh, PA: Toe Tag Pictures, n.d.

The Benny Hill Show. Television. Produced by Associated-Rediffusion/Thames Television. UK: BBC/ITV, 1951–91.

Born of Hope. DVD. Directed by Kate Madison. 2009; Actors at Work Productions. Accessed January 2, 2012. www.youtube.com/watch?v=qINwCRM8acM.

Bundy: A Legacy of Evil. DVD. Michael Feifer. 2009; Santa Monica, CA: Lionsgate Home Entertainement, 2009.

Conan the Barbarian. DVD. Directed by John Milius. 1982; Universal City: Universal Studios Home Entertainment, 2000.

Creepshow. Blu-ray. Directed by George Romero. 1982; Burbank, CA: Warner Home Video, 2009.

Danger: Diabolik. DVD. Directed by Mario Bava. 1968; Hollywood, CA: Paramount Home Entertainment, 2005.

Fantom Kiler. Directed by Roman Nowicki. 1998; UK: Teraz Films, 1998.

Fantom Kiler 2. Directed by Roman Nowicki. 1999; UK: Teraz Films, 1999.

Fantom Kiler 3. Directed by Roman Nowicki. 2003; UK: Teraz Films, 2003.

Fantom Kiler 4. Directed by Roman Nowicki. 2008; UK: Teraz Films, 2008.

Fantom Seducer. Directed by Roman Nowicki. 2005; UK: Teraz Films, 2005.

Friday the 13th. DVD. Directed by Sean S. Cunningham. 1980; Hollywood, CA: Paramount Home Entertainment, 1999.

Giallo a Venezia/Thriller in Venice. VHS. Directed by Mario Mandi. 1979; Video Star.

The Green Goblin's Last Stand. DVD. Directed by Dan Poole. 1992; Burbank, CA: Alpha Dog Productions, 1992.

Il dolce corpo di Deborah/The Sweet Body of Deborah. DVD. Directed by Romolo Guerrieri. 1968; Italy: Cinekult.

Il profumo della signora in nero/The Perfume of the Lady in Black. DVD. Directed by Francesco Barilli. 1974; Rome: Raro Video, 2011.

Kemper. DVD. Directed by Rick Bitzelberger. 2008; Santa Monica, CA: Lionsgate Home Entertainment, 2008.

La ragazza che sapeva troppo/The Girl Who Knew Too Much. DVD. Directed by Mario Bava. 1963; Rome: Sinister Film, 2010.

L'assassino ha riservato nove poltrone/The Killer Reserved Nine Seats. Directed by Guiseppe Benati. Produced by Dario Rossini. 1974.

Le orme/The Footprints. Directed by Luigi Bazzoni. Produced by Marina Cicogna and Luciano Perugia. 1975.

The Lord of the Rings. DVD. Directed by Peter Jackson. 2001; Los Angeles: New Line Home Entertainment, 2002.

Murder Set Pieces. DVD. Directed by Nick Palumbo. 2004; Santa Monica, CA: Lionsgate Home Entertainment, 2007.

Neighbours. Television. Produced by Alan Hardy. UK: BBC1/Channel Five, 1986–.

The New York Centrefold Massacre. DVD. Directed by Louis Ferriol. 1985; USA: Vidimax Teleproductions, 2005.

Paranoia. DVD. Directed by Umberto Lenzi. 1970; New York: Synergy, 2011.

Profondo Rosso/Deep Red. DVD. Directed by Dario Argento. 1975; West Hollywood, CA: Blue Underground, 2011.

Scrapbook. DVD. Directed by Eric Stanze. 2000; Venice, CA: Egami, 2000.

Sei donne per l'assassino/Blood and Lace. DVD. Directed by Mario Bava. 1964; London: VCI Video, 2005.

Star Trek. Television. Producced by Gene L. Coon, John M. Lucas, and Fred Freiberger. New York: NBC, 1966–9.

Un posto ideale per uccidere/Dirty Pictures. Directed by Umberto Lenzi. Produced by Carlo Ponti. 1971.

Xena: Warrior Princess. Television. Executive produced by Robert Tapert and Sam Raimi. Syndication, 1995–2001; DVD. Beverly Hills, CA: Anchor Bay Entertainment, 2003–5.

9

Do Serial Killers Have Good Taste?[1]

Louis Bayman

A wealth of meanings accrues to serial killing, which holds a prominent place in the modern collective imagination. It is a rare extremity of human behavior whose prominence is maintained, in particular, via cultural representation which, in turn, is the main arena in which to elaborate the common ideas, fears, and fantasies that serial killing engenders.

My analysis focuses on a curious facet of this cultural imagination: the recurrent fantasy of the serial killer as *tasteful*. Frequently, representations offer an image of the serial killer as a figure who is as disproportionately interested in culture as culture already is in it. Focusing on cinematic portrayals, my analysis begins with a series of examples that demonstrate the sheer range of representations of the relationship between killers and culture. One lineage of such a fantasy is the Romantic proposition that the killer is an artist (see, in particular, Black (1991) and Schneider (2001)). However the examples below also associate the urge to kill with aspects of everyday life; to the extent that at the same time as they deal with isolated genius or monstrosity, they associate serial killing with questions of normality and with common doubts regarding productivity, purposeful activity, and human physiology.

The way in which killing is connected to art is thus telling, for it expresses an ideological mistrust of lonely pleasure that is not oriented toward the family or capitalist production. What follows is an examination of what this mistrust implies and how it is developed through culture. The way killing is connected to art demonstrates the ambiguous tone in which serial killing is often treated in culture, balancing between horror, admiration, and sarcasm in relation to its moral and ideological, as well as aesthetic, uses. An examination of these ambiguities contributes to debates on how the serial killer implicates a loss of security in notions such as identity (Gomel 2003) and the self (Seltzer 2000; King 2006). My argument is that, although an imaginative invention, the connection of art to killing forms a rich creative source that provides ways to elaborate fears—and fantasies—that are far more common than those that emerge from the never very great possibility of any actual encounter with a serial killer; first, fears of deviance and cruelty, but also of the failure to secure an underlying substance to the rules of social order, of identity and rational activity which would otherwise give meaning to human existence.

Cultured killing

Often the serial killer's relationship with culture is an intimate part of his (for the figure is male in fiction almost as often as he is in real life (see Cameron and Frazer 1987; Cameron 1996)) murderous activities. A fairly generic example is offered by *H6: Diario de un asesino/H6: Diary of a Serial Killer* (2005) which begins with a close-up of a portrait painting, and then throughout the film the main character tortures his victims, taking art photography of them while listening to classical music. *Nature Morte* (2006)—a telling title—teams a cop and an art critic to track down the painter of a scene that could only have been created by the 'Marseilles Monster' serial killer. There exists a common tendency to see the materials of violence and art as indistinguishable. *Antikörper/Antibodies* (2005) opens on a stripe of red paint dripping on the canvas of a religious scene and which is drawn by the killer/artist across his face as he escapes by jumping out of the first-story window, after which the paint smears into his own blood. In *Die Wachsfigurenkabinett/ Waxworks* (1924), the attacker is a frightful exhibit of nineteenth-century folk villain 'Spring-Heeled Jack' come to life to menace the young victim/protagonist, a scribe for the Waxworks shows. The monster emerges in this instance from the imaginative process of the writer (or, in his painting *Self Portrait with Eva Peters in the Artist's Studio* (1918) in which George Grosz paints himself as Jack the Ripper, he is the artist himself (see Tatar 1995)).

An abnormal absorption in art can give something away about the serial killer. In *Svalan, katten, rosen, döden/Swallow, Cat, Rose, Death* (2006), a filmed episode from the Van Veeteren series, the killer is found because he leaves behind his favorite book at the scene of the crime, Baudelaire's *Les fleurs du mal*, which he used in the seduction of his victim. In *M* (1931), the child-murderer's repeated whistling of the theme from Grieg's *Hall of the Mountain King* eventually brings about his recognition and capture. Artistic tastes can also help diagnose the killer's pathological type. The lodger who is the killer in *Le Vampire du Düsseldorf* (1965) (a character based on the mass murderer Peter Kürten) listens to Wagner while preparing his toilette, picks up a dagger, removes the needle from the record, and heads out for a date. In this case, after stopping the record as it builds to a climax, serial killing seems to be explicable as the violent outcome of halted emotion.

Artistic pursuits provide a way to understand serial killing as a particular type of abnormal personality. Interestingly, however, these last two examples refer the killer also to national tradition, *Hall of the Mountain King* from *M* making explicit the Romantic fairytale heritage from which arose the nicknames of the Weimar killers, the 'Vampire' Kürten and his predecessor the 'Werewolf of Hanover' Fritz Haarmann, among others (Tatar 1995, 158–9). In *Le Vampire du Düsseldorf*, the opera, *Lohengrin*, continues a mythological linkage between love and death, and its Wagnerian bombast suggests a Germanic attitude of domination.[2] Alternatively, 'the art of killing' mentioned in *Matador* (1986) is bullfighting, implicitly criticizing Spain's romanticized nationalism as at one with murder. On the other hand, provincial French butcher Popaul's insensitivity to classical French culture (through the writing of Balzac) marks him as a remnant of precivilized humanity in *Le Boucher* (1970).

Aside from attributing serial killing to an abnormal personality—one whose imaginative fixation combines obsessive care with flamboyant whimsy—art also helps define the social and cultural norms to which the serial killer is either a deviant or an over-enthusiastic conformist. The eponymous anti-hero has an artisanal concern for bloody flesh in *Le Boucher*; *Peeping Tom* (1960) is fixated with self-made snuff movies, and the killers inspired by 1950s Wisconsin serial killer, Ed Gein, enact by their gruesome form of transvestitism a particular interest in couture.[3] In this, they exemplify cultural anxieties, respectively, over human carnivorousness, the exploitative aspects of popular pleasure, and gender norms and social personae. On the other hand, the murderous enthusiasm can be for serial killers themselves, that is, the methodical appreciation of famous killers' *modi operandi* which marks the killer in *Copycat* (1995) or—placing a further mirror into the hall of postmodernist self-reflection—the protagonists' taste for slasher movies such as depicted in the *Scream* franchise (1996–). Alternatively, despite the references to pop culture, the films *Henry, Portrait of a Serial Killer* (1986), and *Funny Games* (1997/2007) entirely frustrate the audience's desire to understand the protagonists and ascribe any meaning to the killings they carry out.

These films associate art itself with the drive to kill strangers serially, and by so doing are examples of how culture works to define serial killing and to define normality and deviance as more general categories. They are thus assertions made through culture that it is precisely through his relationship to culture that one can define a serial killer, even if as in *Henry* and *Funny Games* this relationship is a tantalizingly unknowable (dis)engagement. They ascribe a sensibility to the serial killer which may vary from the monstrous, envisaged as domination in *Le Vampire du Düsseldorf*, or as frantic indulgence of childish appetites in *M*, or of insensitivity to the rules of civility as in *Le Boucher*. Alternatively, as with many of Alfred Hitchcock's murderers, representations of the serial killer may involve a nervous sensitivity or gentlemanly connoisseurship combined with sexual frenzy. In each of them, serial killing is represented as a matter of taste.

Taste and terror

Taste works in screen descriptions of killers to offer a vision of what is most basic in humanity—the satisfaction of appetites—in relation to the rules of social order, that is, of how those appetites are managed and developed. The refraction of this relationship into a simultaneously refined and brutal nature is exemplified by Hannibal Lecter, the psychiatrist who sautées human brains in *Hannibal* (2001); described before his first appearance in *The Silence of the Lambs* (1991) to Clarice Starling as "much too sophisticated," but with the threatening addition that "boy, are you ever his taste—so to speak" (Staiger 1993). The jokiness of such a comment also marks a play on the ambivalence of 'taste' as both cannibalistic and cultivated. This jokey ambivalence recurs in *H6* when we cut from a scene of torture to the presentation of a dish that the killer has made with the victim's brains, or in *American Psycho* (2000), whose opening credits begin on what looks like drops of blood but is actually gourmet food garnish (a victim's head later appears in a plastic bag on a freezer shelf behind the ice cream). In the US version of *The Girl with the Dragon Tattoo* (2011), the name of journalist Blomkvist's main suspect is spoken at the point of a close-up over a half-eaten fowl carcass. At the opening of *Henry, Portrait of a Serial Killer* a montage of mutilated bodies is interspersed with the titular killer politely settling his account in a diner. Such still-life or culinary grotesqueness uses serial killing to reveal the fragility of the veneer that the rituals of polite behavior provide to the all-too-human nature of animalistic physicality (Figure 9.1).

FIGURE 9.1 *Taste and killing in* The Silence of the Lambs *(1991).*

Aside from associating mealtime niceness with cannibalism, taste is also used to underline the greater sensitivity that marks the filmic world of the serial killer. In *Matador*, while waiting at a suspect's door, the police remark that "it smells good. Wet paint." Such heightened sensitivity plays an important function in serial killer cinema because it brings the consumption, spectatorship, and perpetration of violence together into one general experience of altered states. In *H6* the killer remembers when he was a boy waiting for a beating as "terror, and yet a strange sort of delight." When asked by Lecter about her first sight of a severed head in *The Silence of the Lambs*, Starling answers that she was "scared at first, then exhilarated." The suave killer Gerald (Basil Rathbone) who arrives in *Love from a Stranger* (1937) declares that his new bride's piano playing "excites my mind, quickens my thoughts, makes my head spin, reminds me of the war . . . the noise changes into music, turning my first terror into ecstasy." The breathless delivery of such lines indicates that taste is a stimulant for bodily arousal, likened to the stimulation achieved when on drugs (which screen killers frequently take and real killers are often presumed to have taken). It can also be a replacement for sex, as in *H6* where the killer's wife will not have sex with him, or in real life diagnoses such as Krafft Ebing's presumption that Jack the Ripper's perversion was that "the murderous act and subsequent mutilation of the corpse were equivalents for the sexual act." Taste thus indicates an indulgence of peculiar appetites and an experience in which the effects of both violence and art, and of sex and drugs, blend into one general non-rational bodily arousal.

Such insistence on taste has relevance to historical debates which often resurface when considering serial killers, and terror more generally in the cinema, specifically those regarding artistic experiences that exist beyond the pleasant or the beautiful.[4] The association of killing to aesthetics goes back at least to the Romantics and their contrarian classification of murder, as put by Joel Black (1991), as an aesthetic act. Thomas De Quincey's (2006, 10–11) 1827 essay "On Murder Considered as One of the Fine Arts" states, for example, that murder "may be laid hold of by its moral handle . . . or it may also be treated *aesthetically* . . . that is, in relation to good taste." In this, the first use of the word 'aesthetically' in English (Black 1991, 2), both aesthetics and murder are understood not for what separates them but for what they have in common.

Killing and art are each seen as states of extremity which serve to bring "the murderer and the writer into the same orbit, for both are interested in pleasure and power, and both seek freedom by outstripping or subverting the social institutions they feel thwart or confine them" (Morrison quoted in DeQuincey 2006, xi). Murder incites appreciation of qualities that can overwhelm—those of disgust, incomprehension, visceral sensation, frenzied excitement. In what Gomel (2003, xv) calls "the violent sublime," the "experience of violence involves ecstasy or intoxication, sometimes paradoxically coupled with revulsion and horror, in which doing harm to another's body becomes an end in itself." Motivated by the experience of heightened states for their own sake, this kind of violence incorporates experiences that can be compared to those offered by art.

Discussion of the sublime, thought of as a significant way of describing the thrills provided by serial killing, by Gomel as well as others, dovetails neatly with discussions of taste. The classical conception of taste in aesthetics is of the rational and hierarchical ordering of bodily responses. Edmund Burke's (1958 [1757], 22) statement of the position (with which he prefaces his discussion of the sublime) runs thus: "Love, grief, fear, anger, joy, all these passions have in their turns affected every mind; and they do not affect it in an arbitrary or casual manner, but upon certain, natural and uniform principles." Taste in this analysis connects the physical organs of perception to culture and the development of reason; a connection which is analogous to the connection of animalistic appetites and refined cultivation in the aforementioned examples of serial killers. The classical conception of taste seems even to be consciously evoked in *Das Parfum—Die Geschichte eines Mörders/Perfume: The Story of a Murderer* (2006), in which the professional Baldini tells the aspiring perfumer Jean-Baptiste Grenouille that he needs "an incorruptible, hard-working organ that has been trained to smell for many decades," and the perfume they analyse is called Amor and Psyche, the complementary affective and rational properties which constitute the classical conception of taste. Yet serial killing upsets the stable ordering of Burke's "certain, natural and uniform principles." Although Grenouille is referred to as "truly an artiste," the first shot of the film is of the sniffing nose of the condemned perfumer on his way to the gallows. The braying hordes who await his punishment for having committed murder to extract his victims' scent confirm a vision in which both the application of Grenouille's refined tastes and the crowd's desire for public spectacle compel lethal violence.

As expressed in the common-sense phrases that there's no accounting for taste, and that *de gustibus non est disputandum*, proverbial wisdom, in distinction to classical aesthetics, maintains a sense of the enigmas of human behavior. It is here that the affinity found between culture and killing can be brought to bear on this discussion of classical aesthetics. Serial killing and taste both confront the need to comprehend *difference* in humanity, and engender elusive desires for accepted points of reference. Taste and serial killing are each employed to exemplify the inexplicable in human behavior, and to confound objective standards and rational processes with the disordering physical experience of compulsive appetites.

Refinement

The serial killer is defined by the peculiar way in which he finds his pleasures. Is there thus no accounting for serial killing, and is it simply the most extreme embodiment of the variety of taste?

Taste *could* be seen as the opposite pole to that which defines the killer as monster: there is a horrific incongruity in *The Silence of the Lambs* when *The Goldberg Variations* play during Lecter's escape; he bites the tongue out of a guard's mouth, spraying his meal and the tape player with blood, then strikes the other in time to the music (the aftermath of which is shown in Figure 9.1). In *H6*, the site of the killer's tortures is the 'Paradise Hotel' he owns, its heavenly name contrasting with its grotty reality and the gurgles of a guest he has poisoned contrasting with the operatic duet that plays on the record player. In the spoof serial killer documentary *C'est arrivé près de chez vous/Man Bites Dog* (1992), the workaday activities of efficiency savings and brute physical labor that characterize the subject's killings contrast with his classical flute practice (a flute which will later find itself inside his murdered accompanist in a revenge attack) and his reciting of a self-penned ode to a pigeon while running naked on the beach. On the other hand, both the violence and the performance in each of these examples are consonant with the egotism that defines the screen killers and demarcates their difference.

This signified difference of the serial killer from both his victim and his principal antagonist can strike an ambivalent moral pose. FBI agent Starling, with her "good bag and . . . cheap shoes," has never seen the Florence Duomo that Lecter reproduces in a painting on his prison wall. Lecter diagnoses her as "a well-scrubbed, hustling rube with a little taste . . . not more than one generation from poor white trash." This achieves a cultural victory to Lecter in his skirmishes with Starling. The end of their second meeting cuts to a woman singing along to "American Girl" on her car radio, the ugly sound of her voice comparing unfavorably to Lecter's refined delivery; she immediately, and almost apparently deservedly, then becomes Buffalo Bill's onscreen victim. The film's serial killers torment the culturally impoverished, with serial killing an act of outlandish cultural assertion against the 'common' and 'tedious' (in Lecter's putdowns) normality of humanity. Buffalo Bill's tastes come across principally as failed New Romanticism as he dances in front of his mirror in semi-transvestitism. Bill's shooting by FBI agent Starling seems a punishment for this unstable masculinity as the blood gurgles from his mouth, resembling the red of his lipstick previously shown in similarly grotesque close-up. The apparent moral lesson would be that while Clarice Starling's down-home plainness beats Buffalo Bill's crazed aestheticism, he remains a "no-one" in comparison with Lecter, as Lecter himself puts it. The film closes on Lecter's final victory, escaped and at large and a seeming confirmation of his ultimate cultural superiority.

The conservative cultural politics of *Silence* differ to the implicit radicalism of *Män som hatar kvinnor/The Girl with the Dragon Tattoo* (2009), in which the (unofficial) investigator Lisbeth Salander is drawn from the urban subcultural underworld of laptop activism. All punky platform boots, black eyeliner and S&M dog collar, her antisocial impoliteness contrasts to the cold detachment of the bourgeoisie in the film and its big capitalist Neo-Nazi killers. Meanwhile in *American Psycho*, yuppie anti-hero Patrick Bateman invests his status in the competitive comparison of the 'tastefulness' of the minutiae of business cards. Bateman's card is overlooked in favor of an associate's, yet he appears to make good his aesthetic failure by later stabbing a tramp whom he declares "reeks of shit." Such physicality contrasts to the ostentatious (if artistically minimalist) ornamentation of his encounters with his peers, while the stabbing achieves a physical dominance over the unfortunate man on the ground in a spatial opposition to the sunlit skyscrapers of high finance that provided the setting for the business card scene. *Silence*, *Dragon*, and *American Psycho* each vary in their critical cultural attitudes, but throughout serial killing manifests the social struggle involved in the only apparently neutral pursuit of taste: either of aesthetes against white trash, a punk youth against representatives of large capitalism, or a white yuppie against a black tramp.

Work, waste, and taste

The representation of the serial killer as motivated either by gentlemanly relish or by greedy self-satisfaction taps into a popular and partly puritan connection of pleasure with social elevation; one that fed the common accusation that Jack the Ripper was either a learned professional or a dissolute aristocrat.[5] The perceived threats of elite privilege, or of the disorderly asociality of sensual delight, show where bourgeois society's suspicions lie. They also indicate admiration of an evasion of ordinariness. Cast free from the labors of workplace discipline, such high-class lifestyles risk the peril of an unbalanced mind—an imbalance often contrasted to the detective proclivities of an uncouth but also working investigator kept earthy by daily routine (*Silence*; *Love from a Stranger*; *The Lodger: A Story of the London Fog* (1927) among others).

Relating taste to the work ethic, Veblen (1934, 15) states how 'man' [sic] is in his own mind "an agent seeking in every act the accomplishment of some concrete, objective, impersonal end. By force of his being such an agent he is possessed of a taste for effective work, and a distaste for futile effort." From this perspective, however, "futile effort" can involve all those activities not tied to the world of exchange and production; including those entailing the enjoyment, pleasure, or destruction in which the serial killer indulges. And yet despite raising the serial killer above the world of ordinary workers, his relation to the workplace is insistently presented as if the murders were an extension of it. The killer in *H6*, for all his Nietzschean talk of breaking out of social rules and man's need to dominate, keeps his victims within the rooms of the hostel he runs; in *Perfume*, despite the Dostoyevskyan overreaching that sees Grenouille variously described as a devil and an angel, his first killing leads him to want to be a perfumer by trade; Bateman's exercises in "murders and executions" belong to an 1980s culture of self-interest that could be called cut-throat; in *Man Bites Dog* the central joke is that Benoit makes serial killing into a daily job; and it is Lecter's role as a psychologist that gives him privileged access to his first victims.

Serial killing is a practice that has been associated with the 'banality' of "modern, repetitive, systematic, anonymous, machine-like, psycho-dispassionate evil" (Seltzer 2000, 99; see also King 2006). Such a vision is connected by Analee Newitz (1998, 42) to the Marxist theory of alienation to show serial killing as a product of a wider deadness:

> When a person is working, he is experiencing what might be called "dead time" because at work, the worker belongs to his employer, the capitalist. . . . Ultimately, the worker experiences himself as "dead" while working, for nothing he does at work enriches his life in any way. However, he does gain his salary, which is paid to him in money—he is therefore rewarded economically for being "dead."

If non-productive time is the only time in which humanity is not alienated, then it follows that productivity is deadness and that fulfilling one's non-alienated, human attributes is, according to the controlling logic of capitalist production, wasteful. It is thus not only in the pursuit of an altered state that killing is connected to sex, drugs, and cultural pursuits, but also in its place in the economy of uselessness. But while art is creative, and sex procreative, killing is destructive, typifying waste most comprehensively.

Extending the Romantic viewpoint, then, the indulgence of tastes in either serial killing or in art could seem to be extravagant rejections of such social deadness. From this stance, the engagement in art enacts in Nietzsche's terms "*ressentiment*"; "a desire to *deaden pain by means of affects*" (quoted in Seltzer 2000, 107). But this also suggests that just as there is an experience of deadness in labor, so there is in art, which, though it may inspire emotions and represent human life, does not possess these, remaining impassive, inanimate, inhuman (properties developed for their ghostly aspects in the Italian *giallo*).

The anonymity and meaninglessness of alienation thus lead to instances in which "the pleasure-killer [can be understood] as one version of the largely extinguished subject: the 'devoided' and predead subject, for whom pleasure has become bound to the endless persecution of pleasure and to the endless emptying or voiding of interiors, in himself and in others" (Seltzer 2000, 100). An example of this simultaneous protest against and embodiment of deadening emptiness is offered in *American Psycho*. In bed, Bateman kills one of two women he has invited to his home for sex while the other escapes. He comes out naked, covered in blood, screaming and momentarily crouched in an almost foetal position. After a chase sequence the second woman, a prostitute, is killed by a chainsaw hurled toward her down a spiral staircase. The camera tracks toward her mutilated body creating an aestheticized stillness that highlights qualities of composition, the pattern of the surrounding staircase, and the vividness of the blood. The next shot is a rough doodle of the image of the murdered prostitute that Bateman is absentmindedly drawing while out for dinner with his girlfriend, apparently daydreaming in silent protest at the situation. The sequence has moved from the bodily immediacy of the postcoital attack, through to aestheticization, and a playful doodle, each emerging from the destruction of a prostitute, a representative of working life and the commodification of human relationships, and each creating heightened moments of sensory arousal that intertwine with the dullness of ordinary life.

With most of the films mentioned here, there is little focus on successful investigation in any conventional sense except in *Silence,* although even in this film the serial killer, whose taste is most fully explored, exists after capture—for the first half of the film he is already inside—and before it, for in the end he enacts his escape. Perhaps then the focus on taste thus helps confound not only rationalization in the sense of Taylorist production but, also, in the more general senses of the rational endeavors of deduction and motivation. In this vein, Gomel (2003, xvii) mentions the sublimity of moments when violence "disturbs a narrative of subjectivity: by undermining causality," citing Hannibal Lecter's remark that "Nothing happened to me, Officer Starling. I happened. You can't reduce me to a set of influences." In fact, when Lecter declares that "A census taker tried to quantify me once. I ate his liver with some fava beans and a nice Chianti," he enunciates a triumph of pleasure, degustatory consumption and disorder over quantification, categorization, and work. Otherwise described as "the profound absurdity of the seriousness with which men take serial-killing" (Dyer 2000, 150), the very concept of serial killing confuses questions of purpose: through seriality, serial killing necessarily offers us a structure, but one that does not point to a particular direction. The pattern of activity offered by serial killing can thus be termed as a rationale without reason, recalling Kantian definitions of art as contra-purposive purposiveness, of willed, conscious human design that lacks definable point.

Does Bateman actually kill anyone in *American Psycho*? The evidence of dead bodies remains unnoticed, Bateman fails to be taken seriously when he confesses, and even he ends up unsure as to the identity of who he believes he has killed. This creates a sense of 1980s America as an environment in which actual human lives are unimportant. The continual motif of Bateman being mistaken for another of his associates also moves uncertainty into the notion of non-entity. Murder is the logical conclusion of this notion, but it is a notion that is also found in the murderer himself, whose identity is constituted by the ephemera of cosmetics, yuppie style, or the lettering of the name on the business card (and not the person to whom it refers). In *Perfume*, a similar motif is that of a lack of a soul: Grenouille realizes that he is "nobody to anyone" and while the smell he seeks in flowers represents the "very soul" of a rose, he himself has no smell. Thus the subject of taste allows serial killer representations to broach the subject of the loss of identity (Gomel 2003) or self (Seltzer 2000; King 2006) which, it has been suggested, is the modern condition responsible for the serial killer's pathology. Such debates have focused on how penetrating others through killing offers "ecstatic moments of intercourse" (King 2006, 122) through which, however, the killer's selfhood is lost. What the above analysis shows is how the screen killer finds just this kind of identity-losing ecstatic intercourse in artistic engagement.

The loss of identity, or even of the soul, puts into play the immateriality not only of knowledge and purpose but of what actually constitutes existence, an immateriality whose tantalizing aspect is heightened by the various art forms in which screen killers are engaged. To grasp "the fleeting realm of scent" is the object of the killer in *Perfume*, and in *Love from a Stranger* the just-arrived gentlemanly lodger claims he is trying "to recapture, not youth, that would be impossible, but the dreams of youth." Both versions of *Girl with* have early sequences of a man looking over the pressed flowers that are a metonym of the niece he has presumed has been killed, while a more aggressive form of 'still life' can be found in the vivisection practised by Norman Bates in *Psycho* (1960). From the photos of the departed that stare back on investigators' walls, to *Man Bites Dog*'s example of the modern desire to exhibit all of life for the camera, photography is used in ways that offer material evidence of the presence of a human being alongside the pastness of the moment in which it was captured. Just as it bypasses certainty and rationality, the taste for art becomes a method of consuming the life it fixes in time, and killing becomes a lunge to possess the ineffable of humanity that it destroys. Art is thus a way of flagging up the fragility of human life that is emphasized by the random destructive terror of serial killing, a fragility which is then extended in these films to be a characteristic also of meaning, identity, or of humanity itself.

Taste and tone

At one point in *American Psycho*, Bateman points a power tool at the back of his secretary's head and tells her that "I guess you could say I want to have a meaningful relationship with someone special." His mocking tone is shared by the film, and yet both his unpretentious secretary and the activity of serial killing actually are the nearest he has to meaningful relationships. In this, the film confuses the boundary between sarcasm and sincerity in a way that embodies the purposeless absurdity discussed above, for one can no longer even tell the difference between irony and truth. As with *Man Bites Dog*'s film-school spoof, *Perfume*'s sarcastic connection of cosmetics and stench, *Matador*'s artifice and De Quincey's urtexts on murder, the connection of killing to taste encourages a combination of heightened style, violent action, and grandiose social commentary with meaninglessness. Although the earnestness of films like *Silence*, *Antibodies*, and *H6* differs to the archness of *American Psycho* and *Man Bites Dog*, even here the serial killers whose tastes they feature give standout detours into sarcasm. Just as it confounds the stability with which civility and identity are held, so does the connection of taste and serial killing destabilize authentic meaning (Figure 9.2).

So, do serial killers have good taste? As far as the adult-orientated, middle-of-the-road 1980s culture goes, Bateman in *American Psycho* does pick the most consummate typifications and professional realizations of the genre, as well as creating a coherent and artistically appropriate soundtrack to his life. When he discusses Huey Lewis and the News he comments that their "Early work was a little too new wave for my tastes" before praising the "clear crisp sound and a new sheen of consummate professionalism" of their mature output. He then hacks, screaming, into his victim, while "Hip to Be Square," in all its 'catchiness', keeps playing: is this an ironic disjuncture or an appropriate example of the very qualities of inauthenticity, distraction, and personalitilessness of which serial killing, in the film, forms part?

The aesthetic of a "crisp sheen" matches with the sharp glint of the axe blade, and a killing to the strains of Phil Collins's "Sussudio" occurs as the

FIGURE 9.2 *Does Patrick Bateman have good taste?* American Psycho *(2000)*.

camera lingers on the cold steel of the knives, coherent with the minimalist white aesthetic of Bateman's flat and providing an aesthetic unity between music, killing, setting, and film style. When Bateman states that the lyrics are "about self-preservation, and dignity," he suggests a sincere empathy for qualities that he does not have in his personal relationships, offering the music a greater meaning that the film does not directly contradict. In *Man Bites Dog*, Benoit's odes to pigeons seem to be self-inflating objects of poetic pretension. And yet pigeons form a continual motif throughout the film, and the final shot, after film crew and serial killer have all died, relays the slow-motion sound of a pigeon to whom Benoit had recited his poem—his last words before his dramatic killing—repeatedly cooing and then flapping its wings bringing the film to an end. What connection is being set up here, what metaphor might it provide in what was surely solely a marker of silliness? For all the violence and excitement that the films generate their ambiguous tones suggest that, as with the killers they represent, the search for any definitively substantial meaning is destined to be in vain.

This discussion of sarcasm and ambiguity in the film style aims to show that despite apparent narrative disavowals of the serial killer's tastes, the films' styles are coherent with the tastes of the killer. As if inverting the over-identification that serial killers are sometimes thought to have with representation, the films themselves seem to embody the contradictions that they assign to the killer—deviant/cultured, detached/overwhelmed, horrific/sympathetic; maintaining the presence of both at once. The aesthetic experience allowed by taste draws the spectator into the same realms of the killer, creating an identification with the killer and an ambiguous attitude toward his crimes.

Serial killer films that deal with taste fit especially well between higher art and popular categories; *Peeping Tom* providing a paradigm of how self-reflexivity—being a film about sexualized violence in film-making—offers a route to cultural rehabilitation. But why should the art films *Henry* and *Man Bites Dog* provide the examples of violent movies for a book on popular cinema (as written by Hallam and Marshment (2000))? To address the 'popular culture' aspect of this collection's title, the films discussed here confuse categories of art and exploitation, and bring the popular pleasures of violence and horror alongside a detachment that encourages social commentary, aesthetic contemplation, and artistic reference. It is no coincidence that a key moment in the consciously impoverished and radically disruptive Brazilian movement of *Cinema Marginal* features a bandit who is among other things a serial killer, *O Bandido da luz vermelha/The Red Light Bandit* (1968). In the cinema, serial killing's tendency to violent frenzied disorder can simultaneously heighten a film's political, artistic, and entertainment ambitions, while blurring the boundaries that might separate them.

Not all serial killer films are preoccupied with taste; but those that are tend to express a sense that there is something aesthetic about killing. At the same time they also suggest that there is something deadening in the indulgence of taste. They broach—although still cannot answer—not so much the meaning of life as the meaning of death. They base the higher states of artistic arousal and appreciation in the immediate, non-rational satisfaction of physical appetite; they show polite manners as a cover for a tendency toward bestial cannibalism; they portray art as isolating and inauthentic, work as alienating, and confuse the ordering of rationality, meaning, and purpose which classical accounts of aesthetics aim to uphold. Insofar as they blur the distinctions between identification and detachment and between high art and populist violence, the films which connect serial killing to taste are overly close to their subjects, embodying ambivalence, and, like taste, combining an extra-rational appetite for sensation with a cultivated, amoral detachment. It is here that one finds the enigmatic centre of both the artworks themselves and the killers that they treat.

Notes

1 I would like to thank Richard Dyer for his insights on the topic and for first putting together a course on serial killing from which many of the ideas here took root, and to the students at King's College, London, who greatly nourished my understanding of the topic. Also Hope Liebersohn, Christopher Muirhead, and Natália Pinazza are to be thanked for their worthwhile contributions.

2 I am grateful to Richard Dyer for this final point.

3 Hannibal Lecter's nemesis Buffalo Bill, *The Texas Chainsaw Massacre*'s (Hooper 1974; Nispel 2003) Leatherface, and more.

4 It is worth noting here that the scientific study of pathology and criminology under the category of sadism is itself a literary reference to the eighteenth-century French writer the Marquis de Sade, whose books are a classic example of art that is neither beautiful nor pleasant.

5 Certainly the idea of a refined aristocracy of taste has in more modern times been subject to a general democratic mistrust of practices of domination and social superiority by critical literature from Veblen (1934) to Bourdieu (1984).

References

Black, Joel. 1991. *The Aesthetics of Murder: A Study in Romantic Literature and Contemporary Culture*. Baltimore: Johns Hopkins Press.

Bourdieu, Pierre. 1984. *Distinction: A Social Critique of the Judgement of Taste*, translated by Richard Nice. London: Routledge and Kegan Paul.

Burke, Edmund. 1958 [1757]. *A Philosophical Enquiry Into the Origin of our Ideas of the Sublime and Beautiful*, edited by J. T. Boulton. London: Routledge and Keegan Paul.

Cameron, Deborah. 1996. "Wanted: The Female Serial Killer." *Trouble and Strife* 33: 21–8.

Cameron, Deborah, and Elizabeth Frazer. 1987. *The Lust to Kill*. London: Polity.

De Quincey, Thomas. 2006. *On Murder*. Introduction by Robert Morrison. Oxford: Oxford University Press.

Dyer, Richard. 2000. "Kill and Kill Again." In *Action/Spectacle Cinema*, edited by José Arroyo, 145–50. London: BFI Publishing.

Gomel, Elana. 2003. *Bloodscripts: Writing the Violent Subject*. Columbus: Ohio State University.

Hallam, Julia, and Margaret Marshment. 2000. *Realism and Popular Cinema*. Manchester: Manchester University Press.

King, Anthony. 2006. "Serial Killing and the Postmodern Self." *History of the Human Sciences* 19(3): 109–25.

Newitz, Annalee. 1998. "Serial Killers." *CineAction* 38: 38–46.

Schneider, Stephen Jay. 2001. "Murder as Art/The Art of Murder: Aestheticising Violence in Modern Cinematic Horror." Accessed July 1, 2012. http://intensities.org/Essays/Schneider.pdf.

Seltzer, Mark. 2000. "The Serial Killer as a Type of Person." In *The Horror Reader*, edited by Ken Gelder, 97–107. London: Routledge.

Staiger, Janet. 1993. "Taboos and Totems: Cultural Meanings of *The Silence of the Lambs*." In *Film Theory Goes to the Movies*, edited by Jim Collins, Hilary Radner, and Ava Preacher Collins, 142–55. Routledge: New York.

Tatar, Maria. 1995. *Lustmord: Sexual Murder in Weimar Germany*. Princeton: Princeton University Press.

Veblen, Thorstein. 1934. *The Theory of the Leisure Class: An Economic Study of Institutions*. New York: The Modern Library.

Filmography

American Psycho. DVD. Directed by Mary Harron. 2000; Santa Monica, CA: Lionsgate Home Entertainment, 2005.

Antikörper/Antibodies. DVD. Directed by Christian Alvart. 2005; Orland Park, IL: Dark Sky Films, 2007.

C'est arrive près de chez vous/Man Bites Dog. DVD. Directed by Rémy Belvaux and André Bonzel. 1992; New York, NY: The Criterion Collection, 2002.

Copycat. DVD. Directed by Jon Amiel. 1995; Burbank, CA: Warner Home Video, 1995.

Das Parfum—Die Geschichte eines Mörders/Perfume: The Story of a Murderer. DVD. Directed by Tom Tykwer. 2006; Universal City, CA: Dreamworks, 2007.

Die Wachsfigurenkabinett/ Waxworks. DVD. Directed by Paul Leni. 1924; New York: Kino Video, 2002.

Funny Games. DVD. Directed by Michael Haneke. 1997; New York, NY: Fox Lorber, 1999.

Funny Games. DVD. Directed by Michael Haneke. 2007; Burbank, CA: Warner Home Video, 2008.

The Girl with the Dragon Tattoo. DVD. Directed by David Fincher. 2011; Culver City, CA: Sony Pictures Home Entertainment, 2012.

Hannibal. DVD. Directed by Ridley Scott. 2001; Beverly Hills, CA: MGM Home Entertainment, 2001.

Henry: Portrait of a Serial Killer. DVD. Directed by John McNaughton. 1986; Orland Park, IL: MPI Media Group, 1998.

H6: Diario de un asesino/H6: Diary of a Serial Killer. DVD. Directed by Martín Garrido Barón. 2005; UK: Tartan Video, 2006.

Le Boucher. DVD. Directed by Claude Chabrol. 1970; Venice, CA: Pathfinder Home Entertainment, 2003.

Le Vampire du Düsseldorf. VHS. Directed by Robert Hossein. 1965; Seattle, WA: Something Weird Video, 2000.

The Lodger: A Story of the London Fog. DVD. Directed by Alfred Hitchcock. 1927; Beverly Hills, CA: MGM Home Entertainment, 2009.

Love from a Stranger. DVD. Directed by Rowland V. Lee. 1937; West Conshohocken, PA: Alpha Video, 2004.

M. DVD. Directed by Fritz Lang. 1931; New York: Criterion, 2004.

Män som hatar kvinnor/The Girl with the Dragon Tattoo. DVD. Directed by Niels Arden Oplev. 2009; Chicago: Music Box Films Home Entertainment, 2010.

Matador. DVD. Directed by Pedro Almodóvar. 1986; Culver City, CA: Sony Pictures Home Entertainment, 2009.

Nature Morte. DVD. Directed by Paul Burrows. 2006; New York: Redemption Films, 2008.

O Bandido da luz vermelha/The Red Light Bandit. DVD. Directed by Rogério Sganzerla. 1968; Versátil Home Video: São Paulo Brazil, 2007.

Peeping Tom. DVD. Directed by Michael Powell. 1960; New York: Criterion, 1999.

Psycho. DVD. Directed by Alfred Hitchcock. 1960; Universal City, CA: Universal Studios Home Entertainment, 1998.

Scream. DVD. Directed by Wes Craven. 1996; Burbank, CA: Walt Disney Studios Home Entertainment Video, 1997.

The Silence of the Lambs. DVD. Directed by Jonathan Demme. 1991; Los Angeles, CA: Orion Pictures Corporation, 1997.

Svalan, katten, rosen, döden/Swallow, Cat, Rose, Death. DVD. Directed by Daniel Lind Lagerlöf. 2006; Fairfax, VA: MHz Networks, 2007.

The Texas Chainsaw Massacre. DVD. Directed by Tobe Hooper. 1974; Universal City, CA: Universal Studios Home Entertainment, 2003.

The Texas Chainsaw Massacre. DVD. Directed by Marcus Nispel. 2003; Los Angeles, CA: New Line Home Entertainment, 2004.

10

Defacing the Acquisitions: A Museal-Analysis of Serial Killing Horror in Cinema

Janice Baker

Thought is primarily trespass and violence, the enemy . . .

GILLES DELEUZE, 1994, 139

Serial killing as a form of cinematic horror is conceived in this essay as a 'shock to thought'; as a sensory violation that affects viewers' subjective reception of the self. Deleuze (1994, 139) notes that a fundamental shock or encounter may be grasped in a range of 'affective tones' which can include suffering as well as sensations of wonder, love, hatred, and so on. Serial killing horror is a trespass or violation of normative experience that disturbs the passivity of thought by stripping familiar relations with the social production of the body. As a cinematic affect, serial murder offers a direct sensation of subjectivity as a process of constant re-assemblage rather than with the body and face constituted as a unified pre-programmed surface upon which organizing traits conform in advance to a dominant reality.

In approaching serial killing as a sensory rupture to common sense understanding of subjectivity, I do not engage with horror as a discursive phenomenon but suggest that such discourse delimits approaches to difference. My interest in the cultural work of cinematic horror is sought in a de-territorializing of the 'rigid' stratification of subjectivity inherent in discursive and structuralist readings of film. Beyond the discursive, and within a poststructural 'self-dismantling', my analysis operates as a dislodging of the viewing passivity inherent in the way psychoanalytical approaches in particular understand and construct the gaze.

In reflecting on the effect of horror on viewing audiences I do not find psychoanalytical interpretation convincing (regardless of whether or not psychoanalysis may be relevant to a textual analysis of a film's narrative plot, character, and *mis-en-scène*). My alternative analysis does not conceive horror as a psychic process of abjection that returns a 'wayward' audience to reason but, rather, it offers the view that certain affective experience can be a split or departure from such a path. This departure from the subjective path of reason gains additional traction when it occurs, as curiously it often does, in a museum; a physical site traditionally associated with the acquisition of art and artifacts for the pedagogic purposes of knowledge production. When uncommon 'things' are done to bodies and faces in a museum, we are moved from a place of taxonomic order and reason into a space of fluid corporeal boundaries and shifting assemblages of organic and non-organic, a site for thinking what is un-thought.

The basis for this approach to horror as a de-territorializing of the body arises from the capacity of film images to powerfully disrupt the authority we give to fixed subjective positions dictating what can and cannot be thought. This stance acknowledges the affective, physiological impact of film and the potency that Deleuze accords to the cinematic image. It is an approach that aligns with film theorists Anna Powell (2005) and Steven Shaviro (2002) who similarly draw on Deleuze in a re-purposing of cinematic horror that frees the film image from the fixity given to it in psychoanalysis. This re-purposing of horror does not dwell on cinematic fantasy and desire as a psychic repression or lack but as a form of perception beyond the dictates of subjective agency. In accordance with this view, Barbara Kennedy (2004, 55) makes an important point in reflecting on the efficacy of a new pragmatic feminist film theory through Deleuze. She writes that, "despite a concern with 'bodies' I am not suggesting a phenomenological account of the cinematic experience . . . [but] a melding of the mind/body/brain with the image, in an assemblage of filmic sensation, where 'affect' affords the ultimate 'material emotion' which is beyond any subjective vision." A sense of this "'material emotion'," of an assemblage outside normative signification of the self, is what concerns me in relation to the way that serial killing horror is treated in cinema.

Death and museums

All manner of museums appear in horror films as locations for serial killing. *House of Wax* (1953) is set in a fictional wax museum. In Dario Argento's *The Stendhal Syndrome* (1996) and Ridley Scott's *Hannibal* (2001) the environs in and around the Uffizi Museum are utilized. *The Relic* (1996) takes place almost entirely within a fictional museum that is loosely modeled on the

American Museum of Natural History. Despite the locale, each of these horror films appeal to an enduring curiosity of cinema audiences to encounter bodies as artifacts and acquisitions that have been artificially or unnaturally reconfigured. Perhaps this appeal is not that far removed from the fascination with undefined objects housed in early *Wunderkammer* and cabinets of curiosity, the European precursors of the modern museum. From the earliest silent films to recent cinema, the violation to bodies in 'serial killer horror' has engaged directly with the audience's sensory perception of being.

The violation to perception of the body in serial killer horror provides a visceral acquaintance with the body disrupted. The event is more than a fictionalized stereotyping of violent crime; what I am interested in is the grip of such films to put viewers viscerally and hence cognitively 'out of joint'. Films that focus on intense repetition of violation demand that the viewer re-address normative cognitive attachment to human limbs, torsos, heads, skin, and the face. The disorientation that ensues interrupts representations that resoundingly associate self-hood with a mind/body/brain that is distinct and separate from the material object world. Anything outside this subjective, 'hooded' unity is normally categorized as Other. Serial murder horror enacted in the museum engages attention otherwise, and in the sensory de-territorializing of idealized representations there arises a sense that images are naturalized via incessant repetition and consequent instalment as sociocultural norms. Thus we have an explanation for the popular appeal and the cultural value of this form of cinematic 'pleasure'.

Serial killer horror as a 'material emotion' diverges from psychoanalytically driven perspectives about horror and deviance that posit film viewers objectifying desire through repressive identification with images on the screen. An example of this form of desire or lack is expressed in Slavoj Žižek's (1991, 86) Lacanian reading of the protagonist's horror in *Vertigo* (1958) as, "the very abyss of the hole in the Other (the symbolic order), concealed by the fascinating presence of the fantasy object . . . figured in the shots accompanying the titles of *Vertigo*, the closeups of a woman's eye out of which swirls a nightmarish partial object." Another example of repressed desire is evident in Barbara Creed's (2004, 46) analysis of the monstrous-feminine in science fiction horror. Aboard a space-ship in *Alien* (1979), for example, "three astronauts explore the gigantic, cavernous, malevolent womb of the mother. Two members of the group watch the enactment of the primal scene in which Kane is violated in an act of phallic penetration-by the father or phallic mother?" Film readings of unconscious repression or lack, such as these by Žižek and Creed, fix subjectivity to an Oedipal triangulation that I suggest, following Deleuze, may actually be eroded by the assemblages created by cinema. These 'anti-Oedipal' assemblages arise from the affects produced when the non-human apparatus of cinema folds with the viewer's visceral response to audiovisual images. This 'new' image of thought escapes the relation between a subject and its object that operates as a core tenet of psychoanalytical and other structuralist and ideological readings of cultural texts. In this 'escape', cinematic assemblages do not function as, for example, representations defined by moral tendencies of good and evil traditionally affixed to the humanist paradigm. Rather, such cinematic assemblages query the very basis upon which we accept that binary representations hold currency as the only way of knowing the world.

As sites for the dissipation of 'totalizing' representations of the world, museums as dangerous locations in fictional texts complicate the logic with which the museum is conceived in scholarly literature. Museums are traditionally associated with the orderly, didactic display of artifacts to advance knowledge from a broadly humanist perspective. Views of the world are formulated around pedagogies of 'good' sense that assume 'irrational' passions of the body are separate from the superior logic of the reasoning mind. In defiance of the authority dualism gives to the faculty of human reason over the 'logic' of material emotion, museums in movies recur as sites that are dangerously 'out of control'. They nurture curses, superstition, the supernatural, and a range of non-human becomings. Within this already Other cinematic site, serial killing horror destabilizes the notion that identity is contained in an immutable subjectivity and should necessarily be represented as a body controlled by reason.

This has interesting implications for perceptions of the museum more broadly. There is a tendency in the critical literature of museology to prevail on the museum's role in the 'death of art', hence the metaphor of the museum as a mausoleum. This discourse locates its origin in the eighteenth-century writings of the French cultural critic Quatremére de Quincy who, dismayed by Napoleon's looting of Rome to furnish the Louvre, conceived that the Museum represented the death of art. He argued that a painting or sculpture no longer has meaning once removed from the site it was originally intended to occupy. The pejorative association of the museum with the death of artifacts is a recurring theme. It held particular appeal for the early twentieth-century avant-garde. Jean Cocteau drolly noted that, "The Louvre is a morgue; you go there to identify your friends" (quoted in Henning 2006, 37). Museums are graveyards according to Marinetti (1973) in "The Founding and Manifesto of Futurism": "We mean to free [Italy] from the numberless museums that cover her like so many graveyards" (quoted in Henning 2006, 38). Theodor Adorno's (1967 [1990], 175) observation is oft-quoted: "The German word *museal* [museum-like] has unpleasant overtones. . . . Museum and mausoleum are connected by more than phonetic association. Museums are like family sepulchres of works of art." Museum-mausoleum discourse finds expression today as a vigilance to expose the museum's past imperial and colonial hegemonic practices. While this attentiveness is important, the metaphor misses the inventive possibilities of the museum experience as an encounter with alterity—just as a focus on serial killer horror as a psychic operation overlooks abjection as an escape from the impasse of a fixed relation between the self and monstrous Other.

Becoming wax

The episodic practice of reconfiguring murdered corpses in wax and displaying these as exhibits is a recurring theme in cinematic representations of the museum. The dominant sign of the corpse in horror tends again to be psychoanalytic. For example, in *Psycho* (1960), Norman Bates steals and preserves his mother's corpse, an act generally interpreted as Norman's ('normal-man's') Oedipal fixation with his mother. To mention just a few of scores of films that focus upon the reconfiguring of corpse's in wax: the popular success of *Mystery of the Wax Museum* (1933) saw it remade in 1953 as *House of Wax* starring Hollywood horror 'celebrity' Vincent Price as an artist who displays his murdered 'treasures' in a fashionable New York wax museum. The killer in *Nightmare in Wax* (*Crimes in the Wax Museum*) (1969) is employed to create special affects in films and is consequently skilled at remodeling his victims for display in the Movieland Wax Museum. A recent incarnation on the theme is an 'updated' *House of Wax* (2005) in which the population of a small Louisianan town are wax-preserved in a museum of horrors by two killer siblings.

In wax museum horror, film audiences share the killer's awareness of the 'real substance' of victims, of the museum's life-like 'acquisitions'. This 'pact' between the killer and audience is not akin to a parallel form of character identification, that is, an explicit representation within the narrative is not imbricated with a film viewer's life. It would be simplistic to think that an audience absorbs a killer's psychopathy or other disorder through the act of garnering some sort of cinematic insight into the killer's mental condition. Rather, the affect is to arouse a sensory vantage point from which to unmoor the viewer's usual anchorage of thought. There is a loosening or overflowing of the 'real' which acts as a form of experiential disjunction. In other words, cinema produces affects otherwise deemed cognitively impossible such as the merging of things in Hitchcock's horror film *The Birds* (1963). Before the birds' first attack, the movement of water, of a bird in the distance, and that of a person on a boat are blended into a single perception which becomes an "entirely bird-centred Nature" (Deleuze 1986, 20). Our sense of things, of subjects, and objects in everyday life, are overcome by the reorganized perception of cinema and its creation of alternate becomings. A zone of indiscernibility is entered; the realm of menace, of waxed, reconfigured bodies of "things, beasts, and persons" reaching toward "that point that immediately precedes their natural differentiation" (Deleuze 2004b, 173).

We experience cinematic affects in many guises such as dynamic 'human' qualities extracted from otherwise static, inanimate objects in the *mise-en-scène* of serial killer horror. The 'sharpness' and glint of a knife, for example, gives it anticipatory value and converts the familiar domestic item into a portent of murder. Likewise, stylistic devices highlight 'waxiness' so that the material acquires an anthropomorphic presence not ordinarily attributed to a non-human substance. Audiences are not immune to this manipulation of material environments; we are not physically detached from the alternative material sensibility of films. In wax museum horror there is an exchange between, as it were, commonly sensed material bodies that are neither natural nor artificial. Identity is not determined by adherence to the substance of 'life', and the certainty that the human is identified as a fixed subjectivity is compromised. What is curious about this cinematic phenomenon is its reflection of a compulsion to experience dissipation from the commonly sensed 'self', to affirm the possibility of reinvention through becomings that are not existentially apart from the Other and the material object world.

In Paul Leni's silent film *Waxworks* (1924), mannequins in wax of Jack the Ripper, Rasputin, and other notorious historical killers are brought to life by a writer imagining scary stories to attract people to visit a wax museum. He succeeds 'doubly' in his task to 'strike fear' as film audiences in the 1920s were shocked to their core by 'close' proximity to murderers and their crimes. Phrases such as 'scared witless' and 'blood chilling' give expression to the direct physiological impact that movies goers have sought since this earliest example of cinematic fantasy/horror. The desire to confront serial killers 'doing' things to bodies—slashing, flaying, torturing, amputating, burning, consuming—reclaims the Otherness of the sensory world. In these ways, Enlightenment understanding of identity as categorically defined through reason may potentially be destabilized. Viewers who choose to experience this kind of cinematic horror are arguably intrigued by assemblages that operate beyond the limit of the signifier, rather than by horror purely cognized as a manifestation of abjection.

For Kristeva (1986), horror is a predominantly psychic operation of abjection. Her conception reduces the 'monstrous' to acts of repressed human desire rather than engaging with the inventive possibilities of a cinematic disruption to the containment of identity as a fixed subject and object position that interests me. As Anna Powell (2005, 16) notes: "Despite Kristeva's suggestive exploration of the fluid nature of abjection, critical readings [based on her work] tend to retain a fixed dichotomy of self and other, as well as gender binaries." For Kristeva, abjection processes everything that threatens the borders of the self. The abject is an experience to put society back on the path of order; a taste of the taboo is sufficient to return individuals to the normalcy of the rational world. She observes that all societies employ notions of the abject to define those things that threaten the meaning of what constitutes the proper, human subject (Creed 2004, 36).

Kristeva views abjection relating to the maternal function and, accordingly, if we direct her theoretical position to the conventional conception of the 'rational' museum, we might interpret cinematic violation of this legacy representing symbolic defiance of patriarchal authority. This discursive framing assumes that the symbolic realm of the father is constantly under threat from an irrational (castrated) mother. Serial killing horror might thus be read as a psychic objectification of an encounter with the abject, unclean woman. This has become a convincing metaphorical trope which finds, for example, Jack the Ripper understood as a 'middle-class' functionary, ridding society of its ills (prostitutes) (Stratton 1996). However, while this type of trophic reading engages with a 'self' that is threatened, it does not to my mind capture the audacity of cinema to annul the 'civilized' world of a restorative mythology to augment a return to reason. It does not accommodate the event of being 'frightened out of our skin' in terms of a desire for new ways of becoming human; for physical renewal, an alternative perception of identity. Ultimately Kristeva's theorization of horror as abjection aligns with fixity to the body/ mind/brain as a grounding for identity and hence an immovable subjectivity.

In line with these reflections, Anna Powell and Steven Shaviro contend that the power of film, its viewing pleasure, lies not in the viewer's psyche but in the body. Shaviro (1993, 148) observes, for example, that David Cronenberg's films generate feelings of fear, anxiety, and mourning not as secondary consequences of some loss or lack, but positively and literally as affections and transformations of the flesh. Anxiety is "a churning of the stomach, a throbbing of the arteries, a tension distending the skull, a series of stresses and shock running the entire length of the body" (Shaviro 1993, 148). The potency lies in direct sensation and is not implicitly circumscribed by a relation to an individual's repressed needs or desires. Shaviro proposes an active and affirmative reading of the cinematic experience that has to do with the body affectively going to the limit of what it can do, beyond the property of the fixed self. This can be conceived as the 'emancipatory' experience I identify with viewing serial killing horror. Serial killing horror operates affectively as a sensory distortion of a viewer's cognitive patterns. The viewer engages viscerally, in the affectively potent mix of the bodily reconfigurations of killers and victims, to become part of the anomaly. Powell (2005, 63) describes that we "become mutant spectators" with monsters/serial killers and "what is initially a cinematic assemblage transmutes into another form of experiential process." This Otherness is what Deleuze (2004a,b) refers to as a "body-without-organs," a body emptied of subjective, repressive content, enabled to experience affectively all matter that surrounds it: "In our assemblage with the screen, the cinematic body-without-organs experiences sounds, textures and rhythms as incorporated vibrations" (Powell 2005, 211).

Art and slashing

The museum environments where victims are slowly and intensely stalked and manipulated in *Dressed to Kill* (1980), *The Stendhal Syndrome*, and *Hannibal* (2001) undo the authority and order expected of a 'rational' museum. The forces and fluxes these films generate do not 'fit' with the familiar recognition of an aesthetic space but, rather, mark an interstitial moment that requires a new sense of logic. When we think along *with* the cinema in this way, we de-territorialize the coordinates of common sense with which we frame recognition through memory. As Deleuze and Guattari (1994, 139) note, the 'something' that causes us to think is beyond that which we already recognize and is a response to an encounter for which there is no pre-existing schema. In this regard, the 'musealization' of serial killer horror destabilizes common sense signification in order to generate movements, sensations, and durations that operate to break sensible attachment to conventional and clichéd representations of the self and Other.

Deleuze and Guattari (2004b, 177) ask ". . . how can we unhook ourselves from the points of subjectification that secure us, nail us down to a dominant reality? Tearing the conscious away from the subject in order to make it a means of exploration." One way horror is crafted to disrupt the 'nailed down' reality of passive viewing is by playing with the status of artifacts within the diegetic narrative world of a film. Museum artifacts acquire agency and exude a living force that disturbs the common sense notion that the material world is static and Other. We see this, for example, in an extended sequence in Brian de Palma's murder thriller *Dressed to Kill* about a cross-dressing therapist who kills his client, Kate. Performing a psychoanalytic reading of this film does not account for the non-organic life of things generated by sensed relations between objects and subjects in the art gallery where Kate is seduced.

Elizabeth Wilson sees the plot of this film as a Freudian narrative of patriarchal authority and familial disintegration, a reading that Jon Stratton (1994, 14) incorporates into his cultural explication of serial killing as a (s)talking of fear in the modern city. But we can move beyond the film as a cultural object of fear to engage with the non-discursive shock of its sensory grip. It is here that we can locate the affective agency of the paintings in the gallery. As Kate wanders the galleries the 'subjects' of paintings participate in the distracted events of her mind; the viewing audience senses the agency of this uncommon subject–object relation. This is not a dualism, it is something else; an assemblage unknown to common sense. The gallery comes to embody Kate's passion through its palpable effect on her. Her thoughts are materialized to include the milieu of things around her. In long, silent sequences in which Kate views artworks, the viewing audience becomes party to this eloquent mental world of the film which merges object and subject awareness together. Consequently, when Kate is murdered there is an abrupt cessation; a visceral jolt. While the shared mental state with Kate is obviously not 'real', the jolt at her death is. Thus it is that cinematic images reassemble perception, they shift our conceptual terrain; there is a de-centering of the faculties that normally congregate to clad us in the notion that we are contained by our individual, subjective sense of the world.

Dismantling the sense of continuous, unified subjectivity is also an effect of Dario Argento's 'slasher' film *The Stendhal Syndrome*. Anna is a detective who hunts and kills a serial killer, then becomes the killer herself. First she is lured into the Uffizi Museum in Florence. Wandering the galleries, the camera's 'eye' drifts among tourists and artifacts, lingering close to paintings including Caravaggio's decapitated *Medusa*. The space becomes imbued with a menace that has a palpable agency for the film's viewing audience. Art acquires a force and movement similar to that encountered in *Dressed to Kill*. The audience is drawn into a multiplicity of viewpoints through a drift back and forth between objects and the expressive world of the characters; a material thinking that conspires to disturb Anna who increasingly suffers from the condition that is the film's title—hallucinations brought on by an intense response to art. The audience becomes part of the conspiracy in a response that is viscerally engaging rather than reasonably discernible.

For example, the viewer 'falls' into paintings with Anna and accompanies her hallucinatory participation in the events visualized in the pictorial plane. She swims 'inside' a seascape by Breugal. In this watery underworld there is an extreme detachment from her human form. Becoming-fish, the viewer encounters Anna's disembodied subjectivity. This disembodiment is sharply brought into focus when Anna 'revives' and she (and the viewing audience) return to 'normal' consciousness. Having fainted, Anna is helped from the gallery floor by the killer she will become. The viewer is also shocked 'back' to human form, but not without having experienced another 'object' point of view, an event of an-other duration. The audience's journey through Anna's disembodiment displaces the idea of the body as an entity with a continuous identity.

Given the opportunity the museum provides for this type of object–subject displacement, it seems fitting that audiences are reacquainted in *Hannibal*, the sequel to *The Silence of the Lambs* (1991), with the cannibal Dr Lecter as a curator researching the Florentine Caponi Art Collection. We are chilled and thrilled at Lecter's reinvention, as we follow him padding barefoot around his lavish Florence apartment. He is an aesthete perfectly at home among classical sculptures, tapestries, and artifacts as he studies images of Dante's *Inferno*. Hannibal, the cannibal, is a Renaissance man; a cannibal for all seasons. His multiple murders amount to an extension of his aesthetic work, and include the graphic disembowelment of an Italian detective who has discovered the curator's less savoury side. The appeal of such gruesome cinematic events is a curious intensity that has less to do with the aestheticization of psychopathy than with the incongruity of the disembodiment Lecter engenders as a felt sensation. Bodies in the affective corpus of Hannibal Lecter are no longer safely contained within a skin. It is the rupture of the body as a recognizable territory of thought that is surely intriguing for viewers, rather than the gratuitous pleasure of watching scenes of brutality.

That killing feeling

Serial killers as fictional characters have been examined as symbols of status, consumption, and the superficiality of late capitalist life (see, for example, Jarvis 2007; Lee, in this collection). The underpinning of this approach is that serial killers are terrifying by their normalcy, which displays a likeness to consumer culture: "The violence of consumerism is similarly hidden beneath a façade of healthy normality" with the mythology of beauty and pleasure that drives consumerism obscuring "widespread devastation and suffering" (Jarvis 2007, 329). Consumption in the capitalist model relies on normalizing and rationalizing the object of consumption, exemplified by texts of popular culture such as Bret Easton Ellis's *American Psycho* (1991). The conflation of bodies and commodities by Ellis's Wall Street 'psycho' Patrick Bateman is palpable through the superficial insights and blocks of inane detail that pepper his narration.

As usual, in an attempt to understand these girls I'm filming their deaths. With Torri and Tiffany I use a Minox LX ultra-miniature camera that takes 9.5 mm film, has a 15 m f/3.5 lens, an exposure meter and a built-in natural density filter and sits on a tripod. I've put a CD of the Traveling Wilburys into a portable CD player that sits on the headboard above the bed, to mute any screams. (Ellis 1991, 304)

With the musealization of serial killing horror, the theme strays from Ellis's critique of capitalism by the substantial fact that museums are *not* ordinary places of 'consumption'. Of course, there are critics who would decree that museums are about commodification and the normalizing of objects, however, while museums frequently have shops, 'blockbuster' exhibitions, and so on, it is an attribute of encounters with artifacts in museums that they do *not* provide the instant gratification of late-capitalist commodification. Krystof Pomian declares it is precisely because objects in museums have absolutely no use that they gain their power as objects full of meaning; the less use, the more meaning (cited in Arnold 2006, 167). Stephen Greenblatt (1991, 52) ties the inability to own objects viewed in the museum as the essence of their arousal of wonder: "Museums display works of art in such a way that no one, not even the nominal owner or donor . . . can actually possess the wonderful objects."

The association of museum objects with impacts outside the realm of commodification connects to the museum's complication of subject and object dualism and the correspondence of this binary opposition with passive thinking. In the musealization of serial killer horror, as we have seen in the above films, subject and object positions are perceived as arbitrary and changeable. Bodies merge with artifacts and take on forms of agency that estrange the binary dualism that separates self from the Other. There is a relation here, more generally, with the fictional presentation of death in museums. Death tends to be accessed as a curious, sensory encounter with transformation rather than finality. This curiosity is articulated by children in fictional texts who delight in encounters with body parts. For example, in *The Relic* school children are excited by the prospect of seeing 'eyeballs in jars', and likewise a child in James Fenton's (1994) poem "The Pitt-Rivers Museum, Oxford" (1982), set in the phantasmagoria that is Oxford's Pitt Rivers Museum, excitedly enquires of an attendant: "Please sir where's the withered hand?"

This engaged response to musealized death is intensively given expression in Robin Jarvis's trilogy for children *Tales from the Wyrd Museum* (1985). In the first of the popular series, a London museum transports children, along with eccentric adults, demonic entities, and teddy bears, into a world at war terrorized by a serial killer in the form of a bug. The Wyrd Museum operates as a sensory experience of temporal disjunction as well as geographic location. As the Museum travels into the past, people and objects experience dislocation in the present. Once again we find a museum operating as a curious and unsettling sensory displacement of bodies, a disembodiment attached to serial killing. In Jarvis's tale, the adult notion of the cuddly, soft toy metamorphoses into a far less innocent taxonomic imaginary. Savage murders are graphically described:

> In the narrow alleyway, Mrs Meacham's terrified screams abruptly ceased. Gurgling with delight, the squander bug scuttled over the body of its slaughtered prey and lowered its already blurring face. A vile lapping sound drifted out into the jet black night and then there was silence. Belial had claimed his first victim. (Jarvis 1985, 210)

This graphic depiction of the first of the creature's many horrific murders makes it apparent that the intensity of suffering and fear described by such fictional texts is not 'felt' as might be supposed. This attends to the argument I have made thus far that serial killing horror appeals as a generative force, as an arousal that escapes normativity.

We might align this point with Brian Massumi's (2002) appraisal of affect where he notes that children find 'sad' scenes in films pleasant, perhaps because they are aroused when they are sad, and arousal is equated with pleasure. He elaborates that "the difference between 'sadness' and 'happiness' is not all that it's cracked up to be" and what is normally indexed as separate is actually connected; "the strength of duration of an image's effect is not logically connected to the content in any straight forward way" (Massumi 2002, 24). If we transpose this to the sensorium of the Wyrd Museum, what might well in other circumstances be understood as 'terror' becomes an embodied encounter with difference. Objects both animate and inanimate, encounter one another in space/time that does not distinguish in any common sense way between human and non-human worlds. The subject/object relation is reframed into more complex configurations than the common sense separation of the human from the non-human body.

Defacing the subject

Through the multiple viewpoints synthesized by the cinema, affective realms such as serial killing horror are created that do not correspond to the logic of familiar, organizing systems of representation, particularly the face.

. . . if human beings have a destiny, it is rather to escape the face, to dismantle the face and facializations, to become imperceptible, to become clandestine, not by returning to animality, nor even by returning to the head, but by quite spiritual and special becomings-animal, by strange true becomings that get past the wall and get out of the black holes . . . eyes you traverse instead of seeing yourself in or gazing into in those glum face-to-face encounters between signifying subjectivities. (Deleuze and Guattari 2004b, 190)

The particular specialty of serial killing violation is to disorient subject and object positions from normative representations of the body. In particular, violation to the face is a recurring feature of disruption. Thus, for example, instead of the human face operating as a marker of permanent identification, in serial killing horror the 'faces' of characters and artifacts melt, peel, are reconfigured, and sometimes consumed. The subject is removed from a face. It is telling that serial killers in films are often portrayed as faceless or as defiling and/or feeding on the faces of others. These films are obsessed with the face, the killer's own and those of victims. Sometimes the faces of killers are disfigured, as happens in wax museums, or else the face is masked.

In considering serial killer horror via the anonymity of the cinematic machine we stray from framing the cinema as a screen or mirror of an individual unconscious. The face cannot reflect or 'mirror' or contain a person's selfhood when it does not exist. Anna Powell (2005, 147) has explored through Deleuze the affinity of faciality and horror to the socialized sense of selfhood: "Not only is the face a frame for social meaning, it is also the 'black hole' of subjective consciousness expressed by the 'third eye' of the camera. Close-ups of the face serve to defamiliarise it as an 'alien landscape'." The agency to become something else is given physical expression by removing the face; to massacre the face is to return to nothing, to a body without dimension that can be reconfigured (Deleuze and Guattari 2004b, 186). It is in this sense that the act of dismantling the face—of de-identifying the human visage—gestures toward a body-without-organs, and consequently a viewer unsettled from their subjective viewpoint as the stance that frames the world.

The immediacy of affecting images, such as a graphic violation to the human face, generates an immediate and unconditioned response without particular reference to the armature of an individual viewer's psychically structured world. This is an example of the potency of affects functioning at a visceral level that is not immediately subject to a viewer's awareness. Claire Colebrook (2002, 38) describes this form of vitality when she notes: "I watch a scene in a film and my heart flinches and I begin to perspire. Before

I even think or conceptualise there is an element of response that is prior to any decision." In moving outside the screen as a mirror of the psyche to non-psychological life, and suggesting the 'transference' of affect between cinema images and viewers in terms of transformation rather than objectifying self-hood, desire acquires an agency or autonomy that differs from the status it receives in representational frameworks. Desire is thought by the body through the senses; it is not innate and not constituted by the discursive realm of recognition and habit, of cause and effect. As Deleuze describes, bodies are not things or facts, but events. In Deleuze's philosophy, desire holds the capacity to 'overcode' or re-territorialize the fixity of discursive designations. Desire operates as a dynamic force of invention and movement outside the coordinates of subjects, objects and persons, and away from repetitive patterns that constrain difference. It is within this paradigm of desire that we can position the affective event of serial killing horror in cinema.

The sensibilities that are manifested through the cinematic image situate the viewer beyond the normative frames of subjective experience. They unfix the individual from occupying a body in which they are separate from the matter of the world. It takes a non-human mechanism such as the cinematic image and its jolt to thought, of which serial killing horror is an example, to suspend preoccupation with representations of 'perfect' and whole bodies clad with the flawless skin of reason.

An early film 'defacing' occurs in *Mystery of the Wax Museum* (1933) when Fay Ray's character hits out to protect herself from her potential killer, causing his mask to crack and fall apart revealing a dreadfully disfigured face. This scene enacted a new and compelling sensibility of terror. In *House of Wax* (1953), a fire destroys the work of a sculptor and leaves him disfigured and unable to work, so he kills in order to continue his practice. Fresh bodies provide multiple models, easy to shape, and mould into life-like statues. The killer takes control of the appearance of things. Watching the faces of wax mannequins melt in the *House of Wax* museum fire is vivid and palpable; graphic visual sequences of dripping flesh and eyes are intense, calling us to turn away and yet we continue to view (Figure 10.1).

In writing about horror and de-facialization in the paintings of Francis Bacon, Deleuze (2005, xv) remarks on the violence of a sensation as opposed to a representation; of the immense pity that confrontation with the meat evokes, or of the face losing its form. He says that "when [it is] narrative or symbolic, figuration obtains only the bogus violence of the represented or the signified; it expresses nothing of the violence of sensation." Herein we can locate the appeal of serial killer horror not as a narrative figuration of the world, although it is also this, but as a direct sensation of the potency required to escape being sucked into the black hole of subjectification.

FIGURE 10.1 *Affective response: Sue Allen (Phyllis Kirk) learns the truth about the Chamber of Horrors—all the waxworks are Professor Jarrod's victims coated in wax.* House of Wax *(1953)*, Warner Bros. *The Kobal Collection.*

The remodeling and masking of faces is closely associated with the excesses of Hannibal Lecter and his acts of cannibalism. His face is hidden by a mask when in captivity; but hidden he is all the more potent and viewers keenly anticipate his metamorphosis. Part of Lecter's pleasure is to strip the faces of his victims, although he does cause one victim to tear off their own face. In what is surely one of the more confronting sequences to appear in mainstream cinema, in a scene from *Hannibal* that echoes the *modus operandi* of the far less sophisticated killer-monster in *The Relic* (1996), Lecter surgically delves behind the face to dine on a living victim's brain. He performs a frontal lobotomy on Justice Department official Paul Krendler while Clarice Starling watches and vomits. He cuts Krendler's brain, sautés it, and feeds it to a semi-comatose Krendler.

The appeal of the musealization of serial killing horror can be sought in the displacement of the assumption that our bodies are fixed to a subjective idea of the self as unchangeable and unchanging. "Dismantling the face is the same as breaking through the wall of the signifier and getting out of the black hole of subjectivity" (Deleuze and Guattari 2004b, 208). Extreme acts of slashing and flensing are part of the production of environments that glimpse the flux of a world comprised of interlinked bodies that experience different events and durations. Events in the museums where serial killers operate do not accord with common sense framing of the world because this form of 'sense' is necessarily based on what has gone before, on repetition framed around recognition. Beyond the psychic framing of serial killing, as an abjection that returns audiences to reason, we can rather create a conceptual framework that acknowledges a rupture to common sense. Within this, serial killer horror disaffects *homo sapiens* trapped in repetition with no recourse to difference. It is the security of repetition without difference that frames us to think ourselves as a body of reason, but this also constrains our thoughts about what a body can be and do. The curious attraction of the schizo-museum, of the musealization of serial killer horror, resides in shifting thought from patterns of normalcy, not least the dictate to frame the self within clichéd representations of the body. Serial killer horror is a sensory experience that violates signification as a human construction confined to the realm of reason. Perhaps, therefore, it is unsurprising that now and then we desire a vicarious waxing, burning, or flensing.

References

Adorno, Theodor. 1967. *Prisms*. Cambridge: MIT Press.

Arnold, Ken. 2006. *Cabinets for the Curious: Looking Back at Early English Museums*. Aldershot: Ashgate.

Colebrook, Claire. 2002. *Gilles Deleuze*. London: Routledge.

Creed, Barbara. 2004. *Pandora's Box: Essays in Film Theory*. Melbourne: Australian Centre of the Moving Image.

Deleuze, Gilles. 1986. *Cinema 1: The Movement*-Image, translated by H. Tomlinson and B. Habberjam. Minneapolis: University of Minnesota Press.

—. 1994. *Difference and Repetition*, translated by P. Patton. London: Athlone Press.

—. 2005. *Francis Bacon: The Logic of Sensation*, translated by D. W. Smith. London: Continuum.

Deleuze, Gilles, and Félix Guattari. 2004a. *Anti-Oedipus: Capitalism and Schizophrenia*, translated by R. Hurley, M. Seem, and H. R. Lane. London: Continuum.

—. 2004b. *A Thousand Plateaus: Capitalism and Schizophrenia*, translated by Brian Massumi. London and New York: Continuum.

Easton Ellis, Bret. 1991. *American Psycho*. London: Picador.

Fenton, James. 1994. *Children in Exile Poems 1968–1984*. New York: Farrar Straus Giroux.

Greenblatt, Stephen. 1991. "Resonance and Wonder." In *Exhibiting Cultures: The Poetics and Politics of Museum Display*, edited by Steven D. Lavine and Ivan Karp, 42–56. Washington and London: Smithsonian Institution Press.

Henning, Michelle. 2006. *Museums, Media and Cultural Theory*. Berkshire and New York: Open University Press.

Jarvis, Brian. 2007. "Monsters Inc.: Serial Killers and Consumer Culture." *Crime, Media, Culture* 3: 326–44.

Jarvis, Robin. 1985. *Tales from the Wyrd Museum*. London: HarperCollins.

Kristeva, Julia. 1986. *Powers of Horror: An Essay in Abjection*. New York: Columbia University Press.

Massumi, Brian. 2006. *Parables for the Virtual: Movement, Affect, Sensation*. Durham and London: Duke University Press.

Powell, Anna. 2005. *Deleuze and Horror Film*. Edinburgh: Edinburgh University Press.

Shaviro, Steven. 1993. *The Cinematic Body*. Minneapolis: University of Minnesota Press.

—. 2002. "Beauty Lies in the Eye." *A Shock to Thought: Expression after Deleuze and Guattari*, edited by Brian Massumi, 9–19. London and New York: Routledge.

Stratton, Jon. 1994. "(S)talking in the City: Serial Killing and Modern Life." *Southern Review* 27(1): 7–27.

—. 1996. "Serial Killing and the Transformation of the Social." *Theory, Culture and Society* 13(1): 77–98.

Žižek, Slavoj. 1991. *Looking Awry: An Introduction to Jacques Lacan through Popular Culture*. Cambridge: MIT Press.

Filmography

The Birds. DVD. Directed by Alfred Hitchcock. 1963; Universal City, CA: Universal Studios Home Entertainment, 2000.

Dressed to Kill. DVD. Directed by Brian De Palma. 1980; Beverly Hills, CA: MGM Home Entertainment, 2001.

Hannibal. DVD. Directed by Ridley Scott. 2001; Beverly Hills, CA: MGM Home Entertainment, 2001.

House of Wax. DVD. Directed by André De Toth. 1953; Burbank, CA: Warner Home Video, 2003.

House of Wax. DVD. Directed by Jaume Collet-Serra. 2005; Burbank, CA: Warner Home Video, 2005.

Mystery of the Wax Museum. VHS. Directed by Michael Curtiz. 1933; Beverly Hills, CA: MGM Home Entertainment, 1998.

Nightmare in Wax (*Crimes in the Wax Museum*). DVD. Directed by Bud Townsend. 1969; Brentwood, NH: Brentwood Home Video, 2008.

Psycho. DVD. Directed by Alfred Hitchcock. 1960; Universal City, CA: Universal Studios Home Entertainment, 1998.

The Relic. DVD. Directed by Peter Hyams. 1996; Hollywood, CA: Paramount Home Entertainment, 1997.

The Stendhal Syndrome. DVD. Directed by Dario Argento. 1996; West
 Hollywood, CA: Blue Underground, 2007.
Vertigo. 1958. Alfred Hitchcock. Universal City, CA: Universal Studios Home
 Entertainment, 2012.
Waxworks. DVD. Directed by Paul Leni. 1924; New York, NY: Kino Video, 2002.

11

"There's Blood on the Walls": Serial Killing as Post-9/11 Terror in *The Strangers*

Philip L. Simpson

As an example of what may be called a 'home invasion' film, Bryan Bertino's *The Strangers* (2008) skillfully leverages American middle-class phobias in the early twenty-first century to produce a chilling viewing experience. In a country still psychologically coming to terms with the collective trauma inflicted upon it by the terrorist attacks of September 11, 2001, recent American horror films such as *The Strangers* speak to the memories of that day, as well as the pervasive dread of another attack, by presenting increasingly nihilistic scenarios of sudden, unexpected doom in ordinary settings.[1] What happens to James Hoyt and Kristen McKay, the attractive young couple in *The Strangers* who are inexplicably terrorized and tortured by three seemingly motiveless masked killers who turn the couple's country home into a self-contained world of terror and death, is certainly one of those scenarios.

In its representation of domestic terror, the film employs a cultural narrative of home invasion generated in late 1960s and 1970s America. The film's oblique allusions to the murders committed by the so-called 'Manson Family' in 1969, one of many key moments signaling the death of the Age of Aquarius,[2] juxtapose the narrative's growing sense of dread and nihilism with its 9/11 subtext. Now, it is acknowledged there is no overt or deliberate referencing of the serial-killing Manson Family or any other historical event in the film; its cinematic agenda is clearly to terrorize its viewers, not politicize them or give them a history lesson. It is further acknowledged that the nefarious deeds committed by the Manson Family pale in comparison to the large-scale horrors and geopolitical ramifications of 9/11. Having said that, however, what links 9/11 and serial murders, such as those committed by the Manson-ites which have been mythologized in the American imagination of nightmare, is their apparent randomness—the sense that the victims happened to be in the wrong place at the wrong time. *The Strangers* also stylistically harkens back to this earlier period of heightened turmoil and paranoia in American society— what might be called 'the years of disillusion'—by borrowing from the popular 1970s 'slasher' genre. While intertextual elements function to create an intense mood of terror that apes popular cinematic (and national) memory, they also serve to defamiliarize prevailing sociopolitical preoccupations. *The Strangers*'s appropriation of a cultural narrative of home invasion and its homage to the 1970s 'slasher' film functions to reframe serial killing as terror in relation to post-9/11 cultural anxieties.

David Schmid (2005, 61) argues that the figure of the serial killer

. . . plays an even more central role in post-9/11 America than it did before the attacks. Its omnipresence as an icon of evil enabled the serial killer to become the lingua franca of both sides of the "war against terrorism." Consequently, rather than the terrorist replacing the serial killer, the two categories overlapped.

Schmid goes on to detail how serial killer films, already a staple of American cinema, proliferated in the wake of 9/11. Moving back through history, before 9/11, the serial killer as multifarious metaphor or catch-basin for the collective fears of a nation served cinema well for decades, embodying the dread of random, violent death long before terrorism became a national phobia. *The Strangers* utilizes the serial killer trope for its anxious subtext that we must defend ourselves against dangerous home invaders even though, sadly, we are doomed to fail. The film depicts an attractive, well-to-do urban couple terrorized in a remote vacation home by three grotesquely masked killers of presumably lower-class, rural origins. This stark contrast between the 'normal' (read: heterosexual) couple and the trinity of lowlife home invaders draws upon the cultural memory of the notorious murders of wealthy actress Sharon Tate and four others in her home by underclass 'hippie' members of the Manson Family in 1969, perhaps the pre-eminent home invaders to shock the American collective consciousness. The class conflict suggested by the 'Manson Murders', which are rearticulated in *The Strangers*, is typical of many horror films of the past four decades in that the 'civilized' protagonists from the city must do battle with a gang of 'primitive' villains from the countryside.

Additionally, the night of terror experienced by James and Kristen illustrates in the starkest way possible the emotional distance between the couple and the anxiety both feel about their respective gender roles in relation to the prospect of marriage. Indeed, what happens to James and Kristen is a re-envisioned instance of a pattern common to 1960s and 1970s horror film identified by Robin Wood (2004, 123), in which such "attacks are linked to, or seem triggered by, familial or sexual tensions." In other words, since Kristen has rejected James's marriage proposal just before the home-invasion begins, the palpable tension between the couple, the failure of their romantic relationship to evolve into legal domesticity, and the failure of each protagonist to fulfill patriarchal gender roles all seem to be an omen of the attack they endure. While both suffer, the onus of the symbolic burden of responsibility for the attack seems to fall heaviest on Kristen because of her rejection of the traditional marriage family structure represented by James's proposal.

Just as in the 9/11 decade, gender construction is an oft-contested site within the topography of 1970s horror cinema; a decade which also witnessed resurgent feminism and gender renegotiation followed by conservative backlash. After all, how many of the stalkers and slashers who haunted the movies in those years were little more than karmic punishment for those characters both male and female (but especially female) who in some way transgressed the gendered boundaries of patriarchal middle-class propriety ascribed to their sex? As a dark exploration of the anxieties of both class and gender, *The Strangers* is the genre heir of 1970s horror that included classic films such as *The Texas Chainsaw Massacre* (1974), *Halloween* (1978), and *The Hills Have Eyes* (1977). *The Strangers*, seemingly designed as a nostalgic reworking of what Christopher Sharrett (1996, 254) calls the "steadily more progressive" nature of 1970s horror films, revisits and redeploys the sense of political class consciousness and gender anxiety that is the hallmark of that era in cinematic horror. The post-9/11 decade in which *The Strangers* exists is broadly similar to the 1970s in that both decades were witness to international tension and escalating wars, so it is not surprising that the film references classic 1970s horror films to address cultural anxieties common to both contexts.

None of the preceding is to suggest that *The Strangers* has any coherent progressive agenda (or for that matter, a coherent reactionary agenda), as Wood (2004) and Sharrett (1996) argue that 1970s cinematic horror often does. Rather, what these diverse narrative and thematic strands do suggest is a strategy on the part of the film-makers to co-opt any one of a series of cultural narratives of fear shaping the sociopolitical, temporal landscape to create a horror film that strikes as many chords of anxiety as possible, in as wide and diverse an audience as possible.

Home(land) invasion and the (foreign) Other

Since the invasion of our homes by violent strangers bent upon terrorizing and then killing us for no apparent reason at all is one of the most terrifying crimes imaginable in modern Western culture, it is no wonder that murderous home invasion has been familiar territory in horror cinema over the past four decades. A representative, but by no means comprehensive, list of such films includes *Straw Dogs* (1971), *Death Weekend* (1976), *Fight for Your Life* (1977), *The House on the Edge of the Park* (1980), *Angst* (1983), *The Fear Inside* (1992), *Fear* (1996), the original *Funny Games* (1997), *If I Die Before I Wake* (1998), *Panic Room* (2002), *Hard Candy* (2005), *Them* (2006), *Inside* (2007), the American remake of *Funny Games* (2007), and, of course, *The Strangers*. Films in this horror subgenre share the common characteristic of hitting us literally where we live through the depiction of the brutal violation of the sanctity of the home. There is a special kind of destabilizing terror unique to this subgenre in that the cozy familiarity of one's own house is suddenly rendered a dangerous, even lethal, space contaminated through the invasion of violent strangers, usually from a marginalized demographic. These films exploit the atavistic fear of being savagely attacked when one is at his/her most vulnerable: at rest, away from the cares and concerns of the outside world, in one's own den. The resulting message to the audience is "Be on the lookout, and prepare to defend the battlements of your home fortress against dangerous strangers." The Strangers will come to you, the home invasion film insists; and when they do, they will be carrying knives, not housewarming gifts. So you had best be ready . . . and part of being ready means you had better put a face to the enemy—a face that will typically belong to someone from an-Other social group. Inevitably, the home invaders in these films embody or signify certain cultural and demographic paranoias relevant to the viewing audience.

It may be more than coincidence that the turbulent decade of the 1970s ushered in a spate of these kinds of home invasion films. Certainly, America in the 1970s felt itself to be under siege by foreign Others, just as it did in the first decade of the twenty-first century. Both decades can be characterized by intensified American xenophobia during a time of increased hostilities with the Middle East. The 1970s was the decade of the Palestinian Liberation Organization (PLO) and its militant arm, Black September; the Munich

Olympics massacre; the Arab oil embargo; hijackings and bombings; and the Iranian hostage crisis. As Tim Jon Semmerling (2006, 8) puts it, "the rising power of the Middle East and the perceived threat of the Arabs became another infamous theme of the 1970s." Fear of the Middle Eastern Other was at a premium then as well as now, leading progressively in combination with fear of random domestic crime to a free-floating paranoia of all strangers.

Additionally, traditional values and metanarratives that had sustained the national self-image for decades—fealty to God and country, the veneration of capitalism, the sanctity of marriage and the so-called nuclear family, the righteous moral foundation of our many wars—were under blistering attack not only from many perceived outside enemies but, most insidiously, from within. Many factors contributed to this sense that cherished American ideals were crumbling, but undoubtedly the national disillusionment of the Vietnam War, and the thwarted promise of the early 1960s it represented, accelerated the over-boiling of collective angst and fury. Courtesy of television reporters, the horrors of the Vietnam War were brought into the American household each and every day at dinner time, a point made by John Kenneth Muir (2002, 27):

> Monks immolated themselves. Soldiers shot innocent civilians in the head. American soldiers burned down villages, and so forth. . . . How could any fiction compare to these apocalypses, all of which were being gleefully shepherded into suburbia by Walter Cronkite, Dan Rather and their ilk?

Accordingly, Muir (2002) argues, cinema reacted to the horrifying headlines of the era by constructing fiction that was far more violent and nihilistic than the daily reality of televised war in order to shock numbed audience sensibilities. In what Muir (2002, 27) calls the "Savage Cinema" of the 1970s, a "primary tenet . . . is that terrible things happen to good people for no larger purpose or reason." What better way to illustrate this terrifyingly existential principle than to show basically decent people terrorized and slaughtered in their living rooms—the living rooms that in the actual world housed for middle-class Americans such dire and perplexing news each and every night through television news reportage. The senseless murders of innocent people depicted in the film narratives of home invasion represent cinematically the anxiety wreaked upon the American soul by the racial, generational, and class fault lines widened by the Vietnam War.

Muir (2002, 27, 29) identifies two of the more notable 1970s home invasion films as examples of the war-inspired "Savage Cinema," *Straw Dogs* and *The Hills Have Eyes* (the latter qualifying as a 'home invasion' movie because the killers besiege the Carter family in their mobile home, an extension of the primary household). As we watch the middle-class American families in these two films complete their transformative arc from helpless victim to empowered aggressor in mortal combat with a ruthless and incomprehensible enemy, it can be argued that these protagonists stand in for the American experience of slogging it through the endless Vietnam War. The potential for savagery in all of us is the theme of the bulk of the 1970s home invasion films, and the war is the subtext. Decades later, while the war/'enemy' is now different, the theme and subtext of the home invasion film remain the same.

The Strangers as a recent entry in the 'home invasion' film subgenre is a chilling horror fiction that nevertheless purports to be based upon 'real events'; a narrative strategy that positions the audience not only to imagine this same horrific scenario happening to real people like themselves but to their own family. While the specifics of the plot do not appear to line up to the details of any particular true crime case, there are loose parallels to the Manson Murders and the more obscure, but equally chilling, 'Keddie Murders' in 1981, in which four individuals were bound and then slashed and bludgeoned to death in a resort cabin in the northern California town of Keddie. The Keddie Murders were unusually violent, with those on the scene reporting extreme blood spatter, and the perpetrators have never been apprehended. The extreme levels of blood-letting associated with both the Keddie and Manson Murders are mirrored in the fiction of *The Strangers*, with the iconic visual of blood spattered on the walls of the desecrated homes an element common to all three. The frantic Mormon boy who calls 911 in the opening moments of the film verbalizes the unspeakable: "There's blood on the walls. . . . There's blood everywhere!" His panic is a representation of the hysteria of those who discovered the bloodbaths at the scenes of the Keddie and Manson Murders.

The *ne plus ultra* of home invasions received extensive national coverage when actress Sharon Tate and four others at her fashionable home in Benedict Canyon in California were slain on August 9, 1969, by youthful followers of 'hippie' cult leader Charles Manson. The following night, members of the Manson Family broke into the Los Angeles home of Leno and Rosemary LaBianca, bound the couple so that they were helpless, and then stabbed them to death. The murder of Tate and the LaBiancas in their own houses demonstrated in absolutely stark and chilling terms that no one, from the richest and most well-known Hollywood stars to the anonymous self-made wealthy class, was safe from lower-class murderers whose hatred of the wealthy heirs to the American dream was spawned in obscurity and squalor. This series of murders and the subsequent high-profile arrest and prosecution of Manson and his handpicked assassins seared itself forever into the national consciousness.[3] Joan Didion (1990, 47) famously wrote that "the Sixties ended abruptly on August 9, 1969, ended at the exact moment when word of the murders on Cielo Drive traveled like brushfire . . . The tension broke that day. The paranoia was fulfilled." The murders were a watershed moment that augured the death of the hope and promise of the nascent youth movement of the 1960s and ushered in the profound disillusionment of the 1970s, a disillusionment rooted in the perceived failure of American institutions (up to and including the Presidency itself) and liberal progressivism to deal realistically with prolonged war, economic recession, long gas lines, and political corruption.[4] Muir (2002, 27) compares the impact of the Manson Murders on the American psyche to that of the Vietnam War. Both events in combination led to the growing American dread of the domestic and/or foreign Other. These Manson Family/Vietnam stories of national horror and disillusionment act as an intertext for *The Strangers* which the film appropriates as a deep structure.

Bertino himself acknowledges that the film is informed by representations of the Manson Murders (in addition to a childhood memory of a stranger and would-be robber knocking at his door asking for someone who didn't live there). He states that much of his inspiration for the story's events came from his boyhood reading of Vincent Bugliosi's book *Helter Skelter* (1974), a true-crime recounting of the Manson Murders from the point of view of prosecutor Bugliosi. Of that book, Bertino says:

> Even now, what grabs me . . . is that it's not the section about who Charles Manson was or what was going on with the family. I was thinking about the Tate murders and realizing that these detailed descriptions had painted a story of what it was like in the house with the victims. But none of the victims knew about the Manson family or why it was happening to them. So, I got really fascinated with telling the victims' tale. And not filling it in with an FBI profile and not filling it in with finding out that somebody's grandmother beat them and now they want to kill everybody. You read obituaries every day where someone is killed for a random reason. Yes, we may eventually find out why, but sometimes they don't. (Quoted in Turek 2008)

The finished film stays true to Bertino's intent to not give the killers a back-story or indeed any recognizable human identity at all, given that their faces remain masked or in shadow for the entirety of the film. The focus, as Bertino says, is entirely on the plight of the victims—just as the first section of Bugliosi's book centers on the Tate and LaBianca murders before anyone ever connected the Manson Family to them. Bertino was not the only one involved in the production of the film to look toward Bugliosi's book as a reference point. Actress Gemma Ward, who plays the masked killer Dollface in the film, says: "To get inspiration for Dollface, I read 'Helter Skelter,' so I could get a feel for twisted girls and how their minds work when they reach a certain point" (quoted in Hollywood Jesus 2009). Some of the film's events do recall the infamous Los Angeles murders, particularly in its depiction of a uniquely terrifying home invasion, the protracted brutalization of the victims, and the discovery of the hideous crime scene early the following morning. (Of course, the Keddie Murders also fit this bill of particulars.) Whatever the film's worldly inspirations, aspects of the film's depicted home invasion are all too familiar to us from news programs and headlines. To be slaughtered by strangers in the presumed safest of safe places, the family home, is a fate so intolerable to the imagination that when such a crime does happen in real life, the local and/or national news media often gives the event full saturation coverage precisely because such a deeply felt taboo has been broken.

The Manson serial murders remain one of the most enduring American national traumas for invoking the specter of seemingly random, senseless murder inflicted upon the unsuspecting innocent in their own homes. It is a template that all too easily complements the fear of 'stranger' or serial murder that would grip the nation later in the 1970s and into the 1980s, largely as the result of the murders committed by individuals such as Ted Bundy, John Wayne Gacy, and Henry Lee Lucas. Manson, Bundy, Gacy, Lucas—names carved like the self-inflicted X on Manson's forehead during his murder trial are bloody swaths across a nation's psyche. These names are immediately recognizable to most and conflated together as heinous villains in the public imagination because of the intensive media coverage dedicated to chronicling their deeds. Because the media construction of these criminals depends so much on whipping up the emotions of fear or dread in the consuming audience, it is not surprising that Manson and his nefarious company find themselves incarnated as avatars in fictional narrative, especially horror, dependent upon these same audience emotions for success. The 1970s 'slasher' cinema genre derives its cachet, in part, from cultural awareness of these *men's* crimes. The formative film during this cycle is John Carpenter's film *Halloween*. Like Carpenter, Bertino depicts a masked killer implacably stalking a likable young heroine throughout the interior spaces of a 1970s family household. Michael Myers (the villain of Carpenter's film) and Myers's innumerable successors are the cinematic doppelgangers of the serial killers haunting the American landscape of nightmares. The 1970s-like setting of *The Strangers* revisits the context of the rise to visibility of the serial killer, as the film deploys the serial killer to work through fear of home(land) invasion in the post-9/11 culture.

Lost in the 1970s: *The Strangers*

From the film's opening moments, *The Strangers* announces its debt to its 1970s genre predecessors through a deliberate invocation of the instantly recognizable opening narration of *The Texas Chainsaw Massacre*. This Tobe Hooper film opens with then-unknown narrator John Laroquette speaking of the tragedy that befell Sally Hardesty and four other youths, which led "to the discovery of one of the most bizarre crimes in the annals of American history—the Texas chainsaw massacre." As Laroquette gravely intones these ominous words, they appear on-screen against a stark black background. This lead-in establishes a pseudo-documentary tone, priming the audience to believe that the film that follows bears a chilling verisimilitude to a supposed real-life atrocity in Texas. Similarly, *The Strangers* opens with words on a black screen and an off-screen narrator vouching for the authenticity, or at least plausibility, of the film's scenario:

> What you are about to see is inspired by true events. According to the FBI, there are an estimated 1.4 million violent crimes in America each year. On the night of February 11, 2005, Kristen McKay and James Hoyt left a friend's wedding reception and returned to the Hoyt family's summer home. The brutal events that took place there are still not entirely known.

In the precise economy of four sentences, the narrator first grounds the narrative in at least some semblance of reality, albeit a paranoid one characterized by a pervasive fear of rampant criminality: the FBI's annual violent-crime statistics. Once this foundation is established, the narrator then locates the film's narrative to a specific time and place, using rhetoric that produces an oddly vertiginous effect. On the one hand, the precisely specified date narrows down the events in the clinical manner of a police case file distinguishing its contents of horror and brutality from that of another crime committed at another time and place. On the other hand, invoking the date of the crime is a rhetorical convention borrowed from the opening of many a fictional police procedural, hard-boiled detective melodrama, or crime thriller. Think of the opening of Alfred Hitchcock's film *Psycho* (1960), for instance, which gives the exact date, day, and even time of the fateful lunchtime tryst between Sam and Lila in Phoenix. The blending of 'fact' and fiction, then, has begun in earnest, only a few seconds into the film. The narrator of *The Strangers* next relays the names of the victims of the violent crime, just as *Chainsaw* warns the audience that horror is about to befall Sally Hardesty and her brother, and ironically contrasts the idyllic night Kristen and James intended to have against the violence of the one they actually had.

Clearly *The Strangers*, like many recent horror films, is a 'retro' piece, moving away from the self-referential, ironic parody of films in the 1990s *Scream* mode, or the fashionably grainy look and rapid-cut editing of the 'torture porn' *Saw* films. Director Bertino says that he wanted his film to look like it could have been shot in 1976. He elaborates:

> What people will see is something incredibly dark and warm. We wanted it to feel like you're inside the house, so we purposely stayed away from greens and blues and bleach bypass and said let's shoot it as clean and real as possible.. . . We tried to break down that fourth wall. I think with so many horror films now you're aware you're watching them. (Quoted in "EXCL" 2007)

In other words, Bertino's film is straightforwardly, unabashedly going for jump-in-your-seat scares rather than knowing laughs. Critics immediately recognized the film for its earnest focus on suspense. Leigh Paatsch (2008) writes:

> First-time writer-director Bryan Bertino wants to terrify his audience with implied threats, rather than horrify them with literal outcomes. This is a gutsy choice to make in the current climate, where pseudo-snuff flicks still dominate horror-release schedules. This is a skilled exercise in straightforward scaremongering, with a knack for making little chills go a long way up your spine.

Paatsch is representative of those critics who warmed to Bertino's decision to approach his subject seriously, with a neoclassical reliance on suspense instead of graphic violence.

Yet for all of the film's purported gravitas and lack of irony, it nevertheless remains, if not a pastiche of earlier work, certainly dependent on its audience's memory of the look of the 1970s and its genre movies, including horror. While set in the contemporary moment, the film by design revisits the era of the 1970s, both in terms of its allegedly 'true story' and cinematic inspirations.[5] The 1970s 'feel' of the film even extends to its primary set, the comfortable vacation home in which James and Kristen suddenly find themselves fighting for their lives. The house is a 1970s brick ranch structure, in essence shifting the story back three decades. The film's production designer, John D. Kretschmer, explains that the selection of such a house was quite deliberate: "It's the kind of house that Bryan [Bertino] and I grew up in—a cozy, safe place that's full of strong memories. This makes the picture even more frightening, because you realize that terror can occur even in your most comfortable environments" (quoted in Hollywood Jesus 2009). Situating the film's look and mood in the 1970s creates a paradoxical brew of nostalgia and dread—nostalgia in that for the film-makers and many in the audience the 1970s was a time of precious childhood memories of growing up in safe homes, but dread in that the decade proved to be so extraordinarily violent both in reality and cinema. Bertino states that in writing the script he was strongly influenced by 1970s horror movies: "The thrillers that inspired me come from the 1970s. So I wanted to create one that explores something that could happen with characters at their most vulnerable, like movies did back then" (quoted in Hollywood Jesus 2009). *The Strangers*'s relatively slow pacing and emphasis on suspense and terror, at least in comparison to today's frenetic editing and gory special effects found in films such as *Saw*, reinforces its retro feel.

The Strangers as retro/post-9/11 horror ratchets up the fear level by portraying an otherwise enviable all-American couple utterly terrorized by faceless strangers, signified as Other. The film is informed by a pathologically paranoid sensibility, in which the cozy home is under constant threat of attack by the Other at any time. James and Kristen, caught up in their own private romantic melodrama, are too lax in their vigilance and thus pay the price. The strangers who torture them are masked grotesques coded as inhuman. The fact that we, the audience, never clearly see the killers's faces beneath their masks (though James and Kristen eventually do) is a clear attempt by Bertino to dehumanize the killers, presumably in order to make them more terrifying.

However, a Marxist reading of the film may posit that the choice of masks worn by the killers indicates possible motive. The sinister masks, in particular the porcelain ones worn by the two female killers, are reminiscent of the carnival, a festive time during which normal social hierarchies are up-ended. The big wide eyes of the Dollface mask and the Betty-Boop quality of the Pin-Up Girl mask connote a degree of innocent revelry and festiveness, which is all the more ironic in contrast to the terror inflicted by the wearers of these masks. By assuming the theatrical masks, they become both actors and participants in their own carnivalesque spectacle—a spectacle that includes turning James and Kristen into reluctant performers. According to Mikhail Bakhtin (1984, 81), the carnivalesque subverts dominant social ideology, or turns the world upside down, by mocking or perhaps even violently attacking its cherished assumptions and institutions. This dynamic of reversal is carried out literally by the masked rural killers who terrorize city-dwellers James and Kristen in a well-tended to vacation home as part of some private game.

James and Kristen, a young and attractive couple of the American upper middle class, are violently deposed from their privileged economic position by a localized uprising of the lower classes as represented by the killing trio. The couple is degraded by the prolonged terror they suffer and the phallic violation of their bodies with knives. Through their festive terrorism of the young couple, the killers construct, however temporarily, what Bakhtin (1984, 6) calls a "second world and a second life" freed from the officially sanctioned constraints of entrenched class, law, hierarchy, privilege, and place.

The masked killers, like many representations of serial killers, especially slashers, generally refuse to speak, thus removing themselves for much of the film from what Jacques Lacan calls in his Seminar IV ("*La relation d'objet et les structures freudiennes*") the Symbolic Order. Through the deliberate loss of language the killers perform their Otherness. As a result of limited signification—one of the killers does not speak at all and the other two speak only minimally—James and Kristen are unable to determine what is happening to them or why. They have no truly meaningful dialogue with their killers. The couple only knows a terrible chain of events has been initiated by Dollface showing up at their door at 4 a.m. asking, "Is Tamara here?" This utterance is not enough to discern the killers' motives, though it does imply that the killers are toying with James and Kristen and thus playing a game by rules known only to the killers. The only 'logic' that Kristen and James will ever discover is deferred until the bitter end, when Kristen bound helpless in her chair begs for an answer as to *why* this is happening to her and James. Dollface replies, "Because you were home." Dollface's answer suggests that Kristen and James are accidental victims, targeted solely because they were home when no one else in the neighborhood was (Figure 11.1).

The audience finds out only slightly more information than James and Kristen do; when the killers leave the bloody house in the bright light of morning, Pin-Up Girl says to Dollface: "It'll be easier next time." The implication is that the killers are neophytes, thus they were not as in control of the situation and the victims as they could have or would have like to have been. The audience is therefore left with the unsettling knowledge that more random murders are to come, and next time the killers will be even more proficient in what they do because of what they have learned from their first experience. Constructed as Other in terms of class, the three killers represent the random, apparently meaningless death so feared by America in the last decades of the twentieth century and into the post-9/11 era.

The Strangers investigates another site of tension within the post-9/11 decade: the divide between the underprivileged and privileged classes. The film portrays its two protagonists, James and Kristen, as heirs to a decidedly upper-middle-class legacy who are victimized by three killers clearly signified

FIGURE 11.1 *"Because you were home": The sole reason for the victimization of James (Scott Speedman) and Kristen (Liv Tyler) in* The Strangers *(2008), Rogue Pictures/Mandate Pictures. Photographer: Glenn Watson. The Kobal Collection.*

as rural in origin. From a sociological perspective, as Koen Raes (1995, 206) writes, "Urban society has always been contrasted to agrarian society," with the city typically coming off as "intrinsically threatening"; however, *The Strangers*, as many horror films do, inverts this comparison and undermines the conventional notion of rural society as a simpler, crime-free place. One might call the narrative sensibility informing *The Strangers* 'pastoral paranoia', in that danger lurks among the rough folk of the country rather than the suburbs and cities. Of course, it may be that provincial violence is a result of contamination, or in other words that the kind of stranger-upon-stranger violence typically associated with urban life metastasizes to the rural, a phenomenon noted by Louis Wirth (1938, 7): "urbanism is not confined to [urban] localities but is manifest in varying degrees wherever the influences of the city reach." This dynamic is manifested in *The Strangers*. When James and Kristen move out from the city and its civilized amenities into the extension or enclave of city privilege, represented by the vacation home isolated in the middle of rurality, that is when they run headfirst into trouble. In the symbolic structure of the narrative, plagued as they are by dysfunction and conflict, this couple haplessly brings the taint of violence trailing after them into what should be their idyllic country bower.

Class conflict is inherent in the narrative structure of the film. When we first see James and Kristen, they are formally dressed in the attire of the well-to-do, they have just left a fabulously furnished wedding reception populated by similarly beautiful and elegant people, and they have access to a vacation home: all markers of a certain degree of family affluence and disposable income. The trio of killers, on the other hand, seem to have no fixed address or possessions other than the truck we see them driving. The opening scene, in which the camera sweeps across a series of potential target homes as the soundtrack reverberates to the choppy sound of the killers' truck driving by the homes, suggests that the trio is always on the move, trolling for victims. Though also dressed up for a special occasion, as it were, the nomadic trio wear clothing that is plainer and shabbier looking, reminiscent of the 'Sunday best' worn by people who don't otherwise have a lot of money to buy newer and better-fitting clothing. Or perhaps the choice of clothing is in deliberate mockery of the finery worn by the killers' 'social betters'. The putative leader of the trio is the Man in the Mask, who with his ill-fitting suit and burlap bag worn over his head clearly resembles a scarecrow, an icon of rurality, crossed with a mockery of urbanity. The workman-like, dilapidated Ford truck he drives stands in contrast to the expensive newer car driven by James. As residents of a lower socioeconomic tier, the killers in their choice of victims seem to be enacting at some level a certain class-based retaliatory agenda, even if their primary motive is murderous thrill-seeking. The conflict between Kristen/James and the Man in the Mask and his two accomplices, Dollface and Pin-Up Girl, establishes a dualistic dynamic between the haves and have-nots. The dynamic ends in the ambiguous triumph of the killers signified as rural (ambiguous in the sense that while James dies, Kristen survives their worst assault).

Put another way, the conflict between Kristen/James and Dollface/Pin-Up Girl/the Man in the Mask is that of hierarchy reduced to what Kenneth Burke (1969, 141–2) calls "blunt antithesis," in which "each class would deny, suppress, exorcize the elements it shares with other classes. This attempt leads to the scapegoat (the use of dyslogistic terms for one's own traits as manifested in an 'alien' class)." In Burke's terminology, then, James/Kristen as an alien class serve as the sacrificial scapegoat for all the heretofore-buried social resentments of the three killers, whereas the three killers as an alien class serve for James and Kristen as a threat against which they must finally unify. This narrative development works through post-9/11 tensions in that there is a need to reorder/redefine the (foreign) Other; 'us' and 'them'. Because each side views the Other in such starkly polarized terms, both sides lose sight of the others' shared humanity. In fact, the film's project is to deliberately render the villains into formless symbols of dread: the titular 'strangers'. But in a way, James and Kristen are as much strangers as the killers. James and Kristen are estranged from each other, they are coming to a strange place where they do not know anybody, and they remain as unknown a quantity to the killers as the killers do to them. So ultimately the film's title itself becomes ambiguous, and suggestive of the existential gap between not only groups of people, but within the group itself, that is, James and Kristen's estrangement from each other as the film opens. Intimacy is as fraught with peril as impersonality.

Kristen's rejection of James's marriage proposal dramatizes another aspect of social preoccupation common to both the 1970s and 2000s: gender role anxiety. By rejecting James, Kristen becomes Other to him, a narrative move in keeping with the patriarchal tendency to conceptualize the female as Other to the male. Kristen's unilateral redefinition of her relationship with James threatens James's very identity as lover and future husband. She begins to renegotiate a new identity, a move which is swiftly countered by the arrival of the killers, who in essence drive her and James back together, however briefly.

Kristen's development recapitulates the larger progression of feminism. The 1960s through to the 1970s, as the timeframe of 'second-wave' feminism, saw many cultural advances in the negotiation of the social roles of women, especially within the traditional domestic space assigned to them by patriarchal ideology. Alice Echols (2003, 3–4), in her book *Daring to be Bad: Radical Feminism in America, 1967–1975*, elaborates:

> In the fall of 1967 small groups of radical women began meeting in the United States to discuss the problem of male supremacy. . . . [W]ithin two years radical feminism had established itself as the most vital and imaginative force within the women's liberation movement. Radical feminism rejected both the politico position that socialist revolution would bring about women's liberation and the liberal feminist solution of integrating women into the public sphere. . . . Radical feminists articulated the earliest and most provocative critiques of the family, marriage, love, normative heterosexuality, and rape. They fought for safe, effective, accessible contraception; the repeal of all abortion laws; the creation of high-quality, community-controlled child-care centers; and an end to the media's objectification of women.

This kind of second-wave critique of patriarchal oppression gave rise to the 'third-wave' feminism of the 1990s onward, in which no one particular definition of feminism is privileged over another and gender roles are noticeably more fluid. As Leslie Heywood and Jennifer Drake (1997, 2) explain, "Because our lives have been shaped by struggles between various feminisms as well as by cultural backlash against feminism and activism, we argue that contradiction—or what looks like contradiction, if one doesn't shift one's point of view—marks the desires and strategies of third wave feminists." Third-wave feminism posits that oppression often depends on one's perspective, but nevertheless it recognizes that as a movement it exists within an environment where a robust neoconservative and fundamentalist advocacy of traditional family values seeks to undo feminist gains and return society to a more traditional patriarchal structure.

Susan Faludi (1991, 9–10) famously calls this 'recovery' attempt a backlash, or "an attempt to retract the handful of small and hard-won victories that the feminist movement did manage to win for women. This counterassault is largely insidious: . . . it stands the truth boldly on its head and proclaims that the very steps that have elevated women's position have actually led to their downfall." Faludi dates the feminist backlash to the decade of the 1980s, and the backlash rhetorical strategies have been in play ever since. The cultural drive to return to conservative notions of gender and anti-feminism has been particularly intensified in the wake of 9/11, or as Faludi (2007, 21) puts it: "Within days of the attack, a number of media venues sounded the death knell of feminism." Diane Negra (2008, 1) further refers to the post-9/11 political project of stepping back feminism as an attempt to stabilize besieged national identity, or a kind of historical reversion.

In microcosm, *The Strangers* plays out this macrocosmic gender tension and political anxiety. Kristen, initially depicted as a vulnerable female, is simultaneously empowered to take charge of her own destiny as a woman and cast into the role of suffering female victim forced *in extremis* to turn helplessly for comfort to the man she just rejected—the film's backlash against her brief empowerment. In the film's opening scenes, Kristen is presented as beautiful and traditionally feminine. Dressed in an elegant evening gown but her eyes swollen with tears, she conveys both femininity and vulnerability. She is rendered even more vulnerable when she removes her gown and sinks nude into a bath as a way to relax from the night's tension. Although her nudity is largely hidden from the camera lens, the titillation factor is high, especially since the scene is followed a few minutes later by a near-sexual encounter between James and Kristen in which James is in the dominant position. Yet paradoxically it becomes clear that it is Kristen who is really in the power position in the relationship with James; in fact, as the film reveals, she has turned down his marriage proposal because she isn't ready for the traditional role of marriage partner and now, as a result of that rejection, faces the possibility of a future without him.

However, Kristen's rejection is not presented as an unequivocal denouncement of marriage or as a reaffirmation of feminine independence. The narrative's stance toward domesticity as the site of danger is undeniable, but so too is a countervailing tendency to lament the contemporary complexities that make marriage such a daunting prospect for young women. Clearly, Kristen is torn as to whether turning down James's proposal was the correct course of action. While James is away getting her cigarettes, she places the engagement ring on her finger, as if privately 'trying on' the idea of marriage. A beneficiary of the progressive advances of feminist empowerment, white, middle-class Kristen is in the process of negotiating her own identities as an independent woman, committed lover, and potential wife. But trying on the ring comes with a price. First, it gets stuck on her finger, representing a kind of domestic trap. This action also immediately precedes (or, in the film's nightmarish logic, triggers) a full-bore onslaught by the killers, thus establishing the home itself as a trap when it comes under siege. For the next several minutes of screen time, Kristen cowers in the house as the killers parade unseen in and out of the house and terrorize her with a barrage of loud knocking, thumps, and peek-a-boo glimpses of their masks through the windows. All of this seems to be both punishment for her ambivalence to marriage and the symbolic outcome of her toying with rejecting the idea of domesticity.

The house, already a site of tension for the couple struggling with their relationship's future, has become a death trap. Kristen and James both attempt to escape from the house on several occasions, but they are always forced back into it in full retreat. Ultimately, when both James and Kristen are bound helpless to chairs and the masked killers stand before them as a kind of tribunal passing a harsh judgment on them, Kristen clasps James's hand and finally reveals to him that she is wearing the ring she earlier refused to wear. It is tempting to believe that the night of terror has shown Kristen just how much she really does love James after all, and that she now wants him to know that before they die. But in the immediate context of the scene, just before the couple is brutally stabbed, this moment does not particularly constitute any lasting commitment to James. After all, she firmly believes they are both about to die. Rather, the moment signifies Kristen's surrender to a fate larger than her, a complete abdication of individual empowerment in a terribly powerless situation. Her final assent to wearing James's ring is followed immediately by what appears to be the brutal murder of both her and James, thus seemingly pronouncing the narrative's last word on the desirability of domesticity. Yet the narrative ultimately spares Kristen while dispensing with James; she is left gravely injured but alive when the Mormon boy finds her in the hallway. The ending confirms what has already become clear as the retrograde narrative progresses: this is really Kristen's story, but that story is one of harrowing punishment for her brief consideration of a lifestyle other than traditional married domesticity. Her 'punishment' positions the audience both to identify with her torment but, at some level, to believe she has brought it upon herself.

As the other key character in this gender morality play, James disappears at critical junctures for long stretches of screen time, leaving Kristen to fend for herself against the invaders. His 'feminizing' is another key trait of post-9/11 culture, in which the perceived failure of traditional American masculine values may have led to the terrorist attacks (Faludi 2007, 20–2). He fails miserably at every level in his performance of patriarchal masculinity: he succeeds as neither lover nor defender of the home. When we first see James, he is emotionally devastated as a result of his marriage proposal being rejected. Consequently, he is pouty, despondent, a little surly, and generally quite passive. As the terrifying morning unfolds, he is reluctantly forced to look for the shotgun his father kept in the vacation home, but he proves dreadfully unable to manage the gun. He isn't sure how to assemble it, load it, aim it, or fire it, thus failing to master this emblem of phallocentric power. Unable to escape the evidence of his ineptitude, he must confess to Kristen that his tales of boyhood hunting with his father were untrue, an admission that almost certainly would have provoked a stronger reaction from Kristen were not the immediate exigencies so pressing. James's clumsiness with the shotgun ends tragically when he shoots at a figure he believes to be the Man in the Mask. Instead, James kills his best friend Mike, who had arrived unexpectedly early to give James a ride home.

James's next desperately contrived tactic, to head out to the barn to call for help on an old radio, also fails. Venturing out of the house, James is first unable to hot-wire the killers' truck in the driveway, thus failing the test of mechanical prowess ideologically assigned to the male sex. James is next ambushed and taken prisoner by the Man in the Mask, failing in *mano a mano* combat and leaving Kristen to fight the killers alone and unprotected. He does not appear again until just a few minutes before the end of the film, and then only to be butchered. Beginning the film as a male suffering from wounded romantic pride and hence a figurative castration, he proves to be metaphorically impotent to prevent any of what happens. In the narrative logic of the film, he is feminized, passive, and ultimately helpless before the brute masculinity embodied by the Man in the Mask. Significantly, he is the one to die while Kristen, though critically injured, survives. He is punished more severely than Kristen for his gender failings within patriarchy. As illustrated by the suffering inflicted upon both James and Kristen, gender role anxiety pervades the film. Ultimately, one is positioned into ambivalence as to whether this film is pro- or anti-traditional family.

Conclusion

The masked killers in *The Strangers* cannot readily be profiled, nor their motives easily understood. What we can infer about them, however, does suggest a strong element of class-based domestic warfare. Their dress and choice of transportation (a pick-up truck) signify them as rural, preying upon the residents in the isolated summer homes of the well-to-do. Dollface offers only this as a reason for murder to Kristen's anguished plea for an explanation: "Because you were home." However, while the victims may be random, surely the purpose behind the murders and the location is not, just as the Manson Murders were not truly random in their targeting of a class of victims; in both cases, killers troll the homes of the upper classes until they find somebody at home to victimize.

The film betrays a deep sense of fear about the murderous potential of the aggrieved rural Other, much like the 1970s horror films tend to do. One key difference, however, lies in the source of horror. In many 1970s films, the horror originated in the home: demon children, or adult killers once victimized by brutal family members. However, in keeping with the generally reactionary, defensive mood of the post-9/11 culture, horror comes from strangers outside the home who lay waste to the traditional defenses erected against such invasion by the privileged class. In doing so, no hope is left, no values remain intact to cling to, no redemption is possible. *The Strangers* ends on exactly this pessimistic, indeed nihilistic note, or rather Kristen's scream of utter agony and horror. The ruin of Kristen and James by murderous strangers is the ruin of us all.

The strangers we fear most—foreign *or* domestic terrorists—do not target individuals like James and Kristen so much as they target symbols or representatives of a certain way of life—that way of life being traditional American values encapsulated in sites of patriarchal capitalism such as family and marriage. Now that we are familiar with the experiential reality of random attacks, dread of the horrific potential in the everyday is epidemic. Making it worse, at some unspoken level we suspect we bring this horror down upon ourselves—that the Other we repress (and oppress) will strike back at the tyranny of normalcy with lethal force. The words of Charles Manson, at his murder trial in 1970, engaged this mainstream fear of the return of the repressed: "You made your children what they are. These children that come at you with knives, they are your children." The Manson Family and the other serial killers who haunt our fiction and our cinema, the strangers who come at us with knives, are reflections of that which we fear most in our culture.

Notes

1 Kevin J. Wetmore (2012) writes of the effect on witnesses of 9/11: "What was ultimately terrifying, for those watching, was the randomness and the anonymousness of the death seen and experienced on that day, and in other disasters and terror attacks since. . . . September 11 results in random and anonymous death in horror cinema, not because of what you did or who you were, but where you were." Wetmore goes on to discuss at length how 9/11 differed from other 'wars', in that for the first time since 1812 a foreign enemy had attacked the United States, or brought the war 'home'. The fear that no one was now safe in their home or domestic spaces, be in their literal homes or their formerly safe workspaces or public spaces, results in, among other phenomena, horror films that emphasize random death at the hand of purposeful killers.

2 Other such moments include the death of Meredith Hunter at the infamous Rolling Stones concert in Altamont in 1969 and the student shootings by the National Guard at Kent State in 1970.

3 Of the Manson Murders and their cultural impact, Greg King (2000, ix–x) writes: "[Sharon Tate's] death one hot summer night in 1969 changed America forever. It touched a raw nerve in a country disillusioned, shocked by the assassinations of John F. Kennedy, Martin Luther King, Robert F. Kennedy, and Malcolm X. The Manson Murders scared the hell out of an entire nation torn apart by war and shattered by riots."

4 Dominic Sandbrook (2012, xii) puts it this way: "One of the things that made the 1970s different from both the 1960s and the 1980s was that for the first time in more than a generation, ordinary Americans genuinely doubted that tomorrow would be better than today."

5 Kevin J. Wetmore (2012) pinpoints nostalgia for earlier decades, especially the 1960s, 1970s, and 1980s, as another hallmark of post-9/11 horror cinema.

References

Bakhtin, Mikhail. 1984. *Rabelais and His World*, translated by Helene Iswolsky. Bloomington: Indiana University Press.

Bugliosi, Vincent. 1974. *Helter Skelter: The True Story of the Manson Murders*. New York: Bantam Books.

Burke, Kenneth. 1969. *A Rhetoric of Motives*. Berkeley: University of California Press.

Didion, Joan. 1990. *The White Album*. New York: Farrar, Straus, and Giroux.

Echols, Alice. 2003 [1989]. *Daring to Be Bad: Radical Feminism in America, 1967–1975*. Minneapolis: University of Minnesota Press.

"EXCL: Never Talk to Strangers." 2007. Accessed May 3, 2013. www. shocktillyoudrop.com/news/950-excl-never-talk-to-strangers.

Faludi, Susan. 1991. *Backlash: The Undeclared War against American Women*. New York: Three Rivers Press.

—. 2007. *The Terror Dream: Fear and Fantasy in Post-9/11 America*. New York: Metropolitan Books, 2007.

Heywood, Leslie, and Jennifer Drake. 1997. "Introduction." In *Third Wave Agenda: Being Feminist, Doing Feminism*, edited by Leslie Heywood and Jennifer Drake, 1–20. Minneapolis: The University of Minnesota Press.

Hollywood Jesus. 2009. "*The Strangers* Production Notes." Accessed May 3, 2013. http://hollywoodjesus.com/movies/strangers/notes.pdf.

King, Greg. 2000. *Sharon Tate and the Manson Murders*. New York: Barricade Books.

Muir, John Kenneth. 2002. *Horror Films of the 1970s: Volume 1, 1970–1975*. Jefferson, NC: McFarland & Company, Inc.

Negra, Diane. 2008. "Structural Integrity, Historical Reversion, and the Post-9/11 Chick Flick." *Feminist Media Studies* 8(1): 51–68.

Paatsch, Leigh. 2008. "*The Strangers*." *Herald Sun (Australia)*, August 14.

Raes, Koen. 1995. "Citizenship, Public Culture and Insecurity: A Plea for the Revaluation of Public Space." *Ethical Perspectives* 2: 199–219.

Sandbrook, Dominic. 2012. *Mad as Hell: The Crisis of the 1970s and the Rise of the Populist Right*. New York: Anchor Books.

Schmid, David. 2005. "Serial Killing in America After 9/11." *The Journal of American Culture* 28(1): 61–9.

Semmerling, Tim Jon. 2006. *'Evil' Arabs in American Popular Film: Orientalist Fear*. Austin: University of Texas Press.

Sharrett, Christopher. 1996. "The Horror Film in Neoconservative Culture." In *The Dread of Difference: Gender and the Horror Film*, edited by Barry Keith Grant, 253–76. Austin: University of Texas Press.

Turek, Ryan. 2008. "Interview: *The Strangers* Bryan Bertino (Pt. 2)." Shock Till You Drop, May 25. Accessed May 3, 2012. www.shocktillyoudrop.com/news/6242-interview-the-strangers-bryan-bertino-pt-2.

Wetmore, Kevin J. 2012. *Post-9/11 Horror in American Cinema*. New York: Continuum. Kindle edition.

Wirth, Louis. 1938. "Urbanism as a Way of Life." *The American Journal of Sociology* 44(1): 1–24.

Wood, Robin. 2004. "An Introduction to the American Horror Film." In *Planks of Reason: Essays on the Horror Film*, edited by Barry Keith Grant and Christopher Sharrett, 107–41. Lanham, MD: Scarecrow Press.

Filmography

Angst. DVD. Directed by Gerard Kargl. 1983; Germany: distributor unknown, 2006.

Death Weekend. VHS. Directed by William Fruet. 1976; Burbank, CA: Warner Home Video, date unknown.

Fear. DVD. Directed by James Foley. 1996; Universal City, CA: Universal Studios Home Entertainment, 1998.

The Fear Inside. DVD. Directed by Leon Ichaso. 1992; Beverley Hills, CA: Anchor Bay Entertainment, 1997.

Fight for Your Life. DVD. Directed by Robert A. Endelson. 1977; West Hollywood, CA: Blue Underground, 2004.

Funny Games. DVD. 1997. Directed by Michael Haneke. 1997; New York, NY: Fox Lorber, 1999.

Funny Games. DVD. Directed by Michael Haneke. 2007; Burbank, CA: Warner Home Video, 2008.

Halloween. DVD. Directed by John Carpenter. 1978; Beverly Hills, CA: Anchor Bay Entertainment, 1997.

Hard Candy. DVD. Directed by David Slade. 2005; Santa Monica, CA: Lionsgate Home Entertainment, 2006.

The Hills Have Eyes. DVD. Directed by Wes Craven. 1977; Los Angeles, CA: Vanguard, 2003.

The House on the Edge of the Park. DVD. Directed by Ruggero Deodato. 1980; UK: Shameless Screen Entertainment, 2011.

If I Die before I Wake. DVD. Directed by Brian Katkin. 1998; Santa Monica, CA: Artisan Entertainment, 2001.

Inside. DVD. Directed by Alexandre Bustillo and Julien Maury. 2007; New York, NY: Dimension Extreme, 2008.

Panic Room. DVD. Directed by David Fincher. 2002; Los Angeles, CA: Columbia Pictures, 2002.

Psycho. DVD. Directed by Alfred Hitchcock. 1960; Universal City, CA: Universal Studios Home Entertainment, 1998.

Saw. DVD. Directed by James Wan. 2005; Santa Monica, CA: Lionsgate Home Entertainment, 2005.

Scream. DVD. Directed by Wes Craven. 1996; Burbank, CA: Walt Disney Studios Home Entertainment, 1997.

The Strangers. DVD. Directed Bryan Bertino. 2008; Universal City, CA: Universal Studios Home Entertainment, 2008.

Straw Dogs. DVD. Directed by Sam Peckinpah. 1971; Culver City, CA: Screen Gems, 2011.

The Texas Chainsaw Massacre. DVD. Directed by Tobe Hooper. 1974; Universal City, CA: Universal Studios Home Entertainment, 2003.

Them. DVD. Directed by David Moreau and Xavier Palud. 2006; Orland Park, IL: Dark Sky Films, 2008.

12

Hunting Minds, Hunting Genes: From Profiling to Forensics in TV Serial Killer Narratives

Sofia Bull

Across the American and British popular 'crime' culture landscapes, the figure of the *profiler* was prominent throughout the 1990s as an exceptional expert investigator called upon to catch the most "elusive" of criminals: the *serial killer*.[1] However, during the latter half of the 1990s another type of expert investigator achieved generic significance: the *criminalist*.[2] The visibility of this cultural figure within serial killer narratives is particularly evident in the context of television. Although profilers are still featured on the small screen, the most successful crime dramas of the early twenty-first century have rather tended to depict *forensic science* as a more reliable and scientifically sound method to neutralize the threat of repeat killings. In this chapter I will map the genealogy of the criminalist with a particular focus on the role played by the immensely popular forensic crime drama *CSI: Crime Scene Investigation* (2000–, henceforth *CSI*).

CSI depicts a team of criminalists working alongside the Las Vegas Police Department to explain all types of suspicious deaths. This article will, however, specifically examine episodes portraying forensic investigations of serial murders, as I attempt to account for the series's rearticulation of the profiling narrative's two central figures: the expert investigator and the serial killer. I aim to show how the meanings and functions tied to these two figures have changed and provide some suggestions as to why these changes have taken place. This is thus a type of genre study: I understand the meanings and functions of these figures as produced by the ways *CSI* stages both generic linkages to, and strategic departures from, earlier serial killer narratives and profiling dramas. Moreover, this is also a discursive analysis of the cultural contexts of the different depictions of these figures. That I take the meanings and functions of these programs to be specific to the cultural context of their production is an acknowledgment that the serial killer is a figure continuously used to stage the fears and anxieties of different sociohistorical moments.

When identifying and discussing the interplay between generic and discursive aspects I largely adhere to television scholar Jason Mittell's (2004, 4) "cultural approach to television genre theory," which suggests that genre categories and elements must be understood as historically situated and discursively constituted.[3] Furthermore, I more generally subscribe to a television studies perspective that understands the medium as participating in contemporary discourses and debates by producing, transforming, and working over culturally current questions, notions, and feelings. In adopting this viewpoint I draw on Horace M. Newcomb and Paul M. Hirsch's theory of television as a cultural forum, as well as Charlotte Brunsdon and Helen Wheatley's respective adoptions of this approach.[4] Both Brunsdon and Wheatley have combined genre and discourse analysis to fruitfully study how particular television programs use certain iconographies, tropes, and themes to "work through" or "worry at" contemporary cultural issues and anxieties.[5]

The study begins by examining how a number of 1990s crime dramas represent the figure of the profiler. I propose that both their portrayal of flawed investigators and emphasis on the unconventional, and potentially problematic, aspects of the profiling method are symptomatic of a wider generic tendency of 1990s crime dramas to pose dynamic questions about the integrity and responsibility of law enforcement representatives. This discussion provides a foundation for the comparative analysis of *CSI*'s depiction of criminalists. I suggest that the turn to forensic science defuses the qualms associated with the figure of the profiler, offering the criminalist as a more objective and trustworthy representative of the law assumed to be needed in post-9/11 society. I go on to demonstrate that *CSI*, in supplementing profiling with forensic science, provides the phenomenon of serial killing with a new framework of explanation: it dramatizes the obsessive urge to kill repeatedly as being caused by genetic 'deviances'. This deflects the blame that profiling narratives previously placed on the social environment and limits the threat by locating it in the individual body. Finally, the chapter ends with an attempt to produce a nuanced understanding of *CSI*'s 'geneticized' serial killer figure, arguing that it raises a set of issues with particular currency in present scientific discourses. I thus conclude that the figure of the serial killer ultimately has retained the same basic generic function as a cultural 'bogeyman' that deals with the specific fears and anxieties of any present moment.

The profiler: Flawed hero of the 1990s

Attempts to outline the history of criminal profiling necessarily result in accounts of the cross-fertilization between real-life applications of this method and its spectacularized presence in both news media and fiction.[6] While early attempts at profiling practices received considerable media attention, popular fascination with the figure of the profiler started to increase significantly in the 1980s, with the work of John Douglas and Robert Ressler at the FBI's Behavioral Science Unit being publicized and fictionalized through Thomas Harris's best-selling crime novels *Red Dragon* (1981) and *The Silence of the Lambs* (1988). In the wake of Harris's novels being adapted into two critically acclaimed films, the hype around the profiler reached something of a fever pitch.[7] Similarly, the United Kingdom had its own profiling craze in the early 1990s, with intense media attention being paid to the practices of clinical psychologist Paul Britton, and the subsequent premiere of *Cracker* (1993–6, 2006): a gritty crime drama depicting the work of a criminal psychiatrist.[8] Criminal profiling has since had a significant presence both in feature films and on television.[9] In 1996, two profiling shows premiered on US television. The first, *Profiler* (1996–2000), was aimed at mainstream audiences and centred on Dr Sam Waters (Ally Walker), a forensic psychologist working for the FBI's Violent Crimes Task Force. The second, *Millennium* (1996–9), was a big budget production created by Chris Carter, after he had achieved auteur status with the success of *The X-Files* (1993–2002), and starred Lance Henriksen as ex-FBI agent Frank Black.

The discursive constitution of the profiling narrative as a genre category meant that a number of visual, narrative, and thematic elements became associated with the figure of the profiler during the 1990s. For example, profilers are generically depicted as solving crimes by inferring facts about a killer's 'psychological profile' (personality, behavioral, and demographic characteristics) from the physical evidence left at the crime scene, on the victim's body, or at any other location where the killer has spent time. Furthermore, they almost exclusively use their skills to catch serial offenders, which allows for behavioral patterns to appear clearer with each new murder. The profiling narratives' dramatization of these tropes has evident generic roots in earlier crime procedurals and serial killer films, but they must also be understood as resulting from the sociohistorically specific tendencies of the television crime genre during the 1980s and 1990s.[10]

Charlotte Brunsdon (1998, 223–43) has shown how a critical portrayal of law enforcement representatives grew common in British crime dramas of the late 1980s and early 1990s, superseding the typically celebratory portrayal of the police force in earlier cop shows. Analyzing three British landmark series, namely *Inspector Morse* (1987–2000), *Prime Suspect* (1991–6), and *Between the Lines* (1992–4), Brunsdon (1998, 224–5, 228) argues that the crime drama increasingly began to question the agency, integrity, and responsibility of the British justice system. By repeatedly staging "the drama of the responsible citizen caught in the embrace of what increasingly seems an irresponsible State" and portraying law enforcement representatives as flawed, unreliable, or corrupt, the crime drama openly started posing questions such as "who can police?" and "who is accountable?"

Brunsdon (1998, 223) has convincingly argued that these issues are nationally specific to the United Kingdom, suggesting that they speak "very directly to the concerns of Great Britain in decline under a radical Conservative government with a strong rhetoric of law and order." While US crime dramas of the 1980s and 1990s cannot be said to have examined the processes of privatization and deregulation in British society, they still displayed similar generic tendencies. In his writings on the shifting ideologies informing the crime genre, John Sumser (1996, 154–61) has argued that series such as *Homicide: Life on the Street* (1993–9), *NYPD Blue* (1993–2005), and *In the Heat of the Night* (1988–95) are examples of how the crime dramas of this period increasingly moved away from the tradition of representing the policeman as "the moral boundary of society." Instead, the crime genre was injected with a new "uncertainty" which, according to Sumser (1996, 160–1), was called forth by a new American self-examination under the Clinton administration and wider efforts to make television programming more realistic and "adult."

This general move toward a heightened sense of uncertainty, and a new willingness to question the reliability and responsibility of law enforcement, is one important context for explaining the popularity of profiling narratives during the 1990s. Profiling narratives typically used different visual and narrative techniques to juxtapose the profiler with 'regular' law enforcement representatives in ways that emphasized the singular status of the profiler as an expert investigator. Although being popularly associated with the law enforcement institution of the FBI, fictional profiling narratives almost always depict the profiler as a marginal figure hunting the serial killer on the outskirts of the official legal system. Dr Eddie "Fitz" Fitzgerald in *Cracker* and Dr Sam Waters in *Profiler* are both formally distinguished from their law-enforcement colleagues by their Doctor titles, and *Millennium* places much narrative importance of Frank Black's status as a retired FBI agent now working freelance.[11] This juxtaposition inscribes the profiler with a number of positive character traits which are suggested as lacking in regular FBI agents, detectives, or policemen: the profiler is usually depicted as intelligent, intellectual, educated, open-minded, thoughtful, and empathic. Hence, within the generic context of law enforcement generally being scrutinized and criticized, the profiler was, at least in part, offered up as a more reliable alternative.

However, the generic inclinations toward realism and ambiguity during this period also meant that the figure of the profiler itself was placed under inspection. Much screen time was typically allotted to the portrayal of the profiler's character flaws and personal problems. "Fitz" in *Cracker* is perhaps the most apparent example of this: while able to be charming and empathic, he often displays strong tendencies toward selfish, destructive, and cruel behavior, and also battles with a severe alcohol and gambling addiction.[12] Furthermore, *Cracker*, *Profiler*, and *Millennium* all portray their main characters as struggling to keep up a functional family life. Both Dr Waters and Frank Black have been forced to move homes and place family members in hiding, in order to protect them from vindictive serial killers.

James S. Herndon (2007, 319) has rightly pointed out that the portrayal of the profilers as imperfect individuals also functions to align them with the serial killers: both are figures that are "obsessed, driven and troubled." This is one of the most familiar generic tropes associated with profiling narratives, and an idea that is central to the depiction of the profiling method: the typically obsessive and empathic nature of the profiler allows her/him to solve the crime by 'entering the mind of the killer' (Cettl 2003, 26–7). In other words, the profiler is portrayed as alone being able to understand the killer's motives, thoughts, fantasies, wishes, plans, and emotions. Furthermore, this process is precisely depicted as highly dangerous in that it destabilizes the profiler's own identity and has the potential of causing serious emotional harm both to the profiler and her/his family and friends.[13] Again, this portrayal of the profiling method as potentially problematic can be understood as part of the crime genre's typically self-critical stance against the institutional crime-solving practices depicted during the 1990s.

Indeed, any potentially uncanny aspects of the profiler's ability to swiftly produce highly detailed insights about the killer were usually played up.[14] Not only do profiling narratives convey the idea that the profiler must rely heavily on intuition (rather than on rational logic), but they also suggest that there might be a psychic component to the profiler's abilities. *Profiler* and *Millennium*, in particular, stage the profiler's insights as bordering on the paranormal. Scenes showing the profiler performing mundane investigative labor (visiting crime scenes, autopsy rooms, or simply pondering over evidence) is often intercut with stylized inserts of the killer's acts or fantasies. The highly expressionistic camera work, lighting, and editing used when dramatizing the process of accessing the killer's mind means that the inserts appear more as fantastic visions, rather than imagined flashbacks. The mystical nature of the inserts is also emphasized through the use of acting techniques that portray the profilers as being physically overcome by these 'visions': both Dr Waters and Frank Black frequently stumble, close their eyes in agony, cry, or become nauseous when experiencing these purported insights into the killer's mind.

Enter the criminalist: Trustworthy scientist

That the profiling method thus became associated with potential identity loss, subjective intuition, and psychic abilities, partly explains the subsequent decrease in the perceived reliability of this particular crime-solving method. Since the late 1990s, profiling has come to be seen as controversial: criticized in both popular and professional discourses for being unscientific and untrustworthy.[15] In addition to the profiling narrative's adherence to the wider generic questioning of the reliability and accountability of law enforcement, this more general loss of trust in the profiling method provides a telling background for *CSI*'s consequent portrayal of the criminalist as a more dependable type of expert investigator.

Brunsdon (1998, 242) has argued that the general medicalization of the crime drama in the late 1990s meant that the genre's dynamic questioning of the institutions of policing was exchanged with a spectacular display of crime scenes and dead bodies depicted as sites that harbored 'the truth'. The crime genre was starting to take cues from the growing success of the hospital drama, portraying medical doctors and scientists as able to produce unquestionable facts. *CSI* is probably the most well-known example of this. Since its premiere on American television in 2000, the series has gained considerable cultural significance. Its depiction of forensic science is largely representative of many subsequent forensic crime dramas, such as the two spin-offs *CSI: Miami* (2002–) and *CSI: NY* (2004–), as well as *Crossing Jordan* (2001–7) and *Bones* (2005–).[16]

The forensic crime dramas generally portray their criminalist heroes as fundamentally different from the figure of the profiler. Unlike the profiler, who identifies too closely with the killer, the criminalist is able to remain objective and distanced. Serial murders are now investigated in a logical and systematic fashion that rejects any elements of intuition or impulse, which means that the criminalists usually avoid any risk of destabilizing their own identities and becoming dangerously submerged in the killer's psychopathy. In addition to this implicit rejection of profiling that is staged in many forensic crime dramas, *CSI* also features episodes that explicitly criticize the method. For example, by depicting narratives in which the criminalists finally solve the crime after other law-enforcement personnel (usually FBI agents) have failed to produce a detailed and correct profile.[17]

The dismissal of the profiling method, in favor of forensics, can be understood as symptomatic of a wider cultural shift. Previous scholarly work done on the revival of the procedural format suggests that the turn to forensics is answering a new cultural call for certainty and governance. A number of scholars have argued that *CSI*'s depiction of forensics, as able to objectively and swiftly produce the truth about the crime, is ideologically invested in the increasingly more prevalent neoconservative tendencies that have followed in the wake of events such as '9/11' and the terrorist attacks in London on July 7, 2005.[18]

Dennis Broe (2004) has, for example, asserted that *CSI* has much in common with shows such as *The Agency* (2001–3) and *Alias* (2001–6) that "romanticised formerly distrusted federal intelligence agencies" in ways that mirror the growing cultural sentiment for a renewed need of government organizations that 'monitor the populace' in order to weed out any threats toward the nation. Broe (2004, 90–7) argues that in the case of *CSI*, "science [is used] as an accurate tool of surveillance" that encourages a renewed faith in law enforcement. *CSI*'s rejection of the figure of the profiler can thus be understood as a way of deflecting and defusing any flaws of law enforcement. The turn to forensics allows for a reinvestment in systems of policing that appears necessary at a time when the Western world is seemingly subjected to outside threats. The fact that television profiling shows so recently pointed out that various governing bodies are defective and unreliable means that forensic crime dramas now have to work hard to reestablish trust in the institutions of policing, and they do so by continuously emphasizing the scientific soundness of the criminalists' practices. By presenting forensic science as always able to establish certain truths, as well as identify, trace, and locate individuals, *CSI* promises to, at least partly, neutralize the felt threats of contemporary society (Figure 12.1).

Martha Gever (2005, 455) has argued that *CSI* is also symptomatic of another cultural turn through which "the search for truth has been relocated . . . from reading minds to reading bodies"; a shift that can be understood as closely interlinked with the wider call for certainty and governance in contemporary society. The most apparent difference between the portrayal of the profiler in the series discussed above and the depiction of the

FIGURE 12.1 *Neutralizing 'threats': Criminalist Greg Sanders (Eric Szmanda) employs forensic science to analyze the physical evidence in* CSI: Crime Scene Investigation *(2000–), CBS-TV. The Kobal Collection.*

criminalists in forensic crime dramas such as *CSI* is that forensic science no longer attempts to access the mind of the killer, but provides a scientific and rational analysis of physical evidence. The strictly scientific nature of the forensic approach to crime solving is dramatized through a narrative focus on the methodical procedure that is 'crime scene investigation', but also through a spectacular visualization of a wide range of scientific and technological tools used by the criminalists.

Profiling narratives and forensic crime dramas both share a focus on the crime scene and the victim's body as sites of significance, but the methods with which they 'read' these clues, and the knowledge they derive from them, are completely different.[19] Criminalists are portrayed as only really interested in the 'pure facts' that presumably can be produced from a scientific analysis of physical evidence. These expert investigators are uninterested in the killer's motives, fantasies, and thoughts; they want to know the 'how', not the 'why'. Instead of attempting to empathically 'enter the mind of the killer', the criminalists are depicted as doing all they can to remain objective. This objectivity is further emphasized by narratively stripping the investigators of private lives: most of the criminalists in *CSI* are 'married to their work' in one way or another, and in comparison with profiling narratives very little screen time is devoted to depicting personal relationships.

On a basic level, *CSI*'s depiction of the forensic scientist can thus be understood as a way of offering simple 'solutions' to the cultural anxieties about uncertainty, irresponsibility, and accountability that was articulated by the profiling narratives of the 1990s, and that has since grown in urgency in the wider cultural context. At a moment when there is seemingly an increased need for governmental power, but where cultural anxieties about the potential flaws of institutions of power still linger, forensic science is portrayed as a framework that will guarantee an objective, fair, and trustworthy mode of surveillance and policing.

The changes within the serial killer narrative is particularly indicative of this wider cultural shift, mainly because the serial killer became so forcefully established as an ultimate threat to society in the late 1980s and early 1990s. This figure has retained its status as a particularly dangerous adversary in *CSI*, even though forensic science is not intimately associated with the figure of the serial killer as is the method of profiling. Forensic science is generally understood as having a much wider field of application, but serial killers are still recurring figures in many of the forensic crime dramas of the 2000s. *CSI* usually features serial killers in at least a couple of episodes each season, and later seasons of the series have included longer narrative arcs focusing on repeat murders.[20] In *CSI* at least, the serial killer functions as a challenge that tests the criminalists' scientific toolbox and results in an even more forceful assertion that forensic science is an institution of policing to be trusted.

The reconfiguration of serial killing: From psychology to genetics

By using certain generic tropes familiar from the wider serial killer genre, repeat killings are constructed in *CSI* as a type of crime that puts forensic methods to a particularly trying test. On the one hand, serial killers are portrayed as anonymous and transient individuals killing strangers without a direct motive; on the other hand, they are depicted as master minds that taunt the investigators by either planting false evidence or meticulously cleaning up crime scenes. In other words, they leave very little usable evidence behind for the criminalists to process, and they thus make it more difficult to identify the killer and establish the events around the crime.

In spite of these difficulties, the criminalists almost always manage to locate at least one significant piece of evidence that in the end will allow them to solve the crime and identify the perpetrator. With the narrative arcs focusing on serial killers growing longer in later seasons of *CSI*, the difficulty of the challenge posed by the figure of the serial killer has increased. This means that the method of forensic science is continuously retested, thus allowing opportunity for new scientific techniques and technologies to be proved reliable. One of the functions of the serial killer is thus to showcase the 'cutting-edge' nature of the criminalists' toolbox, which, by extension, has the basic ideological role of proving that forensic science is a highly reliable method of policing.

Serial killer narratives are specifically used to demonstrate a range of scientific 'tools' that instrumentalize knowledge and practices from the field of genetics, which *CSI* generally presents as being a particularly useful and innovative source for crime-solving methods. The depiction of forensic science as heavily dependent on recent developments in molecular biology is not only conveyed through the narrative importance placed on DNA evidence, but also through a visual language that draws heavily on the iconography of electron microscopes. *CSI* habitually features extreme close-ups, produced though a mix of special effects, that effectively stage a 'shift in scale', suggesting that forensic science is more useful than ever because it is able to locate and analyse evidence that is much smaller than ever before.

Carol Mendelsohn, one of *CSI*'s executive producers, has acknowledged that this approach was consciously adopted to make the series—and its science—appear innovative: "One of the things we did from the start that was unique was that we didn't go big, we went small. We took a fiber and made it look like a redwood forest" (Richmond 2004). Where earlier crime dramas might feature miniscule evidence such as hairs, fibres, or grains of sand, *CSI* goes further, frequently depicting strings of DNA, viruses, molecules, and even atoms. Forensic science is thus dramatized as able to access proof that has previously remained inaccessible to earlier expert investigators, which implicitly holds a promise of neutralizing even those most cunning of perpetrators: genius stranger killers.[21]

The extent to which a molecular framework saturates *CSI*'s discourse on science not only implies that DNA evidence is useful for locating and identifying serial killers, but it also provides a new framework of explanation for the phenomenon of repeat offenders that results in a reconfiguration that geneticizes the figure of the serial killer. In short, *CSI* frequently depicts the murders committed by the serial killer as ultimately caused by some kind of genetic 'deviance' in the individual. Before examining this in more detail, I will first outline the model of explanation for serial murder usually provided by the profiling narratives, as this generic background will help to clarify the cultural function of *CSI*'s genetic framework of explanation.

The dramatization of the profiler as able to catch serial killers by accessing their minds was fundamentally rooted in a psychological or psychoanalytical framework of explanation. This has generic roots in earlier serial killer narratives: the most familiar example is perhaps the final scene of Hitchcock's serial killer classic *Psycho* (1960) where the psychiatrist provides an authoritative explanation of Norman Bates's acts. With the appearance of the figure of the profiler, this framework of explanation became even more central for the narrativization and dramatization of both the serial killer's acts and his/her eventual capture. As Robert Cettl (2003, 28–31) has explained in some detail, profiling narratives tend to devote much attention to the killer's fantasy life, which is depicted as the key to both solving the crime and understanding the cause behind the murderous acts. The portrayal of the profiler as able to enter the mind of the killer is based on an idea that the killer's fantasies are reflected in his/her *modus operandi* and can be deciphered from clues at the crime scene. In accordance with the popular understanding of psychoanalytical theory, these fantasies are usually dramatized as caused by some kind of damage sustained earlier in life. Hence, "the concept of a malfunctioning socialisation process" is crucial for the explanations that the profiling narratives of the 1990s offered in regard to the phenomenon of serial killings (Cettl 2003, 30). The exact type of trauma or socialization failure differs, but common variants depicted in *Cracker*, *Profiler*, and *Millennium* are childhood abuse, the witnessing of violent events, and bad parenting (abuse, neglect, control).

Frequently, the explanations provided are much less particular, rather suggesting that obsessive repeat killings are caused by the dangers of living a modern urban life. In other words, in profiling narratives serial killing is understood as a symptom of the extreme damage potentially inflicted on the individual by the (post)modern social. This view has been summarized by Richard Dyer (2000, 146) when writing about serial killer films and television series:

> Serial killing is often taken to be the crime of our age. It is held to be facilitated by the anonymity of mass societies, and the ease and rapidity of modern transport, to be bred from the dissolution of the affective bonds of community and lifelong families and fomented by the routinisation of the

sexual objectification of women in the media. It is supposedly a symptom of a society in which worth is judged in terms of fame, to the point that spectacularly terrible killing is just a route to celebrity.

This framework of explanation renders the serial killer into a self-reflexive figure though which more general fears about modern society are staged. Whether it is the anonymity and transience of modern urban life, flawed parents, or sexualized violence in the media that is dramatized as being the root cause of the serial killer's obsessive murderous behavior, the psychological explanatory model ultimately places the blame *outside* of the individual killer. The notion that anyone can become a killer under certain cultural circumstances implicates larger societal structures as an accessory to the crimes. In the profiling narratives, the figure of the serial killer was used to worry at economic and social policies. This examination of the failings of society's systems is in line with the wider self-reflexive tendencies of the 1990s crime dramas as outlined above, extending the scrutiny of law enforcement to other aspects of society and its governing forces.[22]

To some extent, CSI follows in this generic tradition. In particular, the more long-running narrative arcs of later seasons tend to include some reference to events in the serial killer's background as formative of his/her acts. For example, in the episode "Living Doll" (S07E24) the criminalists uncover that the so-called Miniature Killer, who they have been hunting throughout Season 7, kills in order to recreate her childhood experience of pushing a younger sister from a tree house, causing her death. However, in line with the series stricter focus on the 'how', rather than the 'why', many of the serial killer narratives in CSI refrain from providing any psychological explanation for the killer's acts. In the majority of the shorter story arcs the killer's *modus operandi* is depicted as significant only in terms of its practicality: the methods of killing are simply chosen because they allow for a quick and convenient kill.[23] Hence, the physical evidence left behind at the crime scene is not depicted as reflecting the killer's elaborate fantasy world, but is simply treated as a physical trace of the events and individuals involved in the criminal acts.

However, there are cases where the criminalists recover DNA evidence that not only functions as proof of the perpetrators' identity, but that is also dramatized as providing a fundamental model of explanation for the act of serial murder. In such episodes, the routine DNA tests (usually performed in order to identify the criminal) reveal some type of genetic anomaly, which is subsequently staged as providing a possible explanation for the serial killer's behavior. The very first example of this is the narrative arc following the investigation into the serial killer Paul Millander, which encompasses three episodes from Seasons 1 and 2.[24] The first two episodes featuring Millander largely adhere to earlier genre conventions: he is depicted as a mastermind serial killer who confounds the criminalists by, for example, planting false fingerprints, and the investigation initially suggests that Millander kills in an attempt to work through a childhood trauma (as a boy, he witnessed the murder of his father and the perpetrators were never convicted because his testimony was deemed unreliable). However, the third episode, "Identity Crisis" (S02E13), adds a biological framework of explanation that is dramatized as identifying a more essential cause of Millander's murderous ways. A series of scientific tests reveal that Millander was born with a genetically rooted 'endocrine ambiguity' that meant that he had an uncertain gender identity: this inherent biological uncertainty is presented as the original cause of both his crazed reaction to his father's death and his ability to trick the criminalists by embodying several different identities.

The conventional psychological framework of explanation is thus not completely rejected by CSI, but it is significantly supplemented by genetic 'deviance' as a more fundamental explanatory model. Implicit in this geneticization of the figure of the serial killer is an assumption that there was perhaps always a biological cause for this behavior, only it was inaccessible as an explanatory framework until the criminalists came along with their cutting-edge scientific toolbox. This reconfiguration of the serial killer must be understood within the wider cultural framework of increased popular interest in determinist and essentialist notions about genes as harboring the 'secret of life itself'. Biological explanations of human behavior in general— and criminal behavior in particular—is by no means new, but has in fact captured the popular imagination throughout most of the twentieth century.[25] However, as shown by Dorothy Nelkin and Susan M. Lindee (1995, 80), "the idea that 'good' and 'bad' character traits (and destinies) are the consequence of 'good' and 'bad' genes" has gained increasing currency and legitimacy due to a number of advances in molecular genetics, and has since the 1990s been circulated in a wide range of popular sources.[26]

One of CSI's later serial killer narratives, namely that featuring the so-called 'Dick and Jane killer' Nate Haskell, is a telling example of how the scientific framework of molecular biology is called upon to legitimize the notion that some people are 'born to kill'.[27] As in the case of Paul Millander, the forensic investigation provides both a psychological and biological framework for Haskell's obsessive personality: he grew up in a home with an abusive father who eventually killed his mother and he is a carrier of the MAO-A gene (also nick-named 'the warrior gene') allegedly making him predisposed toward violent behavior. This biological explanation interestingly reconfigures the traditional psychological explanation, giving it a new meaning as tangible proof of the effects of genetic predispositions, rather than locating the blame outside the individual killer.

In other words, the geneticized serial killer stages the criminal impulse as inscribed in the body of the *individual*. This dramatizes the killer as a deviant Other: a tendency which, at least in part, can be understood as rearticulating generic conventions associated with the figure of the serial killer since long before the profiling narratives. As Cettl's (2003, 7) history of the serial killer film indicates, homicidal monstrousness was in early examples of serial killer films clearly differentiated from humanity by visualizing the Otherness physically. The blatant display of physical difference in monster films was later exchanged for the "doppelganger" motif and the idea of "the killer inside," portraying killers as superficially well adjusted, but hiding a dark secret on the inside (Cettl 2003, 9–14). *CSI*'s portrayal of geneticized serial killers draws from these traditions.

For example, when a serial killer with a split personality is depicted in the episode "Bloodlines" (S04E23), this is explained by identifying him as a "chimera": he has two unique sets of DNA as a result from one twin being absorbed by the other in the womb. This genetic anomaly is, on the one hand, dramatized as the roots of his 'inner evil', invisible to his family and friends who know him as a kind and successful psychiatrist and father. On the other hand, the criminalists' scientific analysis is able to render this abnormality visibly identifiable. The killer's monstrosity is literally brought to the surface in a scene where a criminalist searches his body for signs of struggle: illuminating his skin with UV light, the camera slowly zooms in to reveal a distinct pattern of the so-called Blaschko's lines across his back, which mark him as a biological Other. In the subsequent conversation between the scientist and the killer, these physical signs of genetic anomaly are further identified as markers of monstrosity with reference to the mythological monster from which the name of the condition derives: "The doctors explained it. I'm a creature of myth."

Episodes such as this one suggest that *CSI* uses the figure of the geneticized serial killer to deflect attention from wider social problems, effectively placing the blame on the individual body. Nelkin and Lindee (1995, 91) have already proposed that the popular "interest in 'bad genes'—the genes for deviance—reflects a tendency to medicalize social problems." By reconfiguring the explanatory model used for understanding serial killers and placing the blame on the 'deviant' nature of individual bodies, *CSI* avoids the risk of implicating domestic society, and by extension, the system of government (that the criminalists implicitly are representatives of) as accessories to the crime. At a point in time when society is seemingly subjected to numerous outside threats, like local and international terrorism to mention one example, *CSI*'s geneticization of the serial killer allows for a reinvestment in institutions of policing and surveillance (Broe 2004, 90–7).

Furthermore, by identifying the serial killer as a biological Other, the historic understanding of the serial killer as a domestically produced monster is rejected. Through the process of geneticization, the serial killer is identified as precisely an *outside* threat; in some ways similar to the figure of the political terrorist also frequently problematized as a cultural or national Other in current crime television (Tasker 2012). As such, any implications that Western culture and society produce such monsters are played down and the problem is limited to the biology of the individual body. Hence, the geneticization of the serial killer also implicitly engages with the notion that further scientific developments might not only allow for pre-crime identification of such 'abnormal' individuals, but also for pre-birth intervention or even eradication. Medico-scientific control over the reproduction process could, it is insinuated, perhaps neutralize the threat of repeat killings altogether.[28]

Postscript: The geneticized serial killer and new anxieties

Although the serial killer is now used to a lesser extent to work over and worry at wider social problems such as child-rearing practices and the anonymity of city life, the figure still retains some of this former function in *CSI*. While the series does not question the state of modern urban society, or the responsibility of law enforcement, it raises a different set of dynamic inquiries that have a particular currency for the wider cultural process of geneticization.

As argued above, *CSI* largely heralds an essentialist and determinist view on genetics, and this generally results in a heightened feeling of certainty, instilling trust in the newly scientific law enforcement. Nevertheless, a closer consideration of the exact nature of the genetic anomalies that are depicted as causing the obsessive behavior of the serial killer suggests that the geneticized serial killer conversely questions the viability of some of the most basic assumptions of essentialist genetics. That *CSI*'s discourse on genetics is ambiguous and contradictory is actually not surprising considering that much of mainstream television functions as a cultural forum that voices multiple perspectives and notions in an open manner in order to attract a wide and varied audience (Newcomb and Hirsch 1983). Newcomb and Hirsch's (1983) understanding of television as simultaneously expressing and examining both repressive and reactionary viewpoints, and more subversive and emancipatory affinities, is—I would argue—particularly applicable to a globally popular show such as *CSI*, as a dynamic treatment of contemporary issues enables a wider and more varied audience appeal (Newcomb and Hirsch 1983, 47–8).

Genetic 'deviance' is narratively constructed as determining the behavior of the serial killers in the episodes discussed above, but the particular types of aberration that are featured—namely, 'endocrine ambiguity', 'chimerism', and 'the warrior gene'—evoke more recent scientific discoveries that question essentialist ideas about the DNA molecule as harboring the 'true' identity of individuals and as able to determine future potential. The very notion that an endocrine ambiguity can result in a uncertain gender identity destabilizes the biological understanding of gender as clearly differentiated through X and Y chromosomes, and the chimera's multiple sets of DNA profoundly questions the reliability of forensic DNA which is thought to allow for the identification of each individual through their unique DNA sequence. Furthermore, the narrative arc featuring Nate Haskell continuously juxtaposes the killer with one of the righteous criminalists who, conversely, are also portrayed as having inherited 'the warrior gene', a plotline that repeatedly problematizes the idea that a genetic predisposition to violence actually does equate to a 'natural born killer'.

Much like other popular texts that are part of the genetic imaginary, *CSI*'s discourse on science does depict the gene "as a deterministic agent, a blueprint, a basis for social relations, and a source of good and evil" and thus imbues it with a reassuring promise of "certainty, order, predictability and control" (Nelkin and Lindee 1995, 194). However, the figure of the serial killer also becomes a way for *CSI* to address the possibility that scientific attempts to map the human genome might have failed to fulfil their implicit promise of identifying genes as unique and stable entities that unquestionably determine behaviors and biological processes. The recent discourse around molecular science has increasingly started to redefine the notion of the gene, and by extension a number of fundamental notions of the biological framework for understanding the world (namely, concepts like truth, body, identity, kinship, and even 'life itself').[29] It is this recent process of redefinition that *CSI* worries at when geneticizing the figure of the serial killer.

Hence, while Brunsdon was right when she predicted that the medicalization of the crime drama meant that the genre was moving away from dynamically questioning the institutions of policing, this does not mean that a series like *CSI* completely avoids dealing with contemporary issues altogether.[30] *CSI*'s geneticization of the serial killer results in a dynamic debate that poses new questions, specifically about the stability and certainty of genetic 'information'. The figure of the serial killer thus ultimately retains the same basic function even after it has been reconfigured through the genre's new investment in forensic science, that is, staging cultural fears and anxieties of a specific sociohistorical moment. In addition to expressing worries about current shifts in the wider discourse on genetics, the geneticized figure of the serial killer can also be read as a response to an uncertain 9/11 cultural milieu which, in the aftermath of the earlier backlash against state policing and surveillance (as dramatized in 1990s profiling narratives), now necessarily requires the rationality and order seemingly afforded by forensic science.

Notes

1 Serial murder is famously referred to as an "elusive phenomenon" in the title of criminologist Steven A. Egger's anthology (1990) about serial killers and the social phenomenon of serial murder.

2 'Criminalist' should here be understood as an umbrella term including several different professions working in the field of criminalistics, such as crime scene investigators, forensic scientists, and pathologists.

3 Specifically, my analysis draws on Mittell's (2001, 2004) suggestion that textual analysis can be useful for exploring how stylistic, thematic, and ideological elements of a specific television program functions through complex articulations of generic linkages that must also be understood as intimately tied to shifts in wider cultural discourses. I do, however, abstain from answering Mittell's call for genre studies that take into account the extra-textual practices that constitute genre categories, as this is not an attempt to exhaustively trace or map the history of one genre category.

4 See Newcomb and Hirsch (1983), Brunsdon (1998), and Wheatley (2005, 2006).

5 Like Wheatley, I prefer to use the somewhat odd-sounding terminology of "worrying at," rather than the psychoanalytically rooted "working through," as I find this to be a highly evocative way of describing the open-ended cultural work done by a specific television program. The process of "working through" is, as explained by Freud, a therapeutic technique aimed at eventually 'overcoming' repressed or traumatic experiences, but the concept of "worrying at" indicates the way popular series often present several different notions and viewpoints without achieving one clear conclusion. See Wheatley (2005, 149) and Freud (2001, 155).

6 The method of 'criminal profiling' is usually treated as synonymous with 'behavioral science' or 'forensic psychology' in popular media, even though professional criminologists tend to stress that these are different types of expert knowledge.

7 The adaptations are Manhunter (1986) and The Silence of the Lambs (1991). For a more thorough account on the fictional presence of profiling, see Herndon (2007) and Cettl (2003, 25–31).

8 For more on Paul Britton's career, see Ronson (2010).

9 A selection of the films featuring the method of criminal profiling are: *Se7en* (1995), *Copy Cat* (1995), *Kiss the Girls* (1997), *Fallen* (1998), *The Bone Collector* (1999), *Eye of the Beholder* (1999), *The Cell* (2000), *Along Came a Spider* (2001), *Hannibal* (2001), *Insomnia* (2002), *Murder by Numbers* (2002), *Mindhunters* (2004), and *Taking Lives* (2004).

10 For genre histories on the serial killer film and the crime genre, see for example: Thomas (1999), Wilson (2000), Cettl (2003), Young (2010, 75–80), and Reburn (2012).

11 The same pattern of formally distinguishing the profiler from the 'regular' law enforcement is followed in many profiling films: Will Graham in *Manhunter* is retired and Clarice Starling in *The Silence of the Lambs* is 'just' a student.

12 For a more detailed analysis of "Fitz," see Duguid (2009, 30–47).

13 There are also multiple examples of serial killing films that feature this trope when depicting the method of profiling, including *Manhunter* (1986), *Se7en* (1995), and *The Cell* (2000).

14 Richard Dyer has pointed out that this is equally the case in specialist literature on profiling: John Douglas has, for example, conceded that he would not shy away from any potentially psychic components. See Dyer (2000, 149) and Douglas (1995, 150–1).

15 For examples of the critique voiced against profiling, see Ronson (2010, 1–8), Perri and Lichtenwald (2009), Gladwell (2007, 4), Snook et al. (2007), and Alison et al. (2002).

16 *CSI* has managed to get uncommonly high domestic viewing figures and has also been widely exported. Furthermore, it is one of the most stylistically influential series of the early 2000s: its distinctive cinematography and costly special effects are now more widely associated with the crime genre. Due to this, "CSI" has become an accepted abbreviation for the forensic crime genre category in large. For more detailed discussions of the series's influence, see Cohan (2008), Weissmann (2010), and Kompare (2010).

17 One prominent example of this is the epsiode "Strip Strangler" (S01E23). Reburn (2012, 202) has also rightly pointed out that there are several other fictional films and television shows of the early 2000s that openly criticize the method of profiling.

18 For more detailed discussions on this discursive context of *CSI*, see for example Broe (2004), and several of the articles in Byers and Johnson (2009).

19 For a discussion on this difference, see Reburn (2012, 122).

20 *CSI* is known for having a strict episodic structure, but considered as a whole, the series must rather be identified has having a 'flexi-narrative' structure, combining some longer narrative arcs with stand-alone episodes. Serial killer narratives have from the very first season of *CSI* been the primary example of longer narrative arcs. While in the first few seasons these arcs usually only encompassed a couple of episodes, they later span entire seasons.

21 Even through the figure of the profiler could be said to have given up the brightest spotlight in benefit for the forensic scientist, it should be acknowledged that several successful profiler series has been produced after CSI's premiere, including: *Criminal Minds* (2005–), *Without a Trace* (2002–2009), *Wire in the Blood* (2002–2008). Furthermore, many of the crime dramas contemporary to *CSI* depict a team of investigators that feature one staple profiler. *Waking the Dead* (2000–), *Crossing Jordan* (2001–2007), *Law and Order: Criminal Intent* (2001–), *The Shield* (2002–2008), *Numb3rs* (2005–2010), *Bones* (2005–), and *Dexter* (2006–) all include characters with profiling skills, but without presenting profiling as the main spectacle of the show. This increased tendency to combine profiling with forensic science is, I would argue, indicative of how forensic science, in the wake of *CSI*, has widely become understood as the more reliable method of the two. While this has not completely wiped out the popular interest in profiling, it has generally resulted in placing the figure of the profiler within a stricter scientific framework. In these later series, the method of profiling is portrayed as a more systematic and logical practice, and the intuitive or mystical aspects previously acknowledged in profiling narratives are now played down.

22 It has, however, been argued that the serial killer genre has a wider tendency of deflecting attention from such wider societal issues by limiting the problems to one deviant individual. While this argument provides viable insights into how the serial killer figure functions in individual films, it is less instructive in relation to the profiling series I discuss in this article. As Dyer (2000, 146) argues, the seriality of these narratives enhances the repetitive nature of the concept of serial murder and, in turn, creates a more forceful sense of serial killing not being a singular occurrence but precisely a "symptom of a society." The profiling series not only depicts the individual serial killer as causing death after death, but each episode presents a new killer adding up to a crucial sense of serial murder as a mass phenomenon.

23 See episodes "I–15 Murders" (S01E11), "Strip Strangler" (S01E23), "The Execution of Catherine Willows" (S03E06), and "What's Eating Gilbert Grissom" (S05E06).

24 Namely, "Pilot" (S01E01), "Anonymous" (S01E08), and "Identity Crisis" (S02E13).

25 For an overview of the history of these ideas, see Nelkin and Lindee (1995).

26 *CSI* is far from the first or only popular text that dramatizes the notion that some people are genetically predisposed to become serial killers. For a discussion on other examples, see Nelkin and Lindee (1995, 80, 84–7).

27 Haskell appears in the following episodes: "19 Down" (S09E09), "One to Go" (S09E10), "Doctor Who" (S10E22), "Meat Jekyll" (S10E23), "Shock Waves" (S11E01), "Targets of Obsession" (S11E15), "Father of the Bride" (S11E20), "Cello and Goodbye" (S11E21), and "In a Dark, Dark House" (S11E22).

28 For more discussions on how the essentialist and determinist discourse on genes could motivate "the political control of reproduction as an alternative to social control," see Nelkin and Lindee (1995, 144–8).

29 For more on this cultural process of redefinition, see for example Franklin (2000) and Rose (2007).

30 Brunsdon (1998, 242) did in passing acknowledge that she was unsure whether the "medicalized" crime dramas actually lacked a "structure of anxiety," proposing they might simply be worrying about different issues.

References

Alison, Laurence, Craig Bennell, Andreas Mokros, and David Ormerod. 2002. "The Personality Paradox in Offender Profiling: A Theoretical Review of the Process Involved in Deriving Background Characteristics from Crime Scene Actions." *Psychology, Public Policy, and Law* 8(1): 115–35.

Broe, Dennis. 2004. "Genre Regression and the New Cold War: The Return of the Police Procedural." *Framework* 45(2): 81–101.

Brunsdon, Charlotte. 1998. "Structure of Anxiety: Recent British Television Crime Fiction." *Screen* 39(3): 223–43.

Byers, Michele, and Val Marie Johnson, eds. 2009. *The CSI Effect: Television, Crime and Governance*. Plymouth: Lexington Books.

Cettl, Robert. 2003. *Serial Killer Cinema: Analytical Filmography with an Introduction*. Jefferson, NC, and London: McFarland & Company, Inc.

Cohan, Steven. 2008. *TV Classics: CSI: Crime Scene Investigation*. London: BFI Publishing.

Douglas, John. 1995. *Mindhunter: Inside the FBI's Elite Serial Crime Unit*. New York: Scribner.

Duguid, Mark. 2009. *TV Classics: Cracker*. London: BFI Publishing and Palgrave Macmillan.

Dyer, Rickard. 2000. "Kill and Kill Again." In *Action/Spectacle Cinema: A Sight and Sound Reader*, edited by José Arroyo, 145–9. London: BFI Publishing.

Egger, Steven A., ed. 1990. *Serial Murder: An Elusive Phenomenon*. New York: Praeger Publishers.

Franklin, Sarah. 2000. "Life Itself: Global Nature and the Genetic Imaginary." In *Global Nature, Global Culture*, edited by Sarah Franklin, Celia Lury, and Jackie Stacey, 188–227. London: Sage Publications.

Freud, Sigmund. 2001. "Remembering, Repeating and Working-Through: Further Recommendations of the Technique of Psycho-Analysis (1914)." In *The Standard Edition of the Complete Psychological Works of Sigmund Freud: Vol. XII*, edited by James Strachey and Anna Freud, 145–57. London: The Hogarth Press.

Gever, Martha. 2005. "The Spectacle of Crime Digitized: *CSI: Crime Scene Investigation* and Social Anatomy." *European Journal of Cultural Studies* 8(4): 445–63.

Gladwell, Malcom. 2007. "Dangerous Minds: Criminal Profiling Made Easy." *The New Yorker*, November 12. Accessed June 8, 2012. www.newyorker.com/reporting/2007/11/12/071112fa_fact_gladwell.

Harris, Thomas.1988. *The Silence of the Lambs*. New York: St. Martin's Press.

—. 2000 [1981]. *Red Dragon*. New York: Dell Publishing.

Herndon, James S. 2007. "The Image of Profiling: Media Treatment and General Impressions." In *Criminal Profiling: International Theory, Research and Practice*, edited by Richard N. Kocsis, 303–26. Torowa, NJ: Humana Press Inc.

Kompare, Derek. 2010. *CSI*. Malden, MA: Wiley-Blackwell.

Mittell, Jason. 2001. "A Cultural Approach to Television Genre Theory." *Cinema Journal* 40(3): 3–24.

—. 2004. *Genre and Television: From Cop Shows to Cartoons in American Culture*. New York and London: Routledge.

Nelkin, Dorothy, and Susan M. Lindee. 1995. *The DNA Mystique: The Gene as a Cultural Icon*. New York: W.H. Freeman and Company.

Newcomb, Horace M., and Paul M. Hirsch. 1983. "Television as a Cultural Forum: Implications for Research." *Quarterly Review of Film Studies* 8(3): 45–55.

Perri, Frank S., and Terrance G. Lichtenwald. 2009. "When Worlds Collide: Criminal Investigative Analysis, Forensic Psychology, and the Timothy Masters Case." *The Forensic Examiner* 800: 52–68.

Reburn, Jennifer. 2012. "Watching Men: Masculinity and Surveillance in the American Serial Killer Film 1978–2008." Glasgow Theses Service, http://theses.gla.ac.uk/.

Richmond, Ray, 2004. "The Minds behind the Bodies." *Hollywood Reporter Special Issue: CSI 100th*, November 18. Accessed March 1, 2010. www.hollywoodreporter.com.

Ronson, Jon. 2010. "Whodunit?" *The Guardian*, May 15. Accessed June 8, 2012. www.guardian.co.uk/uk/2010/may/15/criminal-profiling-jon-ronson.

Rose, Nikolas. 2007. *The Politics of Life Itself: Biomedicine, Power, and Subjectivity in the Twenty-First Century*. Princeton: Princeton University Press.

Snook, Brent, Josef Eastwood, Paul Gendreau, Claire Goggin, and Richard M. Cullen. 2007. "Taking Stock of Criminal Profiling: A Narrative Review and Meta-Analysis." *Criminal Justice and Behaviour* 34: 437–53.

Sumser, John. 1996. *Morality and Social Order in Television Crime Drama*. Jefferson, NC, and London: McFarland & Company, Inc.

Tasker, Yvonne. 2012. "Television Crime Drama and Homeland Security: From Law and Order to 'Terror TV'." *Cinema Journal* 51(4): 45–65.

Thomas, Ronald R. 1999. *Detective Fiction and the Rise of Forensic Science*. Cambridge: Cambridge University Press.

Weissmann, Elke. 2010. *The Forensic Sciences of CSI: How to Know about Crime*. Saarbrücken, Germany: VDM Verlag Dr. Müller.

Wheatley, Helen. 2005. "Rooms within Rooms: Upstairs Downstairs and the Studio Drama of the 1970s." In *ITV Cultures: Independent Television over Fifty Years*, edited by Catherine Johnson and Rob Turnock, 143–58. Maidenhead: Open University Press.

—. 2006. *Gothic Television*. Manchester: Manchester University Press.

Wilson, Christopher P. 2000. *Cop Knowledge: Police Power and Cultural Narrative in Twentieth-Century America*. Chicago: University of Chicago Press.

Young, Alison. 2010. *The Scene of Violence: Cinema, Crime, Affect*. London and New York: Routledge.

Filmography

Along Came a Spider. DVD. Directed by Lee Tamahori. 2001; Hollywood, CA: Paramount Home Entertainment, 2007.

Between the Lines. Television. Executive produced by Tony Garnett. UK: BBC, 1992–1994.

Bones. Television. Produced by Kathy Reichs, Emily Deschanel, and David Boreanaz. Los Angeles, CA: Fox, 2005–.

The Bone Collector. DVD. Directed by Phillip Noyce. 1999; Universal City, CA: Universal Studios Home Entertainment, 2001.

The Cell. DVD. Directed by Tarsam Singh. 2000; Los Angeles, CA: New Line Home Entertainment, 2000.

Copycat. DVD. Directed by Jon Amiel. 1995; Burbank, CA: Warner Home Video, 1995.

Cracker. Television. Produced by Gub Neal, Paul Abbott, Hilary Bevan Jones, and John Chapman. UK: ITV, 1993–6, 2006.

Criminal Minds. Television. Created by Jeff Davis. 2005. New York, NY: CBS, 2005–.

Crossing Jordan. Television. Produced by Tim Kring. New York: NBC, 2001–7.

CSI: Crime Scene Investigation. Television. Produced by Jerry Bruckheimer. New York: CBS, 2000–.

CSI: Miami. Television. Produced by Jerry Bruckheimer. New York: CBS, 2002–.

CSI: NY. Television. Produced by Jerry Bruckheimer. New York: CBS, 2004–.

Dexter. Television. Produced by Showtime Networks. New York: Showtime, 2006–.

Eye of the Beholder. DVD. Directed by Stephan Elliott. 1999; Culver City, CA: Sony Pictures Home Entertainment, 2002.

Fallen. DVD. Directed by Gregory Hoblit. 1998; Burbank, CA: Warner Home Video, 1998.

Hannibal. DVD. Directed by Ridley Scott. 2001; Beverly Hills, CA: MGM Home Entertainment, 2001.

Homicide: Life on the Street. Television. Created by Paul Attnasio. New York: NBC, 1993–9.

In the Heat of the Night. Television. Created by John Ball. New York: NBC/CBS, 1988–95.

Insomnia. DVD. Directed by Christopher Nolan, 2002; Burbank, CA: Warner Home Video, 2002.

Inspector Morse. Television. Produced by Zenith Productions/Central Independent Television. UK: ITV, 1987–2000.

Kiss the Girls. DVD. Directed by Gary Fleder. 1997; Hollywood, CA: Paramount Home Entertainment, 1998.

Law and Order: Criminal Intent. Television. Executive produced by Dick Wolf. New York: NBC/USA Network 2001–.

Manhunter. DVD. Directed by Michael Mann. 1986; Beverly Hills, CA: MGM Home Entertainment, 2007.

Millennium. Television. Created by Chris Carter. Los Angeles: Fox, 1996–9.

Mind Hunters. DVD. Directed by Renny Harlin, 2004; Santa Monica, CA: Lionsgate Home Entertainment, 2005.

Murder by Numbers. DVD. Directed by Barbet Schroeder, 2002; Burbank, CA: Warner Home Video, 2002.

Numb3rs. Television. Produced by Ridley Scott and Tom Scott. New York: CBS, 2005–10.

NYPD Blue. Television. Produced by Steven Bochco Productions. New York: ABC, 1993–2005.

Prime Suspect. Television. Produced by Granada Television/ITV Productions. UK: ITV, 1991–6.

Profiler. Television. NBC Studios/Three Putt Entertainment/The Sander Moses Group. New York: NBC, 1996–2000.

Psycho. DVD. Directed by Alfred Hitchcock. 1960; Universal City, CA: Universal Studios Home Entertainment, 1998.

Se7en. DVD. Directed by David Fincher. 1995; Los Angeles, CA: New Line Home Entertainment, 2004.

The Shield. Television. Produced by Michael Chiklis. Dallas, TX: FX, 2002–8.

The Silence of the Lambs. DVD. Directed by Jonathan Demme. 1991; Los Angeles, CA: Orion Pictures Corporation, 1997.

Taking Lives. DVD. Directed by D. J. Caruso, 2004; Burbank, CA: Warner Home Video, 2004.

Waking the Dead. Television. Created by Barbara Machin. UK: BBC, 2000–.

Wire in the Blood. Television. Produced by Philip Leach. UK: ITV, 2002–8.

Without a Trace. Television. Created by Hank Steinberg. New York: CBS, 2002–9.

The X-Files. Television. Created by Chris Carter. Los Angeles: Fox, 1993–2002.

13

Homme Fatal: Illegitimate Pleasures in *Darkly Dreaming Dexter*

David Buchbinder and Ann Elizabeth McGuire

Vengeance is mine; I will repay, saith the Lord.

ROMANS 12.18–20

Garroting, slicing, and vivisecting: how and why do these incite pleasure in the average readership and television audience? For example, Jeff Lindsay's *Dexter* series has come to be seen as intriguing and entertaining, even chic. We may be more disposed to accept, if not actually approve, Dexter's murderous activities because his victims are themselves reprehensible criminals who have, for the most part, molested and killed children and other innocents, and who have got away with it because the law is either ineffectual in its maintenance or full of loopholes in its application; but this alone fails to explain the pleasure and enthusiasm expressed by both readers and viewers with regard to the *Dexter* novels and TV show.

There are distinct and important differences between the novels and the TV show, not only in terms of plot development but also in the positioning of the reader or the viewer in relation to the story being told. Moreover, there are shifts also within the series of novels, most markedly in *Dexter in the Dark*, the third of the books, which seems to venture farther into the realm of the paranormal than the rest of the series. Therefore, for the purposes of this study we will limit ourselves to the first novel, *Darkly Dreaming Dexter*, which sets up the narrative world and the parameters for the rest of the series of novels. The narrative is marked by a series of doublings and dualisms, as we will see.

Dexter: *Homme Fatal*

The title of this chapter is intended also to reflect the duality of *Dexter*. 'Fatal'; means both 'of or pertaining to fate' and 'leading to or causing death', both of which are relevant to the *Dexter* narratives. With regard to the former meaning, Dexter is represented as destined—fated—to kill others because of the traumatic events undergone in a shipping container in which his mother was murdered, and in which the 3-year-old boy remained mired in her blood for two-and-a-half days. That this was a cardinal event in his life determining its future trajectory is underscored by the fact that his brother Brian, likewise trapped in their mother's blood, shares the same pathology. Moreover, Dexter's victims may be thought of as destined for the justice that they escaped in the law courts. That justice is, then, both *illegitimate*—it is not sanctioned by law or by the process of law—and *legitimated*—it deals out 'appropriate' punishment to those who have hitherto escaped it in the normal run of the law.

Dexter may also be described as 'fatal', in that he brings death to those to whom he metes out his peculiarly double form of justice. Indeed, he is occasionally characterized as almost a benediction upon those whom he has marked out for punishment, as is made clear early in the narrative, with his first victim, the paedophile priest:

> And just before I started the serious work Father Donovan opened his eyes and looked at me. There was no fear now; that happens sometimes. He looked straight up at me and his mouth moved.
> "What?" I said. I moved my head a little closer. "I can't hear you."
> I heard him breathe, a slow and peaceful breath, and then he said it again before his eyes closed.
> "You're welcome," I said, and I went to work. (Lindsay 2005, 12)

Thus Dexter combines destiny and fatality.

There is, however, a third meaning, one which is more commonly understood, and is enshrined in the commonly used term *femme fatale*, an expression which has more or less lost its etymological origins in notions of fate and fatality and has come to mean, more simply, a seductress, a woman whose physical and sexual charms are irresistible. Our adaptation and masculinization of the term is intended to suggest Dexter's seductiveness for the reader or viewer; and again it is applicable to his brother Brian, whose appeal, in this case, is limited to Dexter only. As *homme fatal*, then, Dexter may be thought of as the point of convergence of fate, death, and seductiveness.

The erotics of murder/death as pornography

Darkly Dreaming Dexter commences with what amounts to an invocation to the moon. The lunar cycle is connected to Dexter's murder-lust: as the moon reaches its full, so does Dexter experience an increasing need to kill:

> Moon. Glorious moon. Full, fat, reddish moon, the night as light as day, the moonlight flooding down across the land and bringing joy, joy, joy. Bringing too the full-throated call of the tropical night, the soft and wild voice of the wind roaring through the hairs on your arm, the hollow wail of starlight, the teeth-grinding bellow of the moonlight off the water.
> All calling to the Need. Oh, the symphonic shriek of the thousand hiding voices, the cry of the Need inside, *the entity*, the silent watcher, the cold quiet thing, the one that laughs, the Moondancer. The me that was not-me, the thing that mocked and laughed and came calling with its hunger. With the Need. And the Need was very strong now, very careful cold coiled creeping crackly cocked and ready, very strong, very much ready now—and still it waited and watched, and it made me wait and watch. (Lindsay 2005, 1)

That this is almost a sexual tension is suggested at the beginning of the following chapter:

> By four-thirty in the morning the priest was all cleaned up. I felt a lot better. I always did, after. Killing makes me feel good. It works the knots out of darling Dexter's dark schemata. It's a sweet release, a necessary letting go of all the little hydraulic valves inside. I enjoy my work; sorry if that bothers you. Oh, very sorry, really. But there it is. And it's not just any killing, of course. It has to be done the right way, at the right time, with the right partner—very complicated, but very necessary. (Lindsay 2005, 13)

If the act of killing is eroticized in the narrative, the display and visual consumption of death becomes its pornography. When Dexter is first summoned to the site where the Ice Truck Killer's prostitute victim has been discovered, Dexter comments, "It was almost surgical. This guy did very nice work—as good as I could do. . . . I had never seen such clean, dry, *neat*-looking dead flesh. Wonderful" (Lindsay 2005, 25). He continues to admire the killer's work as the deaths continue. However, it is not merely that Dexter gets a thrill from looking at his 'colleague's' fine work: the description of the sectioned bodies and their gradual exposure through unwrapping positions the reader as voyeur and consumer of the sight of death. We too experience a thrill, this one combining the erotic and the repulsive; and, as with any detective novel or thriller, we experience desire—to see more death, in order to observe the protagonist at work.

The familiarity of Dexter

While Dexter Morgan is not in any formal sense a detective, he is recognizably related to the *louche* policeman or detective with whom we are familiar from a myriad cop shows and detective novels. Such a figure is separated by only a hair's breadth from criminality, using methods and dealing with others in ways that are impermissible and illegitimate, in order to obtain legitimate results or to further his own ends. The implication in such narratives is that the business end of policing, because it is always in close proximity to criminality, becomes itself tainted, criminalized to some degree.

While superficially Dexter appears to conform to this model, in fact his trajectory takes him in the reverse direction. Already potentially criminal since boyhood, given his propensity to kill, his presence in the Miami Metro Police Homicide Department both functions as a protective cover for his secret psychopathic tendency, and at the same time helps to shore up the legitimation of his killing as justice rendered where the legal system has failed. Located effectively on the margin between law and order, on the one hand, and brutal criminality and psychopathy, on the other, Dexter's liminality is complex.

In discussing what she calls "psycho-horror" serial-killer fiction, Isabel Santaularia (2010, 58) observes that in this subgenre "the serial killer is the main protagonist and readers/audiences become direct witnesses to his thoughts and murders unmediated by an external agent that posits a moral frame to the serial killer's actions." In this respect, Dexter, as the

Miami Metro Police Homicide Department's blood-spatter analyst, is part of the machinery of authority and of the official processes of detection, which provide the hypothetical moral (and legal) frame; yet, as a serial killer himself within that machinery, Dexter operates outside it in order to restore the justice that the machinery itself is incapable of providing: "In this subgenre, the violence of the serial killer is not only presented as inherent but as somehow justifiable" (Santaularia 2010, 58). Santaularia (2010, 59) goes on to note that "Paradoxically, in some examples of psycho-horror and other serial killer fictions, the construction of the serial killer's masculinity is also related to the preservation of moral values, justice and/or the law and order."

Because the narrator is also the serial killer in *Darkly Dreaming Dexter*, he becomes familiar to us by another route than the figure of the morally dubious law officer. We inhabit his mind, and so perforce must see people and events through his eyes. Additionally, the narrative compels to accept his rationalizations and justifications, even though at a second remove we might have reservations about these, or even reject them entirely. And so a double vision is achieved, whereby we see things as Dexter sees them, but we judge them separately. In sociological terms, Dexter, whom we perceive as marked by a psychopathic tendency toward murder, is 'normalized' in two ways: first, by immersing us, the readers, in his particular logic and way of perceiving matters, and, second, by literally performing ordinariness so that he can survive in a society which would otherwise mark him as a killer.

Indeed, in his article "The Code of Harry: Performing Normativity in *Dexter*," William Ryan Force (2010, 333), speaking chiefly of the Showtime network television series, argues that "Engaged in a heightened self-aware dialog about his performativity, Dexter's narrative voice makes something of a practical sociologist; he reveals the social order's constructedness by demonstrating its mundane accomplishment." He goes on to remark on the "[i]mportant but under-studied elements of social life of those features we dis-attend from: the social accomplishment of an unmarked, mundane personhood" (Force 2010, 333). Force's argument is that, in order to become 'unmarked', that is, a member of the dominant group and hence *unre*mark*able*, Dexter must learn what behaviors are acceptable—and, concomitantly, what behaviors help to mark an individual as Other.

Dexter's doubleness in this respect emerges in his 'daytime'/'night-time' personalities. As the mild-mannered blood-spatter analyst, brother of Deb Morgan, and boyfriend of Rita, Dexter must avoid becoming marked in any way; and herein lies a good deal of the tension in the narrative. At the same

FIGURE 13.1 *Double-life: Despite Dexter's attempts to hide his "Dark Passenger" behind the facade of 'family man', he is (self-) marked as Other. Dexter (2006–), Showtime. Photographer: Jim Fiscus. The Kobal Collection.*

time, however, as the retributive serial killer, Dexter must necessarily accept a marking as Other. Indeed, *he marks himself as Other*, in relation to his victims: despite any protest on their part, he sees himself as qualitatively different from them, as well as Other to the general dominant. In effect, he seeks to *defamiliarize* himself in relation to the common run of serial killers (Figure 13.1).

Queer Dexter

The word 'queer' does not signify only those who identify as non-heteronormative, in sexual terms. Rather, as queer theory argues, 'queer' is intended to render more spacious the possibilities of subjectivity, so as to include both heteronormativity and non-heteronormativity—and, beyond those categories, the wide variety of subject positions available to members of a culture—as equally valid and valorized terms in a discourse. To read queerly, then, is to perceive a range of possibilities of meaning *in addition to* the preferred or ostensible meaning in a text.

In Lindsay's narrative, this can be seen clearly demonstrated in the equivocal valorization of murderous proclivities. Those against whom Dexter sets his hand are judged *fundamentally* evil; but the narrative exonerates Dexter's own murderousness as the consequence of a childhood trauma. The scene of the camping trip in which his adoptive father Harry confronts Dexter about his acts of killing (to this point, only small animals) is framed as the kind of father–son encounter that usually entails a conversation about 'the facts of life'. Indeed, when Harry charges him with having killed the neighbors' dog, Dexter confesses his compulsion to kill in just such terms: "My face is hot, as if Dad had asked me to talk about sex dreams. Which, in a way—" (Lindsay 2005, 38). But 'the facts of life' at the heart of this father–son scene in which Harry gives Dexter a "higher order truth" (compared to the male knowledge of "how to throw a curve ball and how to throw a left hook" [Lindsay 2005, 39]) relate to Dexter's 'difference'. And here we might note again the alignment of the impulse to murder with the sexual urge.

In the conventional scenario of the father–son talk about the 'facts of life', the focus is usually on ensuring that the boy understands the nature and function of human sexuality. This in turn would imply a distinction between heterosexuality and homosexuality, privileging the former over the latter. Notions of 'difference' in this context would refer to the 'normality' of the boy's urges. However, in Harry's conversation with Dexter, the urges are not sexual but lethal; but Harry's remarks starts to sound like the rhetoric of acceptance of *sexual* difference, in relation to the heterosexual/homosexual binary:

> You can't help it. I know that. Because— . . . What do you remember from before?

And when Dexter replies, "Nothing," he responds:

> Good . . . Nobody should remember that. . . . But even though you don't remember, Dex, it did things to you. Those things make you what you are. I've talked to some people about this. (Lindsay 2005, 40)

Of course, Harry is *not* discussing Dexter's sexual orientation or, indeed, the possibility that Dexter has suffered sexual abuse, though, taken out of context, the above passage might suggest that. And Dexter is quite assertive in stating that he is not gay, but rather asexual:

> Whatever made me the way I am left me hollow, empty inside, unable to feel. It doesn't seem like a big deal. I'm quite sure most people fake an awful lot of everyday contact. I just fake all of it. I fake it very well, and the feelings are never there. But I like kids. I could never have them, since the idea of sex is no idea at all. Imagine doing those things—How can you? Where's your sense of dignity? (Lindsay 2005, 14)

Later, he remarks:

> I had no interest in a sexual relationship. I wanted a disguise; Rita was exactly what I was looking for. (Lindsay 2005, 53)

The notion of a woman as a device of camouflage is not a new one, of course: homosexual men have often used this form of heteronormative mimicry as protective coloring. It is interesting, however, that Dexter uses the term 'beard' to describe Rita's function in his life as protective camouflage, since this is precisely the word that is often used in a gay context with exactly the same meaning:

> Rita was merely my beard. A silly kid's costume I wore on weekends to hide the fact that I was the kind of person who did the things that this other interesting fellow was now doing and I wasn't. (Lindsay 2005, 127)

The point to grasp here, then, is not that Dexter is actually or potentially gay, but rather that for him sexual orientation is part of the mimicry, rather than part of the personality. At the same time, however, the sexual ambiguity surrounding Harry's talk with Dexter, and the deliberate use of gay slang to describe what is in effect a heterosexual situation, opens the text to possibilities of meaning that permit its description as queer.

Comedy of manners/revenge tragedy

Ironic, witty and sardonic, Dexter's observations are cutting and, from some perspectives at least, accurate. His double position as both dehumanized and as simulating humanity allows him a unique point of view on social structures, mores, and morality. He becomes the character who, in a conventional comedy of manners, comments on the social—and especially class—foibles of his time. Yet this urbane, civilized, ironically self-distancing voice is that of the perpetrator of brutal acts which are only tenuously defensible in a society in which the model of justice has become rehabilitative rather than retributive. American culture, the text implies, has taken for its motto the French proverb *tout comprendre, c'est tout pardonner* (to understand everything is to forgive everything), with the consequence that moral evil and sinfulness, once absolutes for which the individual bore responsibility, have instead been redefined as psycho-emotional dysfunctions, attributable to causes such as physiology, early childhood experience, social environment, and the like—in any case, to causes outside and bigger than the individual charged with perpetrating anti-social acts or maintaining anti-social behaviors.

The narrative, however, is reluctant to permit such exonerative explanations for the actual and potential victims of Dexter's Harry-sanctioned acts. For instance, when Dexter meditates at the end of a piece of blood-spatter research on the distinction between himself and the criminal he has just identified, a "guy in size 7½ handmade Italian loafers," he observes:

> If I am ever careless enough to be caught, they will say I am a sociopathic monster, a sick and twisted demon who is not even human, and they will probably send me to die in Old Sparky with a smug self-righteous glow. If they ever catch Size 7½, they will say he is a bad man who went wrong because of social forces he was too unfortunate to resist, and he will go to jail for ten years before they turn him loose with enough money for a suit and a new chainsaw. (Lindsay 2005, 51)

We may note here two kinds of distinction. In the first, Dexter characterizes himself as "a sociopathic monster, a sick and twisted demon who is not even human," whereas the other killer, Size 7½, is framed as the victim of history, circumstance, and social environment—in other words, exactly the kind of criminal who gets rehabilitative justice but 'deserves', in Dexter's view and according to Harry's Code, retribution. In the second kind, which remains only implicit, there is a logical disjunction between Dexter's self-portrait explicitly as twisted monster and, as we have seen, the explanation of and justification for his murderousness as lying in the moment in the container when the young Dexter was trapped in his dead mother's blood. Though neither Dexter nor the reader learns this until toward the end of the novel, it serves as a retrospective justification and rationalization of his nature and activities.

Though thus exculpating himself as a special case, Dexter's voice emphatically invites us to take pleasure in justice as *retribution*. His practice—and, for that matter, Harry's Code—is thus the *lex talionis*: the law of an eye for an eye. Rather than inquiring into the nature of a society that is capable of producing monsters like Dexter and those he hunts, the narrative seeks, therefore, rather to legitimate punishment. Underneath the comedy of manners, with its surface wit and humor, and of cultural critique, then, lies the structure of revenge tragedy.

And, as in revenge tragedy (a popular sixteenth- and seventeenth-century theatrical genre that includes, among others, Shakespeare's *Hamlet*), the motivation for crime, for the capacity to do wrong, resides, not in the sociocultural context, but in the subject herself or himself. The glaring paradox in the novel is Dexter's own situation. His mother is presented by his brother Brian as a bad woman:

> I found the old police files. Mommy dearest hung out with a very naughty crowd. In the import business, just like me. Of course, their product was a little more sensitive. . . . My best guess is that Mumsy and her friends tried a little independent project with some product that strictly speaking did not actually belong to her, and her business associates were unhappy with her spirit of independence and decided to discourage her. (Lindsay 2005, 261)

She is also a bad mother, the origin of his pathology, in that she ultimately abandoned her two sons, however involuntarily, thus precipitating the "Traumatic Event" of Dexter's childhood (Lindsay 2005, 263). So Dexter has an alibi for *his* pathology; but his mother does not; nor is one offered for any of the other serial killers. This therefore legitimates his acts at a personal level, given that they are moderated by the Code of Harry, and authorizes also the kind of act central to Dexter's project, which is metonymic of a particular historical conjuncture when justice as retribution became the norm at the level of government, in its concern with terrorism.

Dexter in the context of 9/11

This central divergence between the nature of the events narrated and the pleasure experienced by readers and viewers in consuming them points to a doubleness in these narratives, and to the series of dualities that structure and underlie them. Also of critical interest is the cultural work that such divergences and dualities perform in readers'/viewers' consumption of the *Dexter* stories and TV episodes.

Like many novels, movies and TV shows that appeared after September 11, 2001, the *Dexter* narratives can be understood in part as both reflecting and negotiating that apocalyptic moment and its aftermath. These narratives are not merely accidental in their relation to the events of 9/11 but both address and redeploy them in particular ways. In this context, it is possible to see Dexter himself as an ironic condensation of American anxieties and terrors.

As the monitor of world ethics, the United States constituted itself as the dominant, and therefore, in a special sense, the unmarked: all who deviated from those ethics were Other, and therefore liable to correction and even retribution (for instance, the First and Second Gulf Wars). However, when the nation began to identify itself as victim rather than overseer, following 9/11, the United States came to see itself as othered in some profound way, and sought explanations for that othering. As newly cast in the role of trauma victim by the terrorists' penetration of national boundaries/borders that had never before been successfully attacked, the United States was read as passive, feminine Other. And the attacks were not only literal. The events were construed by the Islamic world as an assault on the moral decadence of the West—the over-sexualized, over-materialistic, corrupted, and therefore also feminized, body of the culture itself.

In the War on Terror, its reaction to its new position as Other, the United States turned to a model of retributive rather than rehabilitative justice. Such a shift involved a newly visible Otherness that was in turn justified by the original process of being othered as innocent trauma victim. As details about Guantanamo Bay and Abu Ghraib emerged, the world's 'policeman' called upon a model of justice hitherto regarded as un-American, which in turn required justification, as the media began to reveal the brutal, often sexualized, ways in which American 'justice' was being enacted in the War on Terror. Whatever the behind-the-scenes *Realpolitik* might have been historically up to this point, the War on Terror and its rationalizations revealed a duality in American self-conceptualization. Ron Suskind makes this clear in his account of an interview with one of President George W. Bush's aides:

> The aide said that guys like me were "in what we call the reality-based community," which he defined as people who "believe that solutions emerge from your judicious study of discernible reality." I nodded and murmured something about enlightenment principles and empiricism. He cut me off. "That's not the way the world really works anymore," he continued. "We're an empire now, and when we act, we create our own reality. And while you're studying that reality—judiciously, as you

will—we'll act again, creating other new realities, which you can study too, and that's how things will sort out. We're history's actors . . . and you, all of you, will be left to just study what we do." ("Faith, Certainty and the Presidency of George W. Bush," *The New York Times Magazine*, October 17, 2004; quoted in Redfield 2009, 49)

The idea that the United States now constitutes "an empire" may well come as news, however unwelcome, to Americans; but implicit in the aide's response is a rejection of the Enlightenment principles that underpin a more considered model of justice, and, indeed, the very foundation of the United States of America itself. 'Reality' now is fluid, dependent on the decisions and activities of those at the very centre of government whence emerged the notion of another empire—an 'Evil Empire'—whose adjudged criminality legitimated the War on Terror. Even the phrase 'War on Terror' indicates a new notion of reality, since 'terror' is abstract, and by its very nature cannot constitute a material target.

The idea that there may be two kinds of reality, one which is accessible to traditional thought nurtured by Enlightenment principles and techniques of analysis, and another, darker, more labile reality which can be identified only by those who are themselves involved in its creation, finds its way into *Darkly Dreaming Dexter*. Dexter's girlfriend Rita, who is familiar with the more conventional notion of reality, articulates a nascent understanding of this other emergent reality:

> I can never get used to seeing . . . I don't know. The underside? The way things really are? The way you [Dexter] see it. . . . We all assume that . . . *things* . . . really are a certain way. The way they're supposed to be? And then they never are, they're always more . . . I don't know. Darker? . . . It's like, everything is really two ways, the way we all pretend it is and the way it really is. And you already know that and it's like a game for you. (Lindsay 2005, 60)

Dexter's capacity to move between these realities makes him interesting—and sinister. It is also the justification for his ironic tone, which in turn suggests that the darker reality is the 'real' reality, which in turn legitimates his illegitimate activities.

Within the frame of the narrative, however, that legitimation is provided by the Code of Harry, Dexter's adoptive father. Realizing that Dexter's traumatic incarceration in the container has made the boy into a killer, Harry determines to make of that tendency an instrument of retribution in instances where the legal and judicial systems have either failed or been evaded in some manner.

Dexter in effect becomes judge and jury—and executioner. Dexter, like the United States itself, has been a victim, which in turn permits—indeed, justifies—his becoming an instrument of vengeance represented as justice.

Darkly Dreaming Dexter can thus be read as the legitimation of retribution at a particular historical moment in a society that many had already begun to think of as feminized—by materialism, by loss of religious faith, by the failure of old values, and, above all, by feminism. In the cultural imaginary, that society was perceived as feminized still further, and perhaps irretrievably, by the events of 9/11, and the penetration of the national body of America by the racial, religious, and moral Other. The author of the blog mensaction.net wrote: "The phallic symbol of America had been cut off . . . and at its base was a large smoldering vagina, the true symbol of the American culture, for it is the western culture that represents the feminine materialistic principle, and it is at its extreme in America" (quoted in Faludi 2008, 9). Susan Faludi (2008, 9–10) comments,

> There is a mystery here: the last remaining superpower, a nation attacked precisely *because* of its imperial preeminence, responded by fixating on its weakness and ineffectuality. Even more peculiar was our displacement of that fixation into the domestic realm, into a sexualized struggle between depleted masculinity and overbearing womanhood. What well of insecurity did this mystery unearth?[1]

Faludi's formulation of the condition of the United States post-9/11 and, by extension, of the Western world indicates a terror that goes beyond the terror of annihilation that the *events* of 9/11 signaled: that is, the collapse and shifting of categories and meanings, and especially of gender categories and meanings, so that the state, hitherto imagined as masculine, powerful, reasonable, and in control, becomes re-imagined as feminine, vulnerable, irrational, and incoherent. The fantasy of a return to a status ante quo, when men were men and women knew their place, gives rise to a desire to remasculinize—not only men and the state, but also the mechanisms by which both of these function, including, in the case of the *Dexter* narratives, the processes of justice. John Mead (2010, 62) describes the fear of a return to a life of quiet desperation:

> This is the story of these men's new lives—the trappings of civilization are no more appropriate to them than they are to Huck Finn: the street smarts of these warriors trump the book-learning of the women and the bureaucrats every time. As the operation winds down, Langewiesche observes the sagging spirits of the "Inner World" as they realize that

they will soon be "returning to a workplace of fluorescent-lit cubicles and network computers—an environment that, paradoxically, was all too much like that of the World Trade Center before the collapse."

If, for many, 9/11 represented an apocalyptic moment in the cultural imaginary of the West, narratives like the *Dexter oeuvre* conceive a *post*-apocalyptic reality in which the attempt to reposition gender categories is founded on the perception and sense of trauma, which in turn precipitates not merely a confusion of sex with death but also a transposition of one with the other. The thrill of sexual intimacy becomes the thrill of that supremely intimate moment when one subject holds the life of another in his hands. The penetration of the body is rendered ambiguous.

Dexter's *Liebestod*

The insistent connection between sex and death may also be described as queer, in that they tend to substitute for or to complement one another at key points in the text. For example, Dexter's empathetic imagining of the Ice Truck Killer's motivation for a change of *modus operandi* makes this explicit:

> To have come so far, all the way to the end, sectioning the leftovers for gift wrapping. And then the sudden realization: *This isn't it. Something is just not right.* Coitus interruptus. (Lindsay 2005, 35)

At other points in the text the connection works the other way. For example:

> Rita lunged forward and leaned her face into my chest. I tightened my arm around her, which brought my hand back into view. Less than an hour ago that same hand had been holding a filet knife over the little janitor. The thought made me dizzy.
> And really, I don't know how it happened, but it did. One moment I was patting her and saying, "There, there" and staring at the cords in my hand, feeling the sense memory pulse through the fingers, the surge of power and brightness as the knife explored Jaworski's abdomen. And the next moment—
> I believe Rita looked up at me. I am also reasonably certain that I looked back. And yet somehow it was not Rita I saw but a neat stack of cool and bloodless limbs. And it was not Rita's hands I felt on my belt buckle, but

the rising unsatisfied chorus from the Dark Passenger. And some little time later—

Well. It's still somewhat unthinkable. I mean, right there on the couch. How on earth did *that* happen? (Lindsay 2005, 148–9)

As in Wagner's opera *Tristan und Isolde*, love—sex—and death become interchangeable in the incandescent moment of the aria known as the "Liebestod," literally 'love's death', or 'love-death'.

Crucially, Harry explains Dexter's difference (or queerness) in terms of his childhood trauma, the details of which he does not reveal:

What happened to you when you were a little kid has shaped you . . . It's going to make you want to kill. And you can't help that. . . . But you can channel it. Control it. . . . There are plenty of people who deserve it, Dex. (Lindsay 2005, 40–1)

Harry, the "wonderful, all-seeing, all-knowing" father (Lindsay 2005, 41), thus not only accepts his adopted son's nature but instrumentalizes it, legitimating the retributive model of justice in this scene on the basis that certain kinds of trauma produce certain kinds of impulses which can be legitimately channeled.

Conventionally, the sexual urge is channeled into socially productive activities—and is regarded as entirely normal and hence normative. However, in *Dexter* the urge is toward death, rather than sex; but is, in a rather perverted way, also channeled into what is defined as a socially productive activity, namely, meting out a vengeful justice in lieu of the state, which has failed in its capacity to recognize evil and punish it appropriately. Metonymically, America as victim is effectively allowed to be remasculinized in ways that seem familiar to us from narratives of the Old West: here, the 'good policeman' gives his *imprimatur* to a regressive form of American justice. The queering of Dexter, as indicated above, does not result in his liberation—his freedom to 'come out'. Instead, it produces a further doubling: Dexter, like the gay man, must 'pass' as normal, much as the actions of an avenging United States must be re-presented as justice.

The pleasure—the *thrill*—in reading Lindsay's narrative thus surely derives in large part from the reader's sense of being scandalized by a story that does not merely indulge in gore and mayhem, but actually finds a legitimating and accepting rationalization of it. This is partly achieved by the mode of narration itself: cool, ironic, detached, cynical, witty, urbane, Dexter's voice and perceptions ingratiate themselves with the reader, and evade any sense of guilt in that pleasurable eroticization of the consumption of blood and death.

Note

1 It is worth noting that Faludi, too, identifies the United States as "imperial."

References

Faludi, Susan. 2008 [2007]. *The Terror Dream: Fear and Fantasy in Post-9/11 America*. Melbourne: Scribe.

Force, William Ryan. 2010. "The Code of Harry: Performing Normativity in *Dexter*." *Crime Media Culture* 6(3): 329–45.

Lindsay, Jeff. 2005 [2004]. *Darkly Dreaming Dexter*. London: Orion Books.

Mead, John. 2010. "9/11, Manhood, Mourning, and the American Romance." In *Reframing 9/11: Film, Popular Culture and the 'War on Terror'*, edited by Jeff Birkenstein, Anna Froula, and Karen Randell, 57–68. New York: Continuum.

Redfield, Marc. 2009. *The Rhetoric of Terror: Reflections on 9/11 and the War on Terror*. New York: Fordham University Press.

Santaularia, Isabel. 2010. "Dexter: Villain, Hero or Simply a Man? The Perpetuation of Traditional Masculinity in *Dexter*." *Atlantis. Journal of the Spanish Association of Anglo-American Studies* 32(2): 57–71.

List of Contributors

Janice Baker is an Alfred Deakin Postdoctoral Research Fellow in the Alfred Deakin Research Institute at Deakin University, Australia. She is affiliated to Deakin University's Cultural Heritage Centre for Asia and the Pacific. Her research is concerned with the application of critical theory to museums, with a particular focus on continental theory. She explores encounters with art and material culture through fictional representations of the museum as a cinematic image. In doing so, Baker seeks to problematize the way subjectivities and difference are conceptualized in the theories, histories, and critiques of museums and museology. She is writing a monograph on the Deleuzian Museum. Her contributions to edited collections include "Anarchical Artifacts: Museums as Sites of Radical Otherness," in *Museum Theory: An Expanded Field* (Blackwell, 2014) and "Flensed," in *Travel and Imagination* (Ashgate, 2013).

Louis Bayman is an Early Career Research fellow at Oxford Brookes, Oxford. He has published a range of articles on popular cinema, melodrama, and aesthetics. He has edited collections on Brazilian and Italian cinema, and is the author of the forthcoming monograph *The Operatic and the Everyday in Post-war Italian Film Melodrama* (Edinburgh University Press, 2014).

Mark Bernard is Visiting Assistant Professor in English and Interdisciplinary Studies at Johnson C. Smith University in Charlotte, North Carolina. His research interests include horror cinema, media industries, home video, and food in film. He is coauthor (with Cynthia Baron and Diane Carson) of a forthcoming book tentatively titled *The Politics of Food and Film* (Wayne State University Press, 2013). He is currently working on a monograph titled *Selling the Splat Pack: The DVD Revolution and the American Horror Film* (under contract with Edinburgh University Press).

David Buchbinder held until 2012 a Personal Professorial Chair in Masculinities Studies at Curtin University, Western Australia. In addition to numerous articles, he has published three books in this field: *Masculinities and Identities* (1994), *Performance Anxieties: Re-presenting Men* (1998), and *Studying Men and Masculinities* (2013). He also edited *Essays in Masculinities Studies 2002*

(2003), a collection of undergraduate essays. In addition, Buchbinder has published widely in the area of Literary and Cultural Studies. Together with Ann McGuire, he is currently exploring the postmodern Gothic and the recent heightened interest in the supernatural.

Sofia Bull has a PhD in Film Studies from Stockholm University, with a thesis titled "A Post-genomic Forensic Crime Drama: *CSI: Crime Scene Investigation* as Cultural Forum on Science." Her research mainly examines popular television, with a particular focus on the representation of science, medicine, corporeality, and the genetic imaginary.

Oliver Carter is Lecturer in Media and Cultural Theory in the Birmingham School of Media, at Birmingham City University. He is convenor of the modules Creativity in the Media, Media Culture, and Popular Culture. He is both a fan and researcher of European cult cinema. His blog can be found at www.olivercarter.co.uk. He is also a contributing author to the book *Media Studies: Text, Production and Context* (Pearson Education, 2009).

Robert Cettl is a freelance author, film-maker, and independent digital publisher. He has an BA (Hons) in Film/Media, a Grad Dip (Information Study), Grad Cert (TESOL), and MTESOL, having taught English in China's Xinjiang province. A former Scholars and Artists in Residence Research Fellow at Australia's National Film & Sound Archive (NFSA), Cettl's published film non-fiction includes *Serial Killer Cinema: An Analytical Filmography* and *Terrorism in American Cinema* (McFarland & Co. Inc, 2003). His digital video feature films are housed in the NFSA. He is a member of the Australian Library & Information Association (ALIA).

Sara L. Knox is Associate Professor in the School of Humanities and Communication Arts at the University of Western Sydney. She is author of *Murder: A Tale of Modern American Life* (Duke University Press, 1998). Her research interests include death, violence and representation, and contemporary cultures of reading. Her most recent articles have been published in *Cultural Studies Review and Mortality*. Her novel *The Orphan Gunner* (Giramondo, 2007) was short-listed for the regional Commonwealth Writer's Prize for first book, and for *The Age* Book of the Year.

Christina Lee is Lecturer in Communication and Cultural Studies at Curtin University, Western Australia. Her main research areas are cultural memory, fandom, and youth cinema. She is the author of *Screening Generation X: The Politics and Popular Memory of Youth in Contemporary Cinema* (Ashgate, 2010) and editor of *Violating Time: History, Memory, and Nostalgia in Cinema* (Continuum, 2008).

Alzena MacDonald is Lecturer in Communication and Cultural Studies at Curtin University, Western Australia. She teaches extensively in the area of Literary and Cultural Studies. Her research interests include representations of crime and horror, popular culture, Indian nationalisms, and postcoloniality.

Ann Elizabeth McGuire is Senior Lecturer in Communication and Cultural Studies at Curtin University, Western Australia. She has taught extensively and passionately in the areas of narrative, semiotics, Gothic and Utopian literatures, and New Media. She has published several works with David Buchbinder. Her current research interests include the increasing popularity of the supernatural in fiction.

Danielle Rousseau is Assistant Professor of Applied Social Sciences at Boston University. She teaches in the Applied Social Sciences program including courses in gender and justice, crime and delinquency, crime and mental health, and research methods. Her current research focuses on gender and justice, race and justice, trauma, hate crime, and crime and popular media. Rousseau's work has been published in the *Journal of Gender, Race, and Justice*; *Law and Society Review*; *The Annals of the Academy of Political and Social Sciences*; and other academic journals and books.

Kumarini Silva is Assistant Professor of Communication Studies at the University of North Carolina—Chapel Hill. Her research is at the various intersections of feminism, identity and identification, postcolonial studies, and popular culture. Her most recent work has appeared in *Social Identities*; *South Asian Popular Culture*; and *Cultural Studies*. Silva is also the author of several book chapters on race, global media, and film.

Philip L. Simpson received his bachelor's and master's degrees in English from Eastern Illinois University in 1986 and 1989 respectively, and his doctorate in American Literature from Southern Illinois University in 1996. He serves as Provost of the Titusville Campus of Brevard Community College in Florida. Before that, he was Professor of Communications and Humanities at the Palm Bay campus of Brevard Community College for eight years and Department Chair of Liberal Arts for five years. He also served as President of the Popular Culture Association and Area Chair of Horror for the Association. He received the Association's Felicia Campbell Area Chair Award in 2006. Simpson currently serves as Area Co-Chair of the Stephen King Area and the Vampire Area for the Association and sits on the editorial board of the *Journal of Popular Culture*. He is the author of *Psycho Paths: Tracking the Serial Killer through Contemporary American Film and Fiction* (Southern Illinois University Press, 2000) and *Making Murder: The Fiction of Thomas Harris* (Praeger, 2010). He has also published numerous essays on film, literature, popular culture, and horror.

Index

421131